Contents

BottomLineInc.com

Bottom Line Books® is an imprint of Bottom Line Inc., publisher of print periodicals, e-letters and books. We are dedicated to bringing you the best information from the most knowledgeable sources in the world. Our goal is to help you gain greater wealth, better health, more wisdom, extra time and increased happiness.

Printed in the United States of America

BLP/am

1

Tax Troubles

The IRS Will Rob Your Heirs

Martin M. Shenkman, CPA, JD, founder of Shenkman Law, a law firm specializing in wealth planning and protection, Fort Lee, New Jersey and New York City. He is coauthor of *The Tools & Techniques of Estate Planning and Powers of Attorney*. ShenkmanLaw.com

---

Don't make the common mistake of neglecting tax planning for your estate just because it's unlikely that the estate will owe estate tax. It's true that few taxpayers will ever face any federal estate tax—that's because the amount exempt from tax has increased to $11.2 million for 2018 ($22.4 million for a married couple after the second spouse dies) or higher when adjusted for inflation in future years. However, the estate and heirs still might owe income tax, reducing the amount that the heirs will inherit, and that's where estate planning can make a big difference.

A combination of wise estate planning now and prudent steps taken by your executor and/or trustee later can save on taxes. *Here's what you need to know about cutting taxes for estates of all sizes*…*

INCOME TAX CAN HIT ESTATES HARD

An income tax return must be filed for an estate for every year that it has gross income of as little as

*Some states have inheritance and estate tax rules that differ from federal rules, so consult a state tax expert.

$600 until the estate is dissolved. The estate's income tax, which applies to income received beginning on the date the person dies, is different from the deceased individual's personal income tax, which applies to income received before the date of death and requires that an individual 1040 return be filed. (The heirs do not owe income tax when they inherit assets, but they may owe capital gains tax when they sell inherited assets such as stocks or property.)

And unfortunately, income tax brackets for an estate return are triggered at much lower levels than for personal tax returns. For example, for the 2018 tax year, the top 37% bracket doesn't apply on an individual tax return until taxable income hits $500,000. But it applies to an estate (and a trust) when its taxable income hits $12,500. An estate's income may include interest and dividends from investments, items owed to the deceased (such as rent), income from a private business, compensation paid by an employer after death and any other income received by the estate.

Generally, you want to reduce the amount of income tax that the estate will owe by reducing the amount of income it will receive and directing that money elsewhere. This may be more complex than it sounds and may include what you can do now and what you should make sure the executor of your estate or trustee of a trust knows to do.

1

WHAT TO DO NOW

•**Consider donating income-producing assets to charity now while you're still alive rather than making bequests to charity in your will.** That's because the rules have changed. It used to be advantageous for an estate to reduce estate tax by making charitable donations. But if an estate doesn't owe estate tax, then no tax deduction will be available for charitable donations made by the estate. By donating now, while you're alive, you can take a tax deduction that your estate wouldn't get—and by reducing the amount of income-producing assets that will be left in your estate, it also will reduce the estate's taxable income. These assets might include stocks, bonds, mutual fund shares and real estate.

If you have already included in your will a bequest to charity and you don't want to redo your will, you may be able to simply tell the charity that you will make a gift to it now in exchange for the charity sending you a letter that waives its right to receive the bequest that is already in your will, acknowledging that the current donation is an advancement of that bequest.

•**Designate individuals as beneficiaries in retirement plans.** Retirement accounts often are the most valuable financial assets owned by an individual, so they should be a key consideration in any estate plan.

If you don't designate individual beneficiaries for your IRA, the IRA may be included in the assets to be distributed according to the provisions in your will…and income tax on it will be due within five years under IRA rules.

In contrast, if you do designate your spouse, children and/or other individuals as beneficiaries of your IRA, they may be able to stretch distributions from it over an entire lifetime, providing them with decades of tax-favored investment returns—a big difference. Keep in mind that unlike with a 401(k), your spouse is not automatically the beneficiary of your IRA.

•**Consider creating a trust.** If you create a trust and designate assets to put into the trust rather than into your estate, the trustee can manage the assets after your death to minimize taxes. You can give the trustee as much or as little discretion as you wish over how to distribute the assets and who receives them. The trustee could, for instance, stretch out distributions from the trust over a number of years and decide which are the most tax-efficient ways to make those distributions. A trustee could be anyone ranging from a spouse or an adult child to a financial institution.

Distributions include the income generated by assets in the trust. Be sure that the trust document permits inclusion of capital gains as a form of income that can be distributed in this way.

Example: The trustee, in conjunction with your heirs, might decide that in certain years it is best to give bigger distributions to young beneficiaries who have minimal income and so are in low tax brackets, such as those beneficiaries who are in college or starting out in their careers, rather than those who are in high tax brackets.

REDUCE FUTURE CAPITAL GAINS TAX

When an heir inherits certain of your assets, such as shares of stock or a piece of art, the asset's tax basis is reset at the market value at the date of your death, instead of your original cost to acquire the asset. Future taxable capital gains or losses when an asset is sold by an heir are determined based on this tax basis, which is called the stepped-up basis if it is higher than your initial cost or the stepped-down basis if it is lower. The tax basis is subtracted from the eventual sale price to determine the capital gain or loss. A stepped-up basis lowers the capital gains taxes that heirs eventually must pay.

Example: A parent buys stock at a price of $20 per share…the share value is $50 when a child inherits the stock…and the child later sells the shares for $55 each. The child's taxable capital gain is just $5 per share, even though the stock price rose by $35 since the parent bought it, because the stepped-up tax basis is $50.

How to make sure capital gains taxes will be minimized…

•**Maximize the advantages of a stepped-up tax basis.** Make sure that your executor or your trustee knows that he/she will need to carefully record the adjusted basis for each asset on your date of death so that your beneficiaries can use that basis whenever they sell assets in the future. This is especially important for valuable items that don't trade regularly, such as real estate, shares in a private business, artwork, antiques and other collectibles that might require an appraisal. An appraisal obtained for a modest price may avoid a costly conflict with the IRS in the future. The executor or trustee also should make sure that your heirs who inherit shares in a mutual fund know to tell the firm that operates the fund to start using the stepped-up basis in its calculations of capital gains for the 1099 form it provides to the IRS each year.

●**Beware the trap of a stepped-down basis.** If the asset that you bequeath to an heir diminished in value from the time you acquired it, it could mean a greater eventual capital gains tax—or a smaller capital loss that is less effective in offsetting capital gains. To avoid this trap, review the assets now that will likely be in the estate and consider selling those that have diminished in value since you acquired them.

Caution: Keep in mind that the strategies described in this article have technicalities that may require advice from a financial professional.

Beware These Tax Scams

Roundup of experts on tax fraud, reported in *USA Today.*

Major tax scams to watch out for in the up-coming filing season: *Phony help-desk calls or e-mails* that seem to come from legitimate firms such as TurboTax but are oddly written and ask users to click links—never reply or click unless you are sure that a notice is legitimate. *Fraudulent e-mails asking for W-2 forms* are going to some corporations. Identity thieves file quickly and create returns that generate refunds so that legitimate returns from victims are rejected—use IRS Form 14039 if you find that a fraudulent return has been filed. *Criminals send e-mails to tax professionals* claiming to be potential clients whose documents can be obtained by clicking on a link. If the tax professional clicks on the link, malware is downloaded to his/her com-

puter. *Crooked tax professionals file returns* designed to get illegitimate refunds that the thieves keep or share with clients.

Tax Scam Alert

Adam Levin, JD, founder of the cyber-security company CyberScout and author of *Swiped: How to Protect Yourself in a World Full of Scammers, Phishers, and Identity Thieves.* Cyberscout.com

The IRS is using private debt collectors to pursue unpaid taxes, which could lead to scams.

What to do: Never provide Social Security numbers or credit card details. The debt collectors are not authorized to take payments. Be especially suspicious if you did not receive an official letter about a debt beforehand. If you get a call, contact the IRS directly at 800-829-1040.

7 Things You Didn't Know Are Taxable

Greg Rosica, CPA, CFA, partner with Ernst & Young LLP in the private client services practice in Tampa. He is a contributing author for the *EY Tax Guide 2017.* EY.com/eytaxguide

Buried treasure…gifts from your employer… and that iPad you got as a gift for opening a bank account—they all have something in common. The IRS defines them as income and expects you to pay federal tax on their cash value.

Americans underreport an estimated $68 billion in personal income annually, sometimes intentionally but often because they don't realize it counts as taxable income. Many establishments such as casinos aren't even required to notify the IRS that you have received income unless the income tops a certain threshold. But in some cases, failing to report taxable income can trigger an audit and/or result in civil penalties ranging from "failure to file" penalties (up to $135 if you are more than 60 days late) to "failure to pay" penalties (0.5% of the amount of unpaid tax per month).

Surprising things that are taxable…

BANK OR CREDIT CARD GIFTS

Many financial institutions offer incentives for opening new accounts, ranging from cash and electronic gadgets to frequent-flier miles. These generally are considered taxable income unless you must spend a certain amount on a credit card or debit card within a limited time period.

Important: Frequent-flier miles and cash back that you receive when you use a credit or debit card are not taxable because they are rebates.

CANCELED CREDIT CARD DEBT

When someone negotiates a settlement with a credit card issuer to pay less than the full amount owed, the IRS treats the forgiven debt as income. So if you owe, say, a balance of $25,000 and the issuer settles for $18,500, the $6,500 difference counts as taxable income.

Exceptions: Credit card debt discharged in a Chapter 11 bankruptcy does not count as income. And in cases of insolvency, you may not have to pay tax on all or possibly any of your forgiven credit card debt. Just before any of the debt is forgiven, if your total debt exceeds your total assets (excluding assets that creditors can't seize, such as 401(k) accounts), you are insolvent by that excess amount. You subtract the insolvency amount from the forgiven debt to get the amount of taxable income. So if your total debt exceeds your assets by $5,000 and your credit card issuer forgives $6,500, you report $1,500 of the forgiven debt as income.

ILL-GOTTEN GAINS

Whether you rob a bank or win an illegal football betting pool at the office, the IRS expects you to pay tax on any ill-gotten gains, although few lawbreakers choose to do so. Although the IRS technically must keep the contents of your tax returns confidential, there are enough legal loopholes that law-enforcement agencies are likely to find out if you are including ill-gotten gains as part of your income. For instance, if the IRS audits you, it is allowed to reveal certain information to law-enforcement authorities that it gathers from outside sources, such as witnesses to your illegal activities.

There's a better way to gain from illegal profits—report other people who are tax evaders. The IRS Whistleblower Office paid out more than $61 million in awards in 2016 to tipsters—they typically get 15% to 30% of the amount the government eventually collects. And yes, any money you get as a whistleblower is regarded as taxable income on your own return.

More information: IRS.gov/about-irs/Whistle blower-Office-at-a-Glance.

EMPLOYER PERKS

Generally, you aren't required to pay tax on gifts you receive from family and friends no matter how much they're worth. But most sizable gifts from your boss or company are regarded as taxable compensation subject to federal and state income tax withholding as well as FICA taxes. This includes everything from golf clubs to the use of a company-owned apartment for a vacation.

Two exceptions: "De minimis" fringe benefits—gifts of minimal value, which some employers define as $75 or less but which the IRS has not defined—generally are not taxable. That includes, for example, a holiday gift basket, group meals and picnics, and local transportation after hours if it is required because of security concerns. Cash and gift cards generally are not included under the de minimis rule—they typically are taxable—but tangible personal property, such as a watch or ring, awarded to employees to recognize their achievements for "length of service" are not taxable if you have been with the company for at least five years and the value of the award is $1,600 or less.

GAMBLING PROCEEDS

The IRS expects you to report all "gambling" winnings, no matter how small, whether they come from church bingo games, raffles, sweepstakes, lotteries, casinos or online sports fantasy betting sites. If you win more than a certain amount, ranging from $1,200 (bingo and slot machines) to $5,000 (poker tournaments and lotteries), the gambling establishment typically withholds a 24% flat tax (slightly down from 25% in 2017) and must notify the IRS…and then you adjust that for your tax bracket when you file tax forms.

The good news: If you itemize, gambling losses are deductible up to the amount of winnings you report as income. You must be able to prove your losses through documentation such as receipts, tickets, payment slips and/or a gambling diary with specific dates, the type of gambling, and the names and addresses of the establishments and the names of other people accompanying you at the establishments.

RENTING OUT YOUR HOME

Services such as Airbnb.com that enable you to rent out available rooms in your house or apartment to travelers have allowed hundreds of thousands of home owners to earn extra income. The IRS considers any short-term rental income taxable if you rent out space for 15 or more days a year. Be aware that additional taxes imposed by your local and state government also may apply.

Example: Chicago, Philadelphia, San Diego and San Francisco are among cities that impose a "transient occupancy" or hotel tax on every short-term rental stay.

You can reduce the taxes you owe on rental income by taking related deductions. In addition to a portion of your own rent or mortgage payments, utilities and insurance expenses, you can deduct items such as the cost of sheets and linens that you designate for the exclusive use of your guests…toiletries for guests…and cleaning fees.

Helpful: Get more strategies at websites of the major online lodging services, LearnAirbnb.com and Community.HomeAway.com.

A TREASURE TROVE

"Treasure Trove" is a fanciful term used by the IRS to categorize any lost or abandoned cash and/or valuables that you find. Precedent for taxing treasure troves dates back to a famous 1964 case in which an Ohio couple bought a used piano for $15 and found $4,467 in cash inside while cleaning it. Recent cases involve fans who have caught historic home run baseballs in stadiums. The balls are taxable based on "fair market value."

How to Fight the IRS

Scott M. Estill, JD, former trial attorney for the IRS. He is author of *Tax This! An Insider's Guide to Standing Up to the IRS.* ScottEstill.com

---

You paid your taxes—but now the IRS says that you owe more. Each year, the IRS sends out millions of notices requesting additional payments from taxpayers who made math errors on their returns…neglected to report certain income…claimed tax credits or deductions that they were not entitled to…or made other mistakes.

But what if your tax return was right and it's the IRS that's wrong?

Taxpayers who receive notices from the IRS tend to just pay what they're told they owe. But most IRS notices are generated by computers—computers that sometimes misinterpret data. And even if a notice was sent by an actual IRS agent, that agent might have misinterpreted the tax code.

Taxpayers truly can take on the IRS. In fact, in June 2014 the IRS adopted a "Taxpayer Bill of Rights," a list of 10 rights—including "The Right to Challenge the IRS's Position and Be Heard."

Here, a five-step plan to fight an IRS notice that you believe to be wrong…

STEP 1: **Look for instructions in the notice itself about what to do if you disagree.** Believe it or not, following these instructions often is all it takes to get a matter cleared up in your favor, particularly when the matter is fairly clear-cut—the IRS thinks you earned more from your employer than you actually did, and you have the W-2 to prove it, for example. But you should follow the instructions exactly.

Typically, you can check a box on the notice stating that you disagree…add a short note explaining why you disagree…attach copies of any supporting documents…then return this section of the notice to the IRS mailing address listed. Send these materials—and any other letters to the IRS—by the deadline via certified mail with return receipt requested.

A short, to-the-point explanation will be more effective here than a long one.

Example: "My total income from ABC Corp was $50,000, not $100,000, and was fully reported on my tax return. Enclosed is a copy of my W-2."

Be sure to keep copies of all your correspondence with the IRS.

STEP 2: Decide whether it's worth hiring a tax professional to assist you. The key factor here is how much money is at stake. If the IRS is asking for a few thousand dollars or less, you're probably better off not hiring an enrolled agent, CPA or tax attorney.

There's a good chance that you would have to pay that tax pro a few thousand dollars to challenge an IRS notice—potentially more with a tax attorney—even if the case appears straightforward. It is not worth spending that much money unless a significantly larger amount is at risk.

STEP 3: Request supervisor involvement. If you receive a notice that rejects your challenge and it mentions a specific IRS employee, call this agent and very politely ask to speak to his/her supervisor—there's probably no point in discussing it any further with the IRS employee mentioned by name, because he is the one who already rejected your written explanation. Don't tell this named IRS employee that you want to talk to his boss because you think his decision was wrong—that would only build antagonism. Instead, frame the situation as a disagreement between honest, well-meaning people, both of whom want the same thing—an "agreed case" where the taxpayer and the IRS see eye to eye about the situation. IRS agents are evaluated in part by their success in obtaining agreed cases, so this is to the agent's benefit, too.

Example: You might say, "Listen, obviously we both think we're right. Can we take this to your supervisor? Maybe we can get an agreed case so that we can keep this out of the appeals process."

The IRS is particularly anxious to make cases go away when the dollar amounts involved are very small—less than $1,000 or so.

When you speak to the supervisor, present your case more or less as you did to the original agent. But if that original agent provided a specific reason why he disagreed with your position, you will also need to specifically explain why the agent was incorrect. (If the notice you receive stating that the IRS still be-

lieves you owe additional money does not mention a specific IRS agent's name, send a certified letter to the address listed requesting that someone at the supervisory level reconsider your case.)

If the IRS doesn't back down after your discussion with a supervisor…

STEP 4: Take your case to the Office of Appeals. The Office of Appeals is an independent unit within the IRS. It will give your case a fresh and fair hearing.

By this point in the process, you might feel that you are presenting the same facts again and again, beating your head against a wall of bureaucracy. Well, that's how you fight the IRS—you keep presenting your case to as many different IRS employees as possible until you find one who agrees with you.

The notices you received from the IRS should include instructions on how to take your case to the Office of Appeals. Otherwise, go to the IRS website (IRS.gov/appeals) for more information about filing this appeal.

STEP 5: Take your case to the US Tax Court as a last resort. If $50,000 or less is in dispute, you can opt to represent yourself in a "small tax case" procedure. This is similar to small-claims court—there is no jury, and your inexperience with courtroom procedures will not be held against you. You just tell your side of the story one more time, present your evidence and answer the judge's questions. The only real downside to a small tax case is that the decision of the Tax Court cannot be appealed.

There's little reason not to go to Tax Court if you're representing yourself and you believe you're right. (If you hire representation, your costs could climb well into four figures, sometimes higher.) All you have to lose is a few hours of your time, travel costs to the closest city where Tax Court is held, a $60 filing fee and potentially some interest charges. But at this point, your matter might not even get to court—an IRS attorney might offer to settle for less than the full amount that the IRS claims you owe before your case is heard.

The notices you receive from the IRS should explain how to bring your case before the Tax Court. Or download the necessary form at USTaxCourt.gov (click on "Forms," then "Petition").

5 Tax Warnings for Widows and Widowers

Amy Wang, CPA, senior technical manager of tax advocacy with the American Institute of CPAs, an accounting industry professional organization that has more than 400,000 members, Washington, DC. AICPA.org

Taxes are not the first thing on someone's mind after the death of a spouse, but they are something that cannot be ignored for long. The recently widowed face special tax considerations, some of which may need to be dealt with well before the next tax-filing deadline.

Five things you need to know about taxes if your spouse recently passed away…or if you are helping a family member or friend whose spouse recently passed away…

●**You might face massive tax penalties if you don't withdraw money from your spouse's IRA by the end of the year.** If your spouse was age 70½ or older at the time of his/her death and had a tax-deferred retirement account, such as a traditional IRA, 401(k) or 403(b), your spouse was obliged to take a required minimum distribution (RMD) from the account each year. (This does not apply to Roth IRAs.) If your spouse had not yet taken the current year's required distribution in the year of his death, then the account's beneficiary—that's often the surviving spouse—must do so on his behalf. The tax penalty for not doing so is a staggering 50% of the amount that was supposed to be withdrawn. That means thousands of dollars could be lost.

Unfortunately, many surviving spouses are unaware of this requirement…uncertain whether the deceased partner made the withdrawal…and/or not aware that the deadline for this withdrawal is the end of the calendar year in which your spouse died, not the April 15 tax-filing deadline.

Exception: The deadine is extended to April 1 of the year following the year in which the account holder turns 70½.

The financial institution that holds your spouse's retirement account can help you determine whether RMDs are up-to-date and, if not, the size of the withdrawal required.

What to do: If the year-end deadline was missed, make the withdrawal as soon as possible. Then file IRS Form 5329, *Additional Taxes on Qualified Plans (Including IRAs) and Other Tax-Favored Accounts,* along with a brief letter explaining what happened and requesting a waiver of the penalty. The IRS sometimes will waive this penalty, particularly if the account owner died late in the year and the beneficiary makes the withdrawal early the following year.

●**You have just nine months to preserve your deceased spouse's estate tax exemption.** Estate tax law offers a way for surviving spouses to preserve their deceased spouses' estate tax exemptions. This essentially doubles the exemption available upon the second spouse's death from $11.2 million to $22.4 million. (These are revised limits for 2018, which are projected to increase slightly in 2019.)

But there's an often-overlooked deadline that must be met if you wish to do this—IRS Form 706, *United States Estate (and Generation-Skipping Transfer) Tax Return,* must be filed within nine months of the date of death. This nine-month deadline often lands before the next tax-filing deadline, so even people who work with professional tax preparers might not learn about it until it is too late.

Some widows and widowers don't bother preserving the exemption of the first spouse to die because the couple's combined estate is less than the basic current exemption. But that's a gamble—your assets could expand to exceed this exemption amount later.

Example: A man dies, leaving a $8 million estate to his wife. The wife does not bother preserving her husband's estate tax exemption—but she lives another 20 years, during which time the couple's assets climb in value to $14 million. Millions of dollars of the family's wealth face federal estate taxes of as much as 40% that could have been avoided by a onetime filing.

●**The timing of real estate sales can have major tax consequences following the death of a spouse.** Some widows and widowers find it emotionally difficult to sell the family home even when it makes little sense to live there alone. If the home's value has climbed significantly since you purchased it, there could be a tax reason not to wait too long. Married couples typically can exclude up to $500,000 of the profits from the sale of a principal residence from their capital gains taxes...while single people can exclude only up to $250,000. Unmarried widows and widowers still can qualify for the full $500,000 exclusion—but only if the home is sold within two years of the date of the spouse's death. Don't cut it too close to this two-year deadline—it might take months to find a buyer and weeks more for a home sale to close.

Other widows and widowers want to sell their homes quickly after the loss of their spouses because it is painful to live in their homes without their life partners...because they need the money... or because they cannot maintain the properties on their own. But selling too quickly sometimes can lead to unnecessary taxes, too. The capital gains tax exclusion can be claimed only if you have used the property as a primary residence for at least two of the past five years...and it has been at least two years since you last claimed this exclusion on the sale of a property. If you do not quite qualify under these rules, it might be worth delaying the sale until you do.

•**You still might qualify for joint tax rates during the years following your spouse's death.** Married couples who file their taxes jointly receive a higher standard tax deduction than single people, plus more favorable tax brackets and higher income limits on many tax deductions and credits. *The death of your spouse does not necessarily mean you no longer qualify...*

•Widows and widowers can file jointly for the year of the spouse's death even if the spouse died very early in the year.

•If there are one or more dependent children in your household, you can file as a "qualifying widow or widower" for two tax years beyond the year in which you were widowed, assuming that you have not remarried. (This provides the same rates and brackets as filing jointly.) After that, you might be eligible to file as a "head of household" if you still are supporting a dependent. The tax brackets are not as favorable with head-of-household status as they are for qualifying widows and widowers, but they are better than for single filers.

•**You generally do not have to pay income taxes on life insurance benefits—with one exception.** If the insurer pays you interest on a policy's death benefits—say, because you agree to a deferred payout or an installment payout—that interest probably is taxable at your income tax rate. Ask your adviser or see IRS publication 525, *Taxable and Nontaxable Income*, for details.

2

Wall Street Swindles

Power Up Your 401k

Ric Lager, president of Lager & Company, Inc., which advises 401(k) plan participants, Golden Valley, Minnesota. He is author of *Forget the Pie: Recipe for a Healthier 401(k)*. LagerCo.com

If you are among the 90 million Americans who invest in a 401(k) retirement plan, you might be surprised by the big opportunities you are missing and the costly mistakes you are making in how you handle that account.

Here are some of the most surprising things you should know about your 401(k)—or a similar 403(b)—whether you have it at a current employer...still hold one from a former employer...are considering shifting it to an IRA...or will be taking distributions soon.

A CURRENT EMPLOYER'S 401(K)

Employees often pay much less attention to the assets they have in their employer-sponsored 401(k) accounts than to the assets they have in IRAs or taxable accounts. In many cases, they think they can rely on the employer to keep them from making big mistakes. That leaves them open to various surprises.

SURPRISE: **Your funds could be switched.** Your employer or 401(k) administrator can drop a fund that you are in and shift your assets to a different fund it chooses. This may happen when a lower-cost fund becomes available...as a way to make the investment menu more attractive by replacing a fund that has done poorly over the past year with one that has done well over that period...or because the management of a fund or the administrator of your 401(k) plan has changed. You typically are notified by mail and/or e-mail at least 30 to 90 days before this switch, known as "mapping," takes effect, but the notifications are easy to overlook.

What to do: Check the new fund's five- and 10-year record rather than just the one-year record, and consider whether there is another fund available that is more attractive.

SURPRISE: **You're in the wrong target-date fund.** A target-date fund—a very popular type of fund in 401(k)s—is designed to shift its mix of investments to reduce risk as the fund's target year gets nearer. Even though it is common for an employee to choose the version of the fund whose target year coincides with his/her planned retirement year, that is not always wise.

For instance, you might end up working several years longer than you expected. Or you might have other sources of substantial income—ranging from a pension and Social Security to money-market accounts and certificates of deposit (CDs)—that you can draw on before you tap the target-date fund. If so, you may want to choose a target-date fund with a later target year (which means that it is weighted more toward stocks).

A FORMER EMPLOYER'S 401(K)

It might make sense to keep your money in a 401(k) even after you have stopped working for the employer that sponsors it rather than roll it over to an IRA.

SURPRISE: **Once you have left the employer, you could withdraw assets from the 401(k) without penalty if you are at least 55 years old—you could not do this until 59½ with an IRA.**

A twist: If this possibility seems enticing and you still are working for the employer that sponsors the 401(k), you might want to think ahead and do a "reverse rollover"—moving assets from a traditional IRA into your current employer's 401(k). That could increase the amount available to withdraw from the 401(k) after you leave your current employer. About two-thirds of 401(k) plans allow these reverse rollovers.

ROLLING OVER A 401(K)

About 60% of all 401(k) participants transfer or "roll over" their accounts into an IRA when they leave a company or retire, but they should first consider some surprising advantages and disadvantages. (For more, see our article at BottomLineInc.com/job401k.)

SURPRISE: **In some cases, you can invest in mutual funds that are closed to new investors if you roll over your 401(k) to an IRA.**

Example: At T. Rowe Price, you can gain access to any fund that is closed to new investors, including highly ranked funds such as Capital Appreciation, Mid-Cap Value and New Horizons.

Caveat: The fund can't be completely closed—it still must be accepting additional assets from investors who have already invested in it.

SURPRISE: **If you are rolling over a 401(k) to an IRA, in some cases—but not all—you must liquidate your mutual funds and then transfer the cash to the IRA, where you can reinvest it.** This is always true if you are rolling over the 401(k) from one investment firm to a different

one, even if the same mutual funds are available in the IRA at the second firm. And it usually is true even if you are staying within the same investment firm for any funds that are not managed by that investment firm.

Examples: If you have a Fidelity fund in a 401(k) that is administered by Vanguard and you want to roll it over to an IRA at Vanguard, you must cash it out first, repurchase the shares at Vanguard and typically pay Vanguard a transaction fee. You also would have to sell your shares if your 401(k) account includes one of the "institutional" class Vanguard funds, which charge extremely low fees, because that class is not available in IRAs. You then could purchase the same fund in a class with higher expenses (but no transaction fee).

What to do: Before rolling over a 401(k) to an IRA, check with the company that will hold your IRA to determine all of the fees and ongoing expenses that will be involved, and take this into account when deciding which funds to choose.

TAKING REQUIRED DISTRIBUTIONS

Many investors assume that the IRS requires them to take required minimum distributions (RMDs) from their 401(k)s starting at age 70½ because they must do that for their IRAs.

SURPRISE: **The rules regarding RMDs are different for 401(k)s and IRAs.** For instance, if you still are working at age 70½, the IRS does not require you to take RMDs from your current employer's 401(k) until you retire or leave the company. For both 401(k)s and IRAs, the amount you take is based on a life-expectancy formula that is calculated each year and on the value of your accounts. But for 401(k)s, you must calculate the RMD formula separately for each 401(k) requiring an RMD and take the appropriate amount from each.

In contrast, for IRAs, you apply the formula to the total amount in all your IRAs—whether you are employed or not—and then you get to choose which IRA or combination of IRAs the distribution comes from. Keep this in mind when deciding whether and when to roll over a 401(k) into an IRA.

Robo-Adviser with Human Help

Barron's. Barrons.com

A human boost has been implemented for robo-advisers. Betterment, a firm that pioneered automated portfolio management services for a cost of 0.25% of invested assets per year, now is offering two service tiers that add human interaction to robotic management. Betterment Premium allows unlimited human interaction for a 0.4% fee for accounts with at least $100,000 invested. Some firms offering robo-advisory services, including Fidelity, have not yet followed suit.

How You Buy Gold Matters

Frank E. Holmes, CEO and CIO of US Global Investors, a San Antonio–based investment-management firm with expertise in gold and other precious metals and assets under management of more than $945 million. He is coauthor of *The Goldwatcher: Demystifying Gold Investing.* USFunds.com.

Barry Stuppler, founder and president of Barry Stuppler & Company, a major US wholesaler of coins and precious metals, Woodland Hills, California. He is a past president of the American Numismatics Association and a current vice president of the Professional Numismatists Guild. MintState Gold.com

Gold may be set to glitter again, according to many "gold bugs." These gold enthusiasts say the best time to buy is when inflation threatens to soar, which may happen as a result of President Donald Trump's plans to ratchet up government spending and recent tax cuts. They also say that gold's recent price below $1,250 an ounce, compared with its all-time high of nearly $1,900 in 2011, makes it a bargain now. Gold doubters, however, say that the improving US economy makes gold unattractive.

Whether you decide that now is a time to invest in gold or you hold off for a while, how you buy gold can be almost as important as when you buy. It's available in a variety of forms including gold coins and bars…funds that own physical gold…and gold-mining companies. Each offers certain advantages and disadvantages. To help you decide, we in-terviewed two leading gold experts—gold bullion dealer Barry Stuppler, who discusses investing in physical gold, and precious-metals mutual fund manager Frank E. Holmes, who discusses investing in various forms of "paper" gold.

INVESTING IN PHYSICAL GOLD

Physical gold is available for investment as coins and bars.

Pros of physical gold: You can keep a close eye on your gold in a home safe or a safe-deposit box, and your gains and losses are directly tied to gold prices rather than to other factors that can influence the success of gold-mining companies, such as management or geopolitics.

Cons: It takes extra work to store and insure gold yourself. It's more expensive and difficult to buy and sell than gold-related stocks or exchange-traded funds (ETFs). And it pays no dividends.

Here are the key strategies…

- **Buy one-ounce American Buffalo coins made by the US Mint and/or Canadian Maple Leaf coins made by the Royal Canadian Mint.** These are among the most widely circulated gold coins… and among the easiest to buy and sell…and both are 99.99% pure gold. There are many other types of gold coins available and gold bars in weights typically ranging from one ounce up to 400 ounces. But the market for any of these is not as large or as liquid, and the fees you pay to buy or sell might be higher.

- **To avoid scams, buy coins from dealers who are members of the Professional Numismatists Guild's Accredited Precious Metals Dealer program.** Although government mints offer special-edition "collectible" gold coins directly as keepsakes and gifts, the markups over the market price of gold are so high that these coins don't make sense as investments. For example, you can buy a 2017 American Liberty 225th Anniversary One Ounce Gold Coin from the US Mint for $1,740 (as of March 2018), about 30% higher than recent gold prices. To buy investment-grade gold, you need to go through a dealer. Transactions with dealers typically are conducted over the phone or via e-mail. Once you agree on a price, you wire the money to a dealer (credit cards are not accepted). Your gold is sent by overnight mail and insured for full value. These dealers will buy your gold back from you as well. For a list of about 20 top dealers, go to APMD Dealers.org/apmd-dealers.

● **Pay no more than a 5%-to-6% premium to the current price of gold…and accept no more than a 1%-to-2% discount to the current price when you sell.** These prices reflect the fees that dealers charge. You can check gold prices at GoldPrice.org.

● **Skip gold jewelry as an investment.** It doesn't reliably track the price of gold, and factors such as the appeal of its design and personal tastes can inflate the price far above the value of the actual gold.

● **Store your gold in a safe-deposit box at a local bank.** Even though home safes are convenient, they might be tempting targets for thieves. Figure on paying at least $50 annually for a safe-deposit box plus insurance premiums of $25 annually for every $5,000 worth of coverage, which you often can get through the company that provides your homeowner's insurance.

● **Be aware of IRS restrictions if you want to keep gold in an IRA or a 401(k).** You're allowed to invest only in gold bars or certain gold coins, which you are not allowed to store in your own home or a safe-deposit box. For more information, go to IRS.gov and search for Publication 590-A and the section called "Investment in Collectibles." Note that even though federal law allows it, most brokerages don't allow customers to keep physical gold in their IRAs. Among the exceptions is Fidelity Investments, which allows you to buy gold coins and/or bars for your IRA if you do so from Fidelity. For details, go to Fidelity.com/trading/investment-choices/gold-silver-platinum.

Tax treatment: Gold in taxable accounts is considered a "collectible," meaning that when it is sold, long-term capital gains are taxed at a special 28% rate (or your tax bracket, if less) rather than at the 0%, 15% or 20% rate that applies to stocks.

INVESTING IN "PAPER" GOLD

If you don't want to own physical gold, you can gain exposure through a variety of securities such as stocks and ETFs…

● **Gold ETFs.** These funds issue shares that represent actual gold owned by the funds. The gold is stored in bank vaults in major cities and is regularly audited.

Pros of gold ETFs: The fund shares are simple and inexpensive to buy and sell through most brokerages in both taxable and retirement accounts. The ETFs track the price of gold closely while sparing you the expense and hassle of storing gold.

Cons: Since you don't own physical gold that you can handle and oversee yourself, you may not get the same sense of security that having physical custody of your asset gives you. And the ETFs pay no dividends.

Recommended: iShares Gold Trust (IAU) has an annual expense ratio of 0.25%—lower than the 0.4% for the much larger SPDR Gold Shares (GLD) ETF. Both ETFs reliably track the price of gold.

Tax treatment: Gold ETF shares are considered "collectibles" just like gold coins and subject to the same long- and short-term capital gains tax rates.

● **Gold-miner ETFs.** These ETFs, which own stocks of various gold-mining companies, have greater potential for big gains and big losses than physical gold or ETFs that invest in gold.

Reasons: Once the fixed costs of mining are covered, even a small move in gold prices can sharply increase or reduce a gold-mining company's profits. Also, the stock prices are sensitive to other company-specific factors ranging from a new gold-mine discovery to management mistakes to the political situations in countries where gold mines may be located.

Pros of gold-miner ETFs: These funds provide greater diversification than investing in a single gold-mining company, and they pay cash dividends.

Con: They are much more volatile than physical gold or ETFs that invest in physical gold.

Recommended: VanEck Vectors Gold Miners ETF (GDX) is the largest and most liquid ETF in its category, holding about 50 large-cap stocks including the top gold miners in the world, Barrick Gold and Newmont Mining.

Recent yield: 0.77%.*

*Yields as of April 12, 2018.

Tax treatment: Unlike physical gold or shares of physical-gold ETFs, these funds are subject to the same short- and long-term capital gains taxes as ordinary stocks.

● **Stock of gold "royalty" companies.** These companies don't mine gold themselves. Instead, they provide capital to gold-mining companies in exchange for a percentage of future sales as royalties.

Pros of gold-royalty companies: They don't have to deal with the huge operating expenses and other liabilities involved in actual gold mining. They pay a cash dividend to shareholders, and their shares tend to be less volatile than gold-mining stocks and gold-mining ETF shares.

Con: You're betting on management's prowess in identifying the most cost-effective gold-producing mines around the world.

Recommended: Franco-Nevada Mining (FNV), one of the oldest royalty companies, has 340 royalty-paying assets in places ranging from Australia and South Africa to the Yukon.

Recent yield: 1.33%.

Tax treatment: Same as ordinary stocks.

Now Anyone Can Own a Piece of a Start-Up

Matthew R. Nutting, JD, a senior counsel at Coleman & Horowitt, LLP, where he advises start-ups and investors on business law, Fresno, California. He was a director of the National Crowdfunding Association and coauthor, with David Freedman, of *Equity Crowdfunding for Investors.* CH-Law.com

You can be a "shark"—the kind of shark that invests in promising small businesses that have not begun offering shares to the public on a stock exchange. And you can be that kind of shark even if you have just a few hundred or a few thousand dollars to invest.

How? Through a new fund-raising option. It allows businesses to raise $1 million per 12-month period from anyone—rather than just from wealthy investors. The option, known as "equity crowdfunding," became available May 16, 2016, under the 2012 federal Jumpstart Our Business Startups (JOBS) Act.

Previously, federal securities law allowed such investments only from "accredited" investors who had to meet certain wealth criteria. Now equity crowdfunding gives you ownership shares in the business, unlike ordinary crowdfunding through sites such as Kickstarter that typically gives you early access to a new product or another reward in exchange for supporting a venture—but no ownership stake.

Examples of businesses that have recently used equity crowdfunding: A Boston University professor's firm is developing an artificial pancreas to help children suffering from diabetes. A Brazilian fashion designer sells high-tech clothing that protects people from mosquitoes carrying the Zika virus. A racehorse owner distributes winnings of horses in his elite stable to shareholders. A design engineer's firm is developing a high-tech bathroom scale that scans your body in 3D so that you can track changes not just in your weight but also in your muscle tone and appearance.

About $130 million has been committed to equity crowdfunding by investors since it became available, and hundreds of investment offerings currently are available. That number is expected to grow into the thousands over the next few years.

Of course, this type of investing can be highly risky and isn't for everyone. The Securities and Exchange Commission (SEC) spent several years coming up with safeguards meant to protect small investors from fraud and/or their own naïveté, but the requirements are not as rigorous as those regulating publicly traded companies. Also, keep in mind that in general, about half of all start-ups fail within the first five years.

Here's how small investors can navigate this new world of speculative investments…

HOW IT WORKS

In equity crowdfunding, you buy shares from business start-ups through crowdfunding websites known as portals. Running a portal typically requires a broker-dealer license, and the brokers must meet extensive SEC regulations on crowdfunding. The portals review the credentials of the start-ups.

The active portals currently include Flash Funders.com…NextSeed.com…StartEngine.com

…and WeFunder.com. And dozens more are on the way. You can register with portals for free to gain access to information about "Regulation CF" (crowdfunding) offerings. It's hard to say whether any particular portals are better than others, but it makes sense to start looking at opportunities at WeFunder.com, which recently had the largest number of offerings, about 58.

Each offering provides an extensive overview of the business, known as a "pitch deck," which includes financial statements and a term sheet with details of the investment offering. The business specifies a target amount that it hopes to raise within a defined period of time…the share price…and the minimum investment that it will accept, which typically ranges from $20 to $2,000.

Example: Beta Bionics, the first to raise $1 million, attracted investments averaging $1,300 from 775 investors. The company created the iLet, a wearable medical device that helps manage blood sugar levels for type 1 diabetics by automatically pumping insulin into the body when needed.

Any crowdfunding money you invest is held in escrow until the date an offering closes. If the company fails to raise its target amount, your money is returned. If it successfully raises the target amount, you typically are sent digital documents detailing your share ownership rather than a stock certificate.

INVESTMENT LIMITS

There are legal limits on how much an investor can put into equity crowdfunding within any 12-month period. Anyone can invest $2,200, including assets from IRAs. Whether you can invest more than that within 12 months depends on an SEC formula that accounts for your income and net worth.

If either your income or net worth (excluding the value of your primary residence) is less than $107,000, you can invest up to the greater of $2,200 or 5% of the lower of those two amounts. If both your income and net worth are above $107,000, you can invest up to 10% of the lower amount. But no one can invest more than $107,000 in a 12-month period.

HOW YOU MAKE MONEY

Unlike ordinary publicly traded stocks, equity crowdfunding stocks are highly illiquid. SEC rules generally do not allow you to sell your shares for one year after purchase unless you are selling to an accredited investor, a family member or in the event of your death or divorce. And there is no large, convenient secondary market, such as a stock exchange, to trade crowdfunding shares, so you may have to find a willing buyer on your own.

There are three other ways to profit…

•**The company you invested in is acquired,** and you get part of the proceeds from the sale or stock in the acquiring company.

•**The company generates enough free cash flow to pay you dividends.**

•**The company launches an initial public offering (IPO)** of its stock that helps boost the value of your own shares.

THE BEST STRATEGIES

These guidelines can help you be a successful crowdfunding investor…

•**Invest for the long term.** Don't expect there to be a good opportunity to sell your shares for at least three to 10 years. It often takes that long for a company to become established enough to attract a takeover offer or declare an IPO.

•**Spread your bets.** Venture-capital professionals routinely invest in a number of different start-ups because they know that few end up taking off. One or two successes can make up for multiple losers.

•**Be sure to get answers to some key financial questions**

Examples: What problem does the product or service solve? How does the company differentiate its product or service from competitors in terms of quality, convenience, ease of use, patents, etc.? What are the company's expenses and profit margins? The answers should be found in the company's pitch deck.

THREE TYPES OF OFFERINGS

So far, most equity crowdfunding offerings fall into one of three categories that appeal to different types of investors…

• **Start-ups that have regional appeal or that serve a narrow audience.** These companies may not have the potential for huge profits, but they offer less tangible benefits to a small investor, perhaps contributing to the investor's community or to a cause that the investor cares about.

Example: StartMart Cleveland operates a 35,000-square-foot coworking space that is raising funds to expand and become an integral part of the revitalization of Cleveland's downtown area.

In addition, some of the Kickstarter type of investment money that has been going to socially motivated causes, where profit is not necessarily the primary goal, may now go to equity crowdfunding of such ventures if they are commercially viable businesses.

Example: Green technology that offers environmental benefits.

• **Collective ownership.** These companies invest in expensive assets that you might not be able to invest in on your own, such as commercial real estate or collectibles. They are likely to pay dividends.

Example: The LRF Thoroughbred Fund is managed by one of the largest Thoroughbred racing clubs, Little Red Feather Racing. Its horses have won 223 races in 1,253 starts and grossed $13.6 million in purses over the past 15 years. Investors receive a share of the purse winnings.

• **Innovative products and services.** These start-ups have the most potential for small investors because they could sell nationally and/or attract the attention of a large company and get a buyout offer.

Examples of equity crowdfunding companies with innovative products…

• **ShapeScale.** Its bathroom scale helps users optimize their fitness routines and determine which exercises and diets are working. The scale takes a 360-degree scan of the body and creates a 3D rendering that can be accessed via a smartphone app.

• **Hopsters.** Here's a craft brewery (which is a popular trend) that offers a brew-your-own-beer experience, bar and farm-to-table restaurant all under one roof. The company's original locations in the Boston area plan to expand out nationally to 16 locations by 2020.

Retirement Income for Life— A Unique Way to Get It

Michael Finke, PhD, CFP, professor and director of retirement planning and living in the personal financial-planning department at Texas Tech University, Lubbock.

D o you think you'll live past 85? If so, there's a surprisingly attractive type of investment you can make now that starts paying off big once you reach that age—and never stops as long as you live. And thanks to a new twist, you can easily dip into your retirement accounts to fund it.

Don't be scared off by its name. It's called a Qualified Longevity Annuity Contract, or QLAC for short. And don't be frightened by the fact that it's an annuity—even though there are many types of annuities that have bad reputations and should be shunned.

Unlike many of those annuities, which can be extraordinarily complex and charge exorbitant annual fees, QLACs are easy to understand and have no annual fees. And your payout amount is fixed and guaranteed, unlike with some annuities that are linked to the performance of stocks.

For many people, a QLAC is the best way to guarantee that they won't run out of money if they live past age 85. And it has big tax advantages (see below).

How a QLAC typically works: You hand over a lump sum of money, which can come from a taxable account or a retirement account such as a traditional IRA or 401(k), to an insurance company that provides the annuity. You don't get anything back at first. But once you turn 85, the insurer starts paying you a guaranteed fixed monthly amount. This amount will depend on your age when you purchased the annuity, how much money you paid, your gender (women will receive a lower monthly amount than men because they tend to live longer) and how high interest rates were when you bought the QLAC.

The payments typically are a lot bigger than what you could earn from a long-term bond portfolio that you might invest in on your own.

THE NEW DIFFERENCE

Why are QLACs such a big opportunity now? In the past, there was a serious drawback to longevity annuities for people who had most of their money tucked away in retirement accounts. That was because upon turning age 70½, all investors in traditional IRAs, 401(k)s and some other accounts are required to begin taking required minimum distributions (RMDs) from those accounts—but if a big chunk of the money in those accounts was tied up in a longevity annuity, these people might not be able to withdraw enough to meet the RMD requirement. The result would be substantial penalties.

New solution: In 2014, the IRS approved a twist on the longevity annuity and called it a QLAC, which too many investors still are not taking advantage of. With this type of longevity annuity, you don't have to start meeting RMD requirements from the portion of the account devoted to the QLAC until age 85, when you will start receiving payouts from the annuity. Even better, the payouts themselves are deemed to fulfill the RMD requirements for the invested amount. (Some investors buy QLACs that start paying out at a younger age, but that is uncommon because it diminishes the size of the payouts and the advantage of delaying RMDs.) Only a limited amount of money can be used to buy QLACs—a total up to 25% of the value of all your retirement accounts or up to $130,000, whichever is less (effective Januay 1, 2018).

KEY ADVANTAGES

Because you are not taking RMDs for all those years between age 70½ and 85, you are not paying taxes on those RMDs. You also benefit from what insurance companies call "mortality pooling," which means that the monthly payout amount that the QLAC offers reflects, in part, the money that the insurer won't have to pay out to QLAC holders who die before age 85.

Example of how much a QLAC might pay out: A 65-year-old man who buys a $130,000 QLAC today can expect to receive about $60,000 in income each year starting at age 85 and then as long as he lives. In comparison, if he invested in a portfolio of 20-year AAA-rated corporate bonds at age 65 and wanted to re-create the same payouts from age 85 to 100, he would have to start out with a $304,000 investment, not $130,000 (thus costing

$174,000 more), assuming a 4% interest rate. Since women live longer, a 65-year-old woman who pays $130,000 for a QLAC today would get $45,000 of annual income.

WHO SHOULD NOT BUY A QLAC

The many advantages don't mean that QLACs are perfect for everyone. *They probably won't work for you if one or more of the following applies…*

●**Because of your health and/or family history, you don't expect to live much past age 85.** (Go to the life-expectancy calculator at SSA.gov to determine how long you are likely to live.) If you die before age 85, your heirs get nothing from a QLAC unless you bought a "return-of-premium" death benefit guarantee (see below under strategies).

●**Your assets total enough that you are sure you will have sufficient money to live on no matter how long you live.** In that case, buying a QLAC would not make sense because you don't need the guaranteed income.

●**Your assets total so little that you are likely to exhaust them before the age of 85.** In that case, buying a QLAC would not make sense because you need the money to live on.

Important: Even if you will have plenty of income from such sources as pensions and Social Security, be sure not to invest so much in a QLAC that you are not able to also maintain a sufficient emergency cash fund.

STRATEGIES FOR BUYING A QLAC

Ways to get the most out of a QLAC…

●**Buy only from a major, highly rated insurance company.** Check quotes for QLACs from various insurers at ImmediateAnnuities.com. Check that insurers' credit ratings are A+ or better at AMBest.com or StandardAndPoors.com. However, if an insurer runs into financial problems and is unable to meet its QLAC payouts, each state has an insurance guarantee fund that takes over the obligation but is subject to coverage limitations.

Example: Florida pays out a maximum of $300,000.

●**Calculate how much a QLAC will cost and end up paying out based on a purchase at differ-**

ent ages. You can do this at Immediate Annuities. com for various annuity providers. The younger you are, the cheaper it is to get a QLAC that offers a certain level of income starting at age 85.

Example: If a 65-year-old man wants guaranteed income of about $32,000 a year, he must pay about $70,000 for a QLAC now. A 70-year-old man would have to pay $78,000 to obtain the same income.

Because it is likely that long-term rates will rise, it may make sense to spread QLAC purchases over several years, perhaps buying one per year over four years. That's because higher rates when you buy a QLAC mean higher payouts.

●**Consider adding riders to your QLAC,** but keep in mind that riders will reduce your eventual payouts. *Common riders…*

Cost-of-living-adjustment (COLA) rider: This adjusts payouts starting in the second year. The rider generally pays for itself within five to eight years after payouts begin, depending on how high inflation is.

Return-of-premium rider: With this, your spouse and other heirs receive the initial amount you invested in the QLAC if you die before you get any payouts. For couples, I often suggest that both spouses get a QLAC, if they can afford to, likely making this rider unnecessary. Costs vary widely.

How to Judge a Financial Newsletter

Mark Hulbert, columnist for *MarketWatch* and founder of *The Hulbert Financial Digest.* HulbertRatings.com

---

After 36 years of objectively comparing the performance of investment newsletters, *The Hulbert Financial Digest* ceased publication in 2016. *We found Hulbert's newsletter rankings to be so helpful over the years that we decided to ask its founder and editor, Mark Hulbert, to tell us how our readers can continue to assess the performance of newsletter advice…*

My first suggestion is, once you have chosen an investment newsletter, sign up for a trial subscription, if available, and "paper-trade" the recommendations over that trial period—that is, carry out the recommended transactions on paper rather than actually investing. Pay close attention not only to whether your overall numbers match those quoted by the adviser but also such details as whether the execution prices you would be able to obtain in actual trading are close to what the newsletter reports.

If paper trading an adviser's portfolio is too cumbersome, there are some rules of thumb that can be helpful…

●**Determine whether the adviser maintains a specific model portfolio.** If it includes numbers of shares or portfolio percentages assigned to each holding, all the better. Other things being equal, if you have doubt about a newsletter's trustworthiness, you should give more credence to the performance numbers from an adviser who does provide this information, since advice this precise makes it difficult to fudge the numbers.

I say this because I have found that outright lying about performance by newsletters is relatively rare. Far more common is spinning the numbers in a way that implies something that is false. It's a good sign when a newsletter's portfolio isn't hypothetical but real world—and when the adviser offers to share brokerage statements with customers.

●**Be skeptical of performance claims that are based on the average return of a list of recommended positions.** That's because the order in which those recommendations were made makes a big difference. It's theoretically possible that you could lose a lot of money by following stocks whose average return is quite impressive. For that reason, a newsletter should report its own performance based on the results that would have been experienced by a subscriber following its recommendations at the times that subscribers received the recommendations.

When the newsletter makes performance claims, does it report the precise period over which the performance was produced and the assumptions used to calculate that performance? The more vague the parameters, the less weight you should give them.

- **Short-term performance is mostly noise.** That means, when choosing a newsletter, you should pay barely any attention to recent performance and focus instead on returns produced over many years. My rule of thumb is 15 years, although there is no magical threshold for how long is enough.

- **If a performance claim seems too good to be true, it probably is.** I'm amazed by some investors' gullibility. Those who are incredibly shrewd elsewhere in their lives can become surprisingly naive in the face of newsletters claiming sky-high returns.

Buy Load Funds Without Paying the Load

Roundup of experts on buying load funds without paying sales charges, reported at Kiplinger.com.

Certain funds charge up to 5.75% commissions each time you buy shares—but you can buy them without sales charges through some discount brokers. Fidelity and Schwab each make several load funds available without a load or transaction fee. All of these funds have strong long-term performance records.

US stock funds: Columbia Disciplined Core A (AQEAX)…JPMorgan Small Cap Equity A (VSEAX).

Foreign stock funds: Oppenheimer International Growth A (OIGAX)…Oppenheimer International Small-Mid Company A (OSMAX).

Bond funds: JPMorgan Core Plus Bond A (ONIAX)…Templeton Global Bond A (TPINX)—Schwab does charge a fee on this fund, but Fidelity does not. All these funds, except Columbia Disciplined Core and Oppenheimer International Small–Mid Company A, are available without load or transaction fees at TD Ameritrade. Only Oppenheimer International Growth A and Templeton Global Bond A are available at Vanguard. A 5.75% savings on a $100,000 investment equals $5,750.

Don't Give Up on Bonds

Randy A. Garcia, founder, CIO and CEO of Investment Counsel Company of Nevada, a financial advisory firm, Las Vegas. *Barron's* has ranked him as the number-one financial adviser in the state of Nevada. ICCNV.com

Greg Miller, CPA, CEO of Wellesley Investment Advisors, a financial advisory firm with more than $2.4 billion in assets under management, Wellesley, Massachusetts. He is comanager of the Miller Convertible Bond Fund (MCFAX) and has been ranked by *Barron's* among the top 100 independent advisers. He is author of *Outrunning the Bear: How You Can Outperform Stocks and Bonds with Convertibles.* WellesleyAssetManagement.com

Many financial advisers have been saying that it's time for investors to dump bonds. They say interest rates, which have generally dropped over the past three decades to very low levels, are likely to rise substantially over the next several years. That means investments previously considered safe could generate losses because the value of bonds and bond funds typically falls as rates rise. And investors in low-yield bonds could miss out on better yields as rates rise. That leaves investors who are seeking reliable income from a safe investment in a quandary.

The solution favored by some advisers: Stick with bonds despite the fears. These bond contrarians say that a major bond meltdown is unlikely…and that a carefully selected portfolio of bonds still can be a wise investment, as long as rates don't jump too sharply.

Their reasoning: If you invest in short- and intermediate-term bonds directly and hold them to maturity, it won't matter if they fluctuate in price because you will get their full value at maturity. And if you own a bond fund run by a smart manager, as long as the rate increase is moderate, losses in share price will be mitigated over time by the rising yield that the fund provides as its holdings mature and the assets are reinvested at higher rates. Moreover, rising interest rates typically signal a healthy economy, which could benefit the stock portion of your portfolio and produce good returns overall. If, instead, the economy falters, that would tend to restrain interest rates and strengthen bond prices, helping offset any stock price weakness.

To explain why bonds might be right for you even in this new rising-rate environment, we spoke with two top financial advisers. Randy A. Garcia, who advocates a 50/50 split between stocks and bonds, explains his reasons below…and Greg Miller explains on page 34 why he keeps 100% of client portfolios in "convertible" bonds—a part-stock, part-bond hybrid.

A 50/50 SPLIT

Over the past several years, some of my clients, many of them retirees, have come to me in a panic over fears that interest rates will zoom higher and their bond portfolios, which represent the majority of their wealth, will drop 30% in value in a year, as some bonds have done at certain times in the past.

Bonds do face some significant risks now, and even investors who follow my firm's advice aren't going to get the kind of capital appreciation that they have become accustomed to getting from bonds in the past. But a bond meltdown is highly unlikely. For that to happen, the Federal Reserve would have to push up short-term interest rates by several percentage points over a very short period of time. But current economic conditions do not warrant that approach. US economic growth, as measured by gross domestic product (GDP), is likely to be around 3% for 2018, and inflation is running close to the Federal Reserve's 2% target. That means the Fed will proceed slowly and cautiously.

In past cycles when rates have risen at a reasonable pace, the total returns on bonds (price changes plus income) have been positive. For example, from 1966 to 1981, the annualized return on intermediate-term US government bonds was 5.8%, although that period was marked by high inflation, which makes this performance less impressive. More recently, as rates rose over a 24-month period between mid-2004 and mid-2006, intermediate-term bonds produced a 4.6% total return.

What this means is that bonds can continue to be the best option to anchor your portfolio and provide income. By dividing your investment portfolio evenly between bonds and stocks, you still can profit from possible continued gains in the stock market but give yourself a cushion in case stocks sag.

Of course, that doesn't mean you just continue to hold your existing bond portfolio. Many investors would be wise to make substantial changes…

•**Eliminate long-term bonds.** The longer a bond's maturity, the more its price will drop as interest rates rise. I prefer bonds with maturities in the three-to-eight-year range, a sweet spot where the risk of rising rates is tolerable for the yield you might get.

Focus on bond asset classes that have historically done well in rising-rate environments. My firm's typical portfolio for clients is currently designed to provide a 2% to 2.5% annual yield, about the same as the Barclays US Aggregate Bond Index (considered a proxy for the total bond market). But because our portfolios contain far less in interest rate–sensitive bonds than the index does, they should produce lower volatility and superior returns in a rising interest rate environment. Our allocations in the bond portion of a 50/50 stock/bond portfolio…

88% in funds focused largely on mortgage-backed securities: These are pools of mortgage loans packaged together into a bond and sold by US agencies such as Ginnie Mae and Freddie Mac. They tend to provide higher yields than comparable government bonds and greater flexibility to take advantage of rising interest rates. Unlike with many other types of bonds, payouts are monthly instead of semiannually and you get partial repayment of your principal each month instead of having to wait until the bond matures. That means that you can reinvest both the interest and principal more quickly into securities with higher rates. *Examples of funds…*

For conservative investors: JPMorgan Core Bond Select Fund (WOBDX) divides its assets among mortgage-backed securities, corporate bonds and US Treasuries.

Recent distribution yield: 2.76%.
10-year performance: 4.07%.*

For moderately aggressive investors: Double-Line Total Return Fund (DLTNX) is run by bond impresario Jeffrey Gundlach. He focuses mostly on mortgage-backed securities with a small exposure to US Treasuries.

Recent distribution yield: 3.42%.
Five-year performance: 2.66%.

US Treasury securities, which are in both of the funds above, aren't immune to interest rate spikes, but they do provide protection against global crises

*Performance figures are through August 31, 2018.

in a way that literally no other investment on Earth has. Treasuries rally strongly in environments when investors panic and abandon stocks.

12% in bank-loan securities: These are short-term, adjustable-rate loans that banks make to corporate borrowers. Unlike conventional bonds, yields typically reset every 90 days, keeping pace with rising short-term interest rates. However, many bank loans are below investment-grade. For safety, I don't overload client portfolios with these securities.

Fund example: Fidelity Floating Rate High Income Fund (FFRHX).

Recent distribution yield: 4.31%.

Five-year performance: 3.53%.

STEADY INCOME: THE CONVERTIBLE BONDS SOLUTION
Greg Miller, CPA, Wellesley Investment Advisors

For many investors in recent months, bond markets have been flat and stocks overvalued. If you want to trim your exposure to stocks but don't want to reinvest the money in conventional bonds, convertible bonds may be a good solution. Convertible bonds are a hybrid investment that, like traditional bonds, offer fixed-interest payments and the return of your principal at maturity (as long as the issuer does not default). But convertibles also give you some potential for stock market gains. If you own a convertible bond issued by a company, you have the option of exchanging it for a specific number of shares of the company's stock once the stock hits a specified price. Because of this conversion option, the value of convertibles tends to rise when the issuer's common stock does. On the other hand, if the price of the common stock falls, you're protected. You can hold on to your convertible bond and continue to get a steady flow of income, as well as the eventual return of your principal, no matter how poorly the stock does (again, as long as the issuer does not default).

Drawbacks: Convertibles typically capture only one-half to two-thirds of the underlying stock's appreciation. They also tend to pay lower interest rates than traditional corporate bonds.

Because convertibles can be complex to analyze and to trade, it may be best to invest through a mutual fund. For a list of convertible funds and their performance, go to Snip.ly/QWNH.

Trading Trick

The Wall Street Journal. WSJ.com

Do not trade stocks when the market first opens. This is the most volatile time of the day, when the gap between what sellers want for shares (the ask price) and what buyers are offering (the bid) generally is much larger than it is as the day progresses. One survey found a bid-ask gap of 0.84 percentage points in the first minute of trading, but only 0.08 percentage points 15 minutes later and less than 0.03 percentage points in the final minutes of the trading day. The difference may be pennies per share, but it adds up if you trade often or buy and sell many stocks.

The smaller the gap, the less the chance of buying for too much or selling below the prevailing price. The tendency was especially harmful to small investors on the morning of August 24, 2015, when the market plummeted within the first six minutes of trading—and then half of the losses were erased within minutes after that.

Guru Funds

Charles Sizemore, CFA, is chief investment officer of Sizemore Capital Management, an investment advisory firm in Dallas. He is coauthor of *Boom or Bust: Understanding and Profiting from a Changing Consumer Economy.* SizemoreCapital.com

"Guru" funds let you invest like a major investor. These fairly new exchange-traded funds (ETFs) track SEC documents that reveal what major investors have recently bought and sold, then mimic those moves.

Options include: Direxion iBillionaire Index ETF (IBLN), which invests in stocks based on the portfolios of legendary investors such as Warren Buffett, Carl Icahn and George Soros...Global XG-uru Index ETF (GURU), which tracks investment moves by top-performing hedge fund managers.

3

Get Back at Big Pharma

How to Save on Generic Drugs

Charles B. Inlander, a consumer advocate and health-care consultant based in Fogelsville, Pennsylvania. He was founding president of the nonprofit People's Medical Society, a consumer advocacy organization credited with key improvements in the quality of US health care, and is author or coauthor of more than 20 consumer-health books.

If you're interested in saving money on your health-care expenses—and who isn't?—using generic prescription drugs is a great approach. Studies show that generic medications are 80% to 85% cheaper than comparable brand-name drugs. And in most cases, the medical benefits are equal.

In recent years, however, the cost of many generic drugs, including some that have been on the market for decades, has increased dramatically. For example, the generic antibiotic tetracycline has recently jumped from approximately four cents per pill to over $4. Other drugs have risen at an even greater pace. There are several reasons for the increasing cost of generics. For example, some large generic drug manufacturers are merging, thus limiting competition…and safety regulations are tightening, forcing manufacturers to adopt better safeguards to ensure quality products. And some companies hike their prices simply to increase their bottom lines, which is what happened with the EpiPen in 2016. Fortunately, there are ways to save on generic drugs. *What I recommend…*

●**Comparison shop.** Pharmacies can charge whatever they want for a generic drug. The problem is, most of us do not compare the prices of generics from one pharmacy to another. But you should! Prices on generic drugs can vary by up to 100% from pharmacy to pharmacy in a local area. And all you need to do is make a few phone calls to compare prices. Don't forget to check out pharmacies at big discount retailers such as Walmart. It has many generics for less than $4 per 30-day supply.

Insider tip: Even within the same chain pharmacies, such as Walgreens, Rite Aid or CVS, prices can vary.

Caution: If you use several different pharmacies, let each of the pharmacists know all the drugs you use, even the ones not filled at that store. They can then check for any interactions between drugs.

●**Look for discount coupons.** Many drug manufacturers distribute discount coupons for generic medications. This is their way of getting you to use their drug, but if it works for you, take advantage of the savings. The easiest way to get these coupons is by searching online for "discount coupons for (insert the name of the drug)." Savings can be 50% or more but are generally not usable if combined with any drug insurance you may have. You can also use discount coupon websites, such as GoodRx.com, RxPharmacy Coupons.com or BlinkHealth.com, for discounts ranging from 50% to 95%. These coupons can be used at most pharmacies throughout the country.

Insider tip: Using discount coupons while you're still paying off your drug insurance deductible is a great way to get more for your dollar!

●**Buy by mail.** Most prescription drug insurance plans offer mail-order delivery, which is almost always cheaper than other options and handled by a reputable company. I get three different generic drugs in 90-day supplies (90 tablets per order) by mail order and save 33% over what I'd pay at my local pharmacy. So if you take a drug regularly, ask your doctor to send the prescription to your mail-order pharmacy.

Caution: To ensure quality, use only mail-order pharmacy programs affiliated with major insurers…and avoid online pharmacies, including some Canadian sites. Many have been found to be disreputable, sending wrong pills, wrong dosages and wrong quantities.

Natural Heartburn Remedy

Joan Wilen and **Lydia Wilen,** folk-remedy experts and the authors of *Bottom Line's Treasury of Home Remedies & Natural Cures.* BottomLineStore.com

Chew one to two teaspoons of uncooked oat flakes before swallowing. Oatmeal may help absorb the stomach acid that contributes to heartburn.

Get Your Drugs at 50% Off—or Even Free

Edward Jardini, MD, a family physician at Twin Cities Community Hospital in Templeton, California. He is the author of *How to Save on Prescription Drugs: 20 Cost-Saving Methods.*

Anyone who regularly uses prescription medication knows how pricey drugs can be. Fortunately, there are places where you can buy your drugs for less—or even get them for free. The key is knowing where to look.

Important: Although most low-cost drug programs have income eligibility requirements, do not assume that you won't be accepted into a program just because your income is officially too high. Many programs will consider applications on a case-by-case basis.

Best resources for finding low-cost or free medications…

DRUG DISCOUNT NETWORKS

Some groups connect patients with public and private assistance programs that provide discounted or free drugs to eligible patients. *These include…*

●**Partnership for Prescription Assistance** (888-477-2669 or PPArx.org). This large collaborative network of professional medical organizations, including the American Academy of Family Physicians, and private groups links patients with more than 475 public and private patient assistance programs that offer more than 2,500 drugs at reduced cost or no charge. Income qualifications vary by state.

PHARMACEUTICAL PATIENT-ASSISTANCE PROGRAMS

Major pharmaceutical companies have their own patient-assistance programs that provide many—though not all—drugs for a discount, or even for free, to people who cannot afford them. Eligibility requirements vary—even families earning up to $70,000 a year can qualify. Some companies evaluate the applications on a case-by-case basis.

For a comprehensive directory of patient assistance programs, visit pparx.org or call 888-477-2669. To determine the manufacturer of a particular drug, ask your pharmacist or go online. *Among the pharmaceutical companies with programs…*

●**AstraZeneca's AZ&Me Prescription Savings Program** (800-292-6363, azandmeapp.com).

●**GlaxoSmithKline** (888-825-5249, GSKforyou. com).

●**Lilly TruAssist Patient Assistance Program** (Eli Lilly) (800-545-5962, LillyCares.com).

•**Merck Patient Assistance Program** (800-727-5400, MerckHelps.com).

•**Novartis Patient Assistance Foundation** (888-669-6682, Pharma.us.novartis.com, click on Our Products).

•**Pfizer Helpful Answers** (844-989-7284 [PATH], PfizerRxPathways.com).

Some pharmaceutical companies also offer coupons that can be printed from their websites, as well as discount card programs offering savings on some products. Check the drug manufacturer's website for details.

Expired Drugs Are Still Good

Sharon Horesh Bergquist, MD, a physician with Emory University in Atlanta. She is assistant professor of medicine at Emory University, Atlanta. DrSharonBergquist.com

Do not throw away prescription and over-the-counter drugs just because they are past their expiration dates. These dates are not when the drugs will go bad—they are merely the dates beyond which the drugmakers no longer guarantee full potency. While there is a lot of variability among different drugs, drugmakers tend to be overly conservative with these potency guarantees because they don't want to go to the expense of testing drug longevity over longer periods.

A 20-year Food and Drug Administration study found that 88% of the 122 medicines that were properly stored and tested still were perfectly fine a full year after their expiration dates, and the average expiration date could be extended by five-and-a-half years.

Expired drugs do not "spoil" as some expired foods do. There has not been a single confirmed case of an expired medication becoming toxic. The only potential risk from using an expired medication is that the drug might have lost some of its potency. A past-its-use-by-date pain medication might retain only 90% or 95% of its original potency, for example.

But using expired drugs is not worth the risk for lower potency when your life depends on the potency of the medication.

Examples: Replace your EpiPen when it reaches its expiration date if you have a potentially lethal allergy. Replace your nitroglycerine pills when they reach their expiration date if you have them for a serious heart condition.

Store medications in a cool, dry place out of direct sunlight. A bedroom drawer or kitchen cabinet can be a good spot (though not the kitchen cabinet above the stove). Do not store medications in the bathroom, where heat and humidity can reduce their useful life.

Medicine is especially likely to remain effective if it is in tablet or capsule form. Ointments, creams, liquid medications and any medications requiring refrigeration are significantly less likely to remain viable long after their expiration dates.

Don't Buy Your Drugs Here

Secret-shopper and online surveys and analyses by *Consumer Reports*, ConsumerWorld.org and MarketWatch.com.

Costco usually is the least expensive place to buy prescription medicines. Walmart, Target and Kmart also have low prices. CVS was the most expensive drugstore chain for the drugs being studied, followed by Rite Aid. Over-the-counter medicines also cost less at big-box retailers than at drugstores.

Read the Fine Print Without Glasses

Joan Wilen and **Lydia Wilen,** folk-remedy experts and the authors of *Bottom Line's Treasury of Home Remedies & Natural Cures.* BottomLineStore.com

When you want to read the fine print (and you forgot your reading glasses), try this: Make a fist, leaving a small hole between your palm and pinky. Bring your fist up to your eye, look through that small hole and focus on the letters or numbers you want to read. For some unknown reason, the small channel of light entering your eye clears your vision.

You can also puncture a small hole in a piece of paper with a pen point. Hold the paper hole to your eye, focus on the number and see it come into view—larger and sharp.

How to Repair Broken Eyeglasses

Neil Hounchell, former owner of National Eyewear Repair, a Phoenix-based company that offered a repair-by-mail service for eyeglass wearers outside the Phoenix area.

Many eyeglass repairs are best left to optometrists or other eyeglass-repair professionals, but some can be tackled quickly and cheaply on one's own…

•**Loose hinges.** Eyeglass hinges often become stretched out over time. When that happens, the eyeglass arms no longer fit snugly against the temples, and the glasses become prone to sliding down the nose or falling off entirely.

What to do: Though this may be a temporary measure until you can get to an optometrist, many people find it works so well that they don't bother seeing a professional. Take a pair of very small rubber bands, and slide one up each arm of the glasses until the rubber bands rest in the V-shaped gaps formed between the frame and arm when the arms are not fully extended. (Crafts stores often sell very small rubber bands.)

These rubber bands will serve as springs, pushing the arms of the glasses tighter against the temples. If you don't like the way they look on your glasses, use a marker that matches the color of the eyeglass frame to color the rubber bands before sliding them into place. They might not be noticeable at all.

•**Lost screw for the hinge.** The tiny screws that hold eyeglass hinges together occasionally fall out—and they're so small that they often get lost.

What to do: The eyeglass repair kits sold in dollar stores, discount stores and elsewhere typically contain a small screwdriver and an assortment of tiny replacement screws. But there's no guarantee that any of these screws will be the right size for your glasses. If you use one, check it each day for the first week or so to confirm that it has not started to come loose. If this tiny screw is even a fraction of a millimeter narrower than the original one, it could fall out, too.

If you don't have a screw of the appropriate size, a paper clip can serve as a temporary substitute. Feed one end of the paper clip through the hinge, then use a pair of needle-nose pliers to bend it just above and below the hinge so that it can't fall out. Use a wire cutter (often built into the same needle-nose pliers) to trim off the excess paper clip metal.

•**Lens that pops out of rimless or semi-rimless frames.** Rimless and semi-rimless frames typically use a thin monofilament—essentially a piece of fishing line—to hold lenses in place.

What to do: After a lens pops out, loop a piece of ribbon around the monofilament, then use this ribbon to gently pull the monofilament aside so that you can slip the lens partially into place in the frame. Next, slide the ribbon down the length of the monofilament, gently tugging the monofilament into the groove on the edge of the lens as you do so. When the monofilament is completely in the grove, pull the ribbon free. If the ribbon is too tightly trapped between the monofilament and the lens to remove it without popping the lens back out, use scissors to cut the ribbon near where it passes between the monofilament and lens to make it easier to work free.

Two repairs NOT to do…

•**Do NOT use superglue on broken plastic frames.** Mainstream glues generally will not repair a plastic eyeglass frame for long, and the residue this glue leaves behind will make it harder for a professional to later repair the glasses.

•**Do NOT use lens-scratch repair kits.** There are products available that claim to remove eyeglass lens scratches. But they will either do a poor job removing scratches or will distort your vision when you look through the lens.

4

Insurance Scams

7 Surprising Things That Could Get Your Homeowner's Insurance Canceled

Laura Adams, senior insurance analyst at Insurance Quotes.com. She is host of the free weekly *Money Girl* podcast. QuickandDirtyTips.com/money-girl

Y ou might not be surprised if your homeowner's insurance premium is increased after you file a costly claim. But did you know that the insurer might go a step further and cancel your coverage or refuse to renew it? And it isn't just claims that can torpedo a policy. Insurers sometimes terminate a policy or raise premiums to prohibitively high levels for much more surprising reasons—ranging from a drop in your credit score to your purchase of a trampoline to a broken gutter.

Having a policy terminated can be more than a minor inconvenience. When you seek to replace your policy elsewhere, other insurers might quote very steep premiums or decline to offer coverage at all. That's because when an insurer terminates a policy, the insurer typically notes that it has done so in a database that other insurers check before

approving applicants. That policy termination can scare off other issuers.

Here, seven surprising reasons your homeowner's insurance could be terminated or your premiums pushed up...

THINGS SEEMINGLY UNRELATED TO YOUR HOME (OR TO YOU)

• **Credit score.** A drop in your credit score could result in nonrenewal of your policy or a dramatic increase in your premiums. How dramatic? In 37 states, people with poor credit pay more than twice as much as people with excellent credit, on average, according to a 2014 study. Only a small number of states, including Hawaii, prohibit homeowner's insurance issuers from considering credit scores. (Credit scores also seem to have little effect on homeowner's insurance in Florida.) Insurers have determined that people who are responsible with credit also tend to be responsible with home maintenance and make fewer claims.

If your insurer tells you that your credit score is among the reasons your policy is not being renewed or your rates are rising, examine your credit report for any inaccurate information that might be unfairly pulling down your score. (You can obtain a free copy of your report each year at the website AnnualCredit Report.com.) If you find inaccuracies, inform your insurer of this and ask whether it would reconsider its decision if you get the problem sorted out. If not, resolve the credit problem as quickly as possible and then ask to be "re-rated" by the insurer.

Helpful: If there is no easy way to improve your score, apply for homeowner's coverage through small and midsize regional homeowner's insurance issuers, which are less likely to check scores. An insurance-shopping website, insurance broker or your state department of insurance could help you locate these smaller issuers.

•**Driving infractions.** Believe it or not, speeding tickets can affect your homeowner's insurance. Insurers have concluded that irresponsible drivers tend to be irresponsible home owners, too.

There are no hard-and-fast rules here, but if you get more than two moving violations that put points on your driving record in a year—or even one serious citation such as for a DUI—you could have trouble maintaining your homeowner's insurance at a reasonable rate. It's worth investigating whether your state offers any way to quickly remove some of the bad-driving "points" that will appear on your record, such as by taking a driver-safety course. It's these points—not the violations themselves—that can catch the notice of homeowner's insurance providers.

•**Insurance claims by your home's previous owners.** If the home's previous owners filed multiple claims, that could increase the risk that your policy will not be renewed if you make even one or two claims. This is particularly likely if the claims are similar and point to a serious underlying problem with the home, such as wiring issues that have led to multiple fires.

What to do: If you have owned your home for less than seven years, request the property's Comprehensive Loss Underwriting Exchange (CLUE) report. You can obtain this report for free as often as once per year at PersonalReports.LexisNexis.com (select "Personal Property Report" under "FACT Act Disclosure Reports"). If you discover multiple claims by the prior owners, you should consider that an additional reason to pay for covered repairs of modest size out of pocket rather than file claims. (By law, CLUE reports can in-clude claims only up to seven years old—less in some states—so if you have owned your home longer than that, there's no reason to check for former owners' claims.)

Helpful: Before purchasing a home, insist that the seller provide you with the property's CLUE report. This report could point to underlying problems.

THINGS THAT MIGHT SEEM INCONSEQUENTIAL

•**Small claims.** It isn't just big claims that scare off home insurers. Repeated small claims can lead to termination, too. Insurers sometimes consider policyholders who file repeated small claims to be nuisances who are not worth the trouble.

What to do: Increase your deductible to at least $1,000 and preferably $2,000 or $2,500 to remove the temptation to make small claims. Use the money this saves you in premiums to pay for minor home repairs.

•**Asking questions.** Calling your insurer to discuss the possibility of making a claim could lead to an entry in your CLUE report. Having a number of CLUE entries that your insurer deems excessive can cause nonrenewal.

Do not contact your insurer to discuss a potential claim unless it is extremely likely that you actually will make a claim. If you feel you must call your insurer to discuss the possibility of making a claim, speak in hypothetical terms and make it very clear that you are not currently making a claim.

Example: "I'm not filing a claim, but in theory, if someone had the following happen, would it be covered?" There is anecdotal evidence that phrasing things this way reduces the odds that the call will be logged into your CLUE file, though it still is possible.

•**Home-maintenance issues visible from the road.** Your insurer might be watching you. Insurers sometimes conduct unannounced drive-by inspections of properties. If your property is deemed to have maintenance issues, you might receive a letter threatening cancellation or nonrenewal if repairs are not made within 60 or 90 days.

Inspectors often focus on things such as missing shingles or broken gutters that can lead to greater home damage and insurance claims, but even basic upkeep issues such as an unmowed lawn could trigger unwanted insurer attention. To insurers, such things can be signs that the home is not being well-maintained in other, more important ways.

Warning: It is especially important for landlords to keep the portion of property that is visible from the road well-maintained—drive-by inspections of rental properties are particularly common.

●**Trampolines, tree houses, swimming pools and dog breeds that are considered dangerous.** Many home owners do not realize that their policies require them to inform the insurer if they obtain one of these potential liability risks. Some policies prohibit these things altogether or have detailed rules that must be followed if they are obtained—perhaps a fence is required around a pool, for example. Read your homeowner's policy carefully before obtaining any of these things.

Similar: Many homeowner's policies restrict or prohibit renting out the home, such as through Airbnb. Violating this rule could result in policy cancellation or nonrenewal.

Easy Way to Calculate Life Insurance Needs

The New York Times.

Take your salary and multiply it by 20—if your salary is $50,000, that means you need $1 million in insurance. Buy a 20-year term policy for that amount. Term insurance is the least expensive kind and is pure insurance—not an investment or savings account. In most cases, it is the best type to have to protect your loved ones against an economic loss, which is the purpose of life insurance.

Collect on a Lost Life Insurance Policy

Jim Miller, an advocate for older Americans, writes "Savvy Senior," a weekly information column syndicated in more than 400 newspapers. He is based in Norman, Oklahoma. SavvySenior.org

Every year, hundreds of millions of dollars in life insurance proceeds go unclaimed because the beneficiaries simply don't know that the policies exist. If you suspect that your deceased parent, spouse or other relative may have had a policy naming you as a beneficiary but you are not sure how to find it, here are some strategies and resources that can help you search, assuming that you have access to these sources of information…

●**Personal records.** If the person died recently, start by checking his/her will and estate papers and then searching for a policy in drawers, files and a safe-deposit box if one exists. Also look for records of premium payments or bills from an insurer. Ask the deceased person's former insurance agent, financial planner, employer and/or accountant whether there were any life insurance policies. And review the deceased's recent income tax returns looking for interest income or interest expense for a life insurance policy—some insurance policies include investment accounts.

If you suspect that an insurer underwrote a policy, contact the insurer's claims office and ask—in most cases, the insurer will tell you without requiring proof of your relationship to the deceased.

●**Policy-locator service.** The National Association of Insurance Commissioners (NAIC), an insurance regulatory support organization, recently created a national policy-locator service. If you request a free search at Locator.NAIC.org, the NAIC asks its 463 member insurance companies to search records for any life insurance policies in the name of the deceased. If any are found, the insurer will contact you within 90 days and request information about your affiliation with the deceased before giving you pertinent information about the policy.

●**Unclaimed property.** If your deceased relative died more than two years ago, his insurance benefit may have already been turned over to the unclaimed property office in the state where the policy was purchased. The National Association of Unclaimed Property Administrators website (Unclaimed.org) has links to all state programs that will allow you to do a free search for such benefits online.

●**Claiming benefits.** Once you have found a policy, contact the insurance company to ask what information it needs to process your claim.

Medicare Hospital Trap

Philip Moeller, author of *Get What's Yours for Medicare.* He is a research fellow at Sloan Center on Aging & Work at Boston College and writes a column at PBS.org called "Ask Phil, the Medicare Maven." GetWhatsYours.org

Not every patient in a hospital has been admitted to the hospital. Hospitals, under pressure to reduce their readmission rates, recently have been holding an increasing percentage of patients "for observation" rather than formally admitting them—including patients who are in the hospital for days.

That lack of a formal hospital admission can have devastating financial consequences for Medicare patients who require rehabilitation in a nursing home following their hospital stays. Original Medicare will pay for up to 20 days of rehabilitation at a skilled nursing facility—if the nursing home stay occurs immediately after the patient was admitted to a hospital for a minimum of three consecutive midnights. Patients given observation status do not qualify under this rule and might have to pay thousands of dollars out of pocket as a result. A federal law that took effect in 2016 requires hospitals to notify patients that they have been given observation status—previously, patients often did not learn about this until they received their bills, if at all.

If you or a loved one is given observation status and a nursing home stay could follow, ask the doctor whether he/she can change this status decision...contest the decision with the hospital's ombudsman...and if that fails, follow the appeal

instructions on the Medicare "summary notice" that arrives in your mail every three months, assuming that you receive medical treatment.

Long-Term-Care Warning

Phyllis Shelton, president of LTC Consultants in Nashville, which trains long-term-care insurance agents. She is author of *Protecting Your Family with Long-Term Care Insurance.* GotLTCI.com

A move to a foreign country can devastate a person's long-term-care (LTC) insurance benefits. Many LTC policies do not cover foreign care at all, and those that do tend to significantly restrict benefits, sometimes slashing them to half what the policy would pay in the US...or to just one year of coverage. Even those restricted benefits might be difficult to use abroad if the policy pays for only licensed caregivers and there is no licensing procedure in the country.

For details concerning how much your LTC insurance covers in countries outside the United States, look for a heading labeled "International Benefits" (or something similar) in your policy or check the sections of the policy that list exclusions.

If your policy does not offer extensive foreign benefits, you still could retire overseas and then return to the US if you require extensive long-term care.

The Federal Long Term Care Insurance Program, which is available to current and retired federal and postal employees as well as members of the military, offers relatively strong international coverage. It provides up to 80% of the policy's normal benefit amounts when policyholders seek care outside the US.

John Hancock policies provide 100% of the normal benefit amount abroad, but for only one year. Genworth policies tend to cover up to four years of nursing home coverage abroad with benefits capped at 50% of the normal benefit amount...and one year of home health care capped at 25%.

Drug Not Covered? Challenge the Rejection

Kiplinger.com

If Medicare will not cover a drug you need, challenge the rejection. Make a note of the drug name and dosage you were prescribed, the name of the pharmacy that declined to fill the prescription and the date on which you tried to fill it. Call your Part D plan, and ask for a coverage determination, which explains the decision in writing—the plan usually has 72 hours to provide one, or you can ask for an expedited 24-hour response. If the plan says the drug is not on its formulary or is restricted in some way, ask for an "exception"—which your doctor must be willing to back up by saying in writing why this drug and no other is the one you must take. If your doctor's letter does not get you approval, you have 60 days to ask for a "redetermination." Nearly 80% of initial denials ultimately were approved in 2013 (latest data available).

If You're a Widow or Widower...

Stephen Brobeck, senior fellow, Consumer Federation of America, a nonprofit association of nearly 300 consumer groups, Washington, DC. ConsumerFed.org

Widows and widowers are charged higher auto insurance premiums than married people—14% higher, on average. Among major insurers, only State Farm seems not to consider marital status when setting premiums. Insurers explain the disparity by saying that married people are more likely to be safer drivers than single people. Widows and widowers should inform their insurance agents that they are single because a spouse has passed away and ask for any discount given to married people. Insurers sometimes are willing to be flexible.

Create a Visual Home Inventory

Jeff Wignall, a professional photographer who has photographed home, municipal and estate collections for home owners, municipalities and insurance companies. He is author of more than 15 books, including *The Photographer's Master Guide to Color*. He was a longtime contributing editor to *Popular Photography* magazine. JeffWignall.com

As your insurance company will tell you, having a comprehensive visual record of your home's contents in the event of a fire, natural disaster or someone burglarizing your home is one of the best ways to prove that those things were in your home. A visual inventory will speed payment on your insurance claims and likely result in higher payment because you have a more detailed and comprehensive tally.

You can use any still camera or video camera, including your cell phone camera, shooting a mix of video and stills. It is a good weekend project, working a few hours per day.

●**Shoot exterior views,** either still or video, to demonstrate the "before" condition of your home and your landscaping. First take an "establishing" shot that shows the home and surroundings. Then take individual shots of expensive items such as barbecue grills, lawn furniture and exterior lighting fixtures. Then head into your garage or shed to shoot yard tools and equipment such as mowers, snowblowers and generators. Anything you can move to the driveway, such as your car or bicycles, can be shot there.

●**Shoot an overall shot of each room on video,** and then create a record of items with still photos.

●**Document individual items.** Expensive items such as electronics, jewelry and collectibles/antiques should be photographed individually and from various angles. With electronics, be sure to show brand and model. Open drawers (your silverware drawer, for instance) and jewelry boxes to show the contents. If you collect books, shoot wide views of each bookshelf, then take individual shots of rare volumes. Stamp and coin collections can be scanned on a flatbed scanner—the same one that you use to scan documents for your computer (a simple flatbed scanner sells for between $50 and $100, but many all-in-one printers have a scanning function built in).

•**Create a simple studio.** To speed the shooting of small items, make a simple studio space using a sheet of white poster board as a background. I simply tape the poster board to a wall and curve it down to the surface of a card table to make a seamless background. Use light from a nearby window or simple desk lights or your camera's built-in flash.

•**Don't forget closets.** Take wide views but also include individual shots of designer items (and labels). To get a good shot, hang an item on the back of a closet door or lay it on a bed.

•**Make copies.** Once your record is complete, download all of the videos and photos to your computer and then burn multiple DVD copies (and/or save to the cloud) and store your discs off premises.

For free online help: The Insurance Information Institute provides links to free software (and apps for iPhones, iPads and Android devices) sponsored by insurance providers that will guide you through creating and updating a visual inventory at KnowYourStuff.org.

5

Medical Miseries

Need an MRI? Shop Around for the Best Price

Bill Kampine, SVP of Healthcare Bluebook, a Nashville-based health-care price- and quality-transparency company that provides price-transparency tools to employers and consumers. HealthcareBluebook.com

The same MRI can cost $400 at one facility and $4,000 at another. The high-priced providers get away with this because few patients shop around for a better price. Doing so could save you a fortune if you do not have health insurance or have not met the deductible of a high-deductible insurance plan. *To get a good price, follow these steps...*

1. Ask your doctor's office for the "CPT" (Current Procedural Terminology) code for the MRI you require.

2. Type "MRI" and your city or state into a search engine to locate nonhospital scan providers in your area. These almost always charge much less than hospital imaging departments.

3. Call every nonhospital MRI provider in your area, and ask for the MRI price. Provide the CPT code, and note whether you have health insurance or Medicare coverage. (Insurance coverage could affect the price, and you need to find out if the facility is "in-network.") If you don't have insurance,

ask for the facility's cash-pay price and whether it offers a prompt-pay discount if you pay the entire amount at the time of service.

4. Find out what's a reasonable price at my site, HealthcareBluebook.com, or use FAIRHealth Consumer.org's free "Estimate Your Healthcare Expenses" tool.

If all the prices you have been quoted are higher, expand your search to include MRI providers in surrounding areas. Driving 100 miles might save you hundreds of dollars, maybe thousands.

5. Confirm that the facility is of reasonable quality. It probably will be—studies have found no correlation between price and quality in this area. But to be sure, ask the facility—Do you have a "3.0 Tesla" (or "3T") MRI machine? This is the current industry-standard technology, so not having one suggests that the facility is not up-to-date. Are you in-network with the major insurance provider(s) in the area? Ask this even if you do not have insurance—being in-network with major insurers suggests that the facility does competent work.

OTC Hack for Toenail Fungus

Study by researchers at US Air Force 375th Medical Group, Family Medicine Residency Program, Belleville, Illinois, published in *Journal of the American Board of Family Medicine.*

Vicks VapoRub fights toenail fungus. It can help fight a stubborn toenail condition called ony-chomycosis, which is caused by a fungus. Among patients who rubbed Vicks into infected toenails every day for 48 weeks, 83% had improvement in the nails' appearance, and the fungus was eliminated in 28%.

Contact Lens Eye Emergency

Karen Larson, former editor of *Bottom Line/Personal.* Bottom LineInc.com

I ripped a soft contact lens trying to take it out of my eye. I wasn't sure if a piece of the lens still was in my eye or not. Two days later, on a Sunday morning, a painful, swollen eye prompted me to go to Urgent Care and subsequently to an ophthalmologist's office. Sure enough, pieces of contact lens were stuck under my eyelid.

This problem is relatively common, says Peter Michalos, MD, the ophthalmologist who fished the pair of lens fragments out of my eye. He is an associate professor of clinical ophthalmology at Columbia University who also has a private practice in Southampton, New York. *He says that contact lens ripping is most likely when we keep our contacts in too long, as well as when we…*

●**Spend long hours in air-conditioning in the summer or outdoors in the winter.** Both situations can dry out eyes and contacts.

●**Take long airplane flights.** Air is extremely dry on most airplanes.

●**Age.** Once we enter our 50s or 60s, we produce fewer tears.

To reduce the odds that a dry soft contact lens will rip, put a few drops of contact lens rewetting solution in each eye before taking out lenses, advises Dr. Michalos. If you struggle to get eyedrops into your eyes—if you have arthritis or tremors, for example—Dr. Michalos recommends a $10 gadget called Eye Drop Helper (available at EyeDrop Helper.com). Use rewetting solution, not traditional eyedrops—traditional eyedrops contain chemicals that reduce the amount of oxygen that gets through contact lenses.

If a soft contact does fall apart in your eye, you'll probably have to see an ophthalmologist. Lens fragments tend to migrate toward the back of the eye, where it is difficult for lens wearers to retrieve them on their own.

Dentist Says Time for X-Rays?

Jay W. Friedman, DDS, MPH, a Los Angeles dentist who received the 2012 John W. Knutson Distinguished Service Award in Dental Public Health from the American Public Health Association. He is author of *The Intelligent Consumer's Complete Guide to Dental Health.*

Some dentists recommend patients get dental X-rays every year—even though the vast majority of patients can go two to three years between X-rays. There are only a small number of legitimate reasons why new X-rays might be prudent after just one year…

●**Your dentist saw some sign that a problem could be developing on last year's X-rays.** He/she might have made a note on your chart to "watch this" and want to take an X-ray to see if the situation is growing worse and requires action.

●**You have developed new symptoms.**

Dental insurance plans typically will pay for "bitewing" X-rays (showing the upper and lower back teeth in a single view) every year, so some dentists reason that skipping them deprives patients of a service they could have without any out-of-pocket costs. (Other types of dental X-rays might be covered less frequently.) Dental practices have a financial incentive to take annual X-rays, too—doing so significantly increases the income they generate from patients with healthy teeth and gums. Few dentists set out to overtreat or overcharge patients, but many were trained to take new X-rays each year, and in this fee-for-service profession, they have little motivation to question whether that's really necessary.

Unfortunately, patients who do not have dental insurance might have to pay perhaps $60 to $80 for a set of bitewing X-rays and potentially more for other types of X-rays. Taking unnecessary X-rays also subjects patients to unnecessary radiation. The amount of radiation received from typical dental X-rays is small, but the effects of radiation exposure are cumulative.

What to do: If you have had dental X-rays taken within the past two years and your dentist recommends taking another set, ask why they are needed. Turn down these X-rays if the dentist cannot point to a specific reason such as those noted earlier.

Save on Pet Meds

Consumer Reports. ConsumerReports.org

Don't pay extra for pet medicines from your vet—markups can be more than 100%. If your pet is taking a medication that also is prescribed to humans, as is often the case, you might be able to have the prescription filled inexpensively at a chain drugstore, supermarket pharmacy or big-box retailer. To find free or discounted programs for vaccines, spaying and neutering, microchip implants and pet supplies, go to HumaneSociety.org and type "afford" in the search box.

Physicians on Probation

Consumer Reports. ConsumerReports.org

Thousands of practicing physicians in the US are on probation for offenses ranging from unprofessional treatment of patients to drug addiction and sexual misconduct. Doctors' disciplinary records are

kept in a database called the National Practitioner Data Bank, which is not open to the public. Patients must ask state medical boards for data.

6 Common Medical Tests Most People Don't Need

Tanveer P. Mir, MD, immediate past chair of the Board of Regents of the American College of Physicians and medical director of palliative care and ethics at Florida Hospital, Orlando. She is board-certified in internal medicine, geriatrics and hospice and palliative medicine and formerly served as associate chief of geriatrics and palliative medicine at North Shore-Long Island Jewish Medical Center, New York.

You expect your doctor to order tests during routine checkups or to investigate unexplained symptoms. But do you need all of those tests? Maybe not.

The American College of Physicians and other groups have joined a project called Choosing Wisely that uses evidence-based medicine to identify tests, treatments and medical screenings that most people don't need. *Common offenders…*

CT SCANS FOR HEADACHES

If you start getting migraines or pounding headaches, you'll want to know why. So will your doctor.

Result: About one in eight patients who sees a doctor for headaches or migraines winds up getting scans.

Yet CT scans find abnormalities in only 1% to 3% of cases—and many of those abnormalities will be harmless or have nothing to do with the headaches. The scans are highly unlikely to change your diagnosis or affect your treatment options. But doctors order them anyway.

The tests create their own problems. Excess radiation is one concern. So is the likelihood that a scan will reveal "incidentalomas," a somewhat tongue-in-cheek name for unimportant abnormalities that can lead to additional (and unnecessary) tests.

Bottom line: CT scans are rarely needed because doctors can readily diagnose headaches just by talking with patients and taking detailed medical histories.

Who might need it: You might need a scan if your headaches are accompanied by neurological symptoms (such as a seizure or fit, change in speech or alertness or loss of coordination) or if you suffered from an accident that involved a sharp blow to the head.

PREOPERATIVE CHEST X-RAY

If you've ever had an operation, you almost certainly had one or more chest X-rays. Many hospitals require them to "clear" patients for surgery.

What are the X-rays for? No one really knows. They have become a part of the presurgical routine even though a study published in *JAMA* found that only 2% of the X-rays provided useful information for the surgeon/anesthesiologist. Most patients don't need them.

Bottom line: If you're generally healthy, tell your doctor you don't want the X-ray.

Who might need it: Patients who have been diagnosed with heart or lung disease or who are having surgery on the heart, lungs or other parts of the chest should get the X-ray. So should those who are older than 70 and haven't had a chest X-ray within the last six months (the likelihood of an abnormal X-ray is higher in these people).

HEART DISEASE STRESS TEST

If you're between the ages of 40 and 60, there's a chance that you've had (or been advised to have) an exercise stress test to determine your risk for heart disease and heart attack. A 2010 study that looked at nearly 1,200 people in this age group found that nearly one out of 10 had been given a stress test.

Unless you're having symptoms of heart disease—such as chest pain and shortness of breath—a stress test will probably be useless. The cost is considerable—you can expect to spend $200 to $300.

Stress tests tend to produce unclear results. This can lead to additional tests, including coronary angiography—an expensive test that exposes you to as much radiation as 600 to 800 chest X-rays.

Bottom line: You're better off reducing your particular risks—giving up smoking, controlling hypertension and lowering cholesterol—than getting a stress test.

Who might need it: Agree to an exercise stress test only if you're having symptoms of heart disease or your doctor suspects that you already have heart disease.

IMAGING FOR BACK PAIN

There's a good chance that your doctor will order an MRI or a CT scan if you complain of sudden back pain. Yet 80% to 90% of patients will improve within four to six weeks. You might need an imaging test when symptoms are severe or don't improve, but there's no reason to rush it—or to expose yourself to unnecessary radiation from a CT scan.

Bottom line: Don't agree to a test that's unlikely to change your diagnosis or treatment options. Since most back-pain patients will recover with physical therapy, over-the-counter painkillers and other "conservative measures," imaging tests usually are unnecessary.

Who might need it: A scan typically is warranted if your doctor suspects a compression fracture from osteoporosis…you have burning pain down a leg that doesn't improve…or you're also having numbness, muscle weakness, a loss of bowel/bladder control or other neurological symptoms.

PELVIC EXAM

Some gynecologists and primary-care physicians believe that a pelvic exam is a good way to detect ovarian cancer or problems with the ovaries, uterus, vulva or other pelvic structures. It's usually combined with a Pap test to screen for cervical cancer.

A study published in *JAMA* concluded that routine pelvic exams are unlikely to detect ovarian cancer. Nor are they likely to help women with uterine fibroids or cysts.

Bottom line: The routine pelvic exam is a low-yield test that should be discontinued, particularly because it makes women anxious and uncomfortable.

Important: Don't forgo regular Pap smears—you can get them without having a pelvic exam. Women 30 years old and older should have a Pap smear—along with testing for the human papillomavirus (HPV), which is done at the same time—every five years. For those with a family history of cervical cancer or other risk factors, the Pap test should be repeated every three years.

PSA TEST

For a long time, men were routinely advised to have this blood test, which measures prostate-specific antigen (PSA) and screens for prostate cancer. Now the American Cancer Society and some other groups advise against it.

The test can't differentiate harmless cancers (the majority) from aggressive ones. Studies have shown that men who test positive are only marginally less likely to die from prostate cancer than those who were never tested...and they're more likely to have biopsies, surgeries and other treatments that will make no difference in their long-term health, that pose serious risks of their own and that cause unnecessary anguish.

Bottom line: Men between the ages of 50 and 74 should discuss the test and the possible risks and benefits with their doctors.

Who might need it: Those with a family history of prostate cancer—particularly a cancer that affected a close relative, such as a sibling or parent—may want to get tested.

Don't Trust the Thyroid Test

Pamela Wartian Smith, MD, MPH, MS, codirector of the Master's Program in Medical Sciences with a concentration in metabolic and nutritional medicine at Morsani College of Medicine, University of South Florida. Dr. Smith also is director of the Michigan- and Florida-based Center for Personalized Medicine. She is author of *What You Must Know About Thyroid Disorders & What to Do About Them.* Center ForPersonalizedMedicine.com

The standard test for low thyroid might not provide a clear answer. You could test normal but still have thyroid function that's at the lower end of the range—which, for some people, is enough to cause problems.

Low thyroid is diagnosed with a simple blood test for thyroid-stimulating hormone (TSH). If you have low thyroxine, a thyroid hormone, your body will produce high levels of TSH to compensate. Peo-

ple with significantly elevated TSH—say, a reading of 5.0 mIU/L (milli-international units per liter) or higher—have obvious hypothyroidism.

What if you test within a normal range but still are having symptoms? It doesn't mean you're imagining things. Laboratories have different reference ranges, the measurements that are considered normal. In 2004, endocrinologists suggested a change in the normal range so that a TSH reading of 2.5 was the upper limit. But for some people, normal isn't optimal. I've found that patients can suffer from thyroid-related symptoms even when they "pass" the TSH test.

This is why it is very important to have a complete thyroid panel done when you see your doctor and not just a TSH and free T4. An entire thyroid panel includes TSH, free T3, free T4, reverse T3 and thyroid antibodies.

This Meal Is the Worst for Your Health

Lindsay Moyer, MS, RDN, senior nutritionist, Center for Science in the Public Interest, Washington, DC, and co-author of the group's Xtreme Eating 2016 list, quoted at WebMD.com.

The worst meal for your health is *The Whole Hog Burger* with 2,850 calories. Sold by Uno Pizzeria & Grill, the burger contains four meats—beef, sausage, bacon and pepperoni—plus three cheeses. It is served with fries and onion rings, but those calories are not included in the count. The burger contains 62 grams of saturated fat and nearly 9,800 milligrams of sodium.

Other foods rated especially bad for health: Dave & Buster's Short Rib and Cheesy Mac Stack, a 1,910-calorie beef sandwich topped with macaroni and cheese that comes with a side of tater tots...and *Buffalo Wild Wings Dessert Nachos,* a 2,100-calorie fried flour tortilla with ice cream, cheesecake bites, and chocolate and caramel sauce.

Bison Burgers Are Better

Wayne Askew, PhD, professor emeritus, division of nutrition, University of Utah, Salt Lake City, quoted in *Self* magazine.

Order bison burgers instead of beef. Bison usually is grass-fed, not grain-fed, so it contains more healthful omega-3 fatty acids than beef does, and it has more iron.

Women Need to Know Stroke Risks

National survey of 1,000 women by The Ohio State University Wexner Medical Center, Columbus.

Few women understand their unique risk factors for stroke. Only 11% of those surveyed knew that being pregnant, having lupus or migraine headaches or taking oral contraception or hormone replacement therapy are stroke risk factors specific to women. And only 10% knew that hiccups combined with atypical chest pain can be an early warning sign of stroke. Some risk factors, such as high blood pressure and smoking, are the same for both men and women.

Vitamin D for Prostate Cancer

Bruce Warren Hollis, PhD, a professor of pediatrics, biochemistry and molecular biology at Medical University of South Carolina, Charleston, and coinvestigator of a study of 37 men scheduled for elective prostatectomies, presented at the 249th National Meeting & Exposition of the American Chemical Society.

Vitamin D may eliminate the need for prostate cancer surgery, reports Bruce Warren Hollis, PhD. A man who is diagnosed with low-grade prostate cancer can consider taking 4,000 IU of vitamin D a day during a one-year waiting period. It slows the progression of low-grade prostate cancer and even may reverse it—eliminating any reason to remove the prostate.

How it appears to work: Vitamin D fights inflammation within the prostate gland.

20-Second Stroke-Risk Test

Yasuharu Tabara, PhD, associate professor, Center for Genomic Medicine, Kyoto University Graduate School of Medicine, Japan, and lead author of a study published in *Stroke*.

Balance on one leg for at least 20 seconds. Difficulty balancing may mean that tiny strokes or bleeds have already occurred, increasing your risk for more serious strokes.

Recent finding: Among those who had two or more tiny strokes, about one-third had trouble balancing.

The Danger After a Colonoscopy

Karen Larson, former editor of *Bottom Line Personal*. BottomLineInc.com

What's the best part of a colonoscopy? When it's over, of course. But for someone I know, the end of a colonoscopy was just the start of a medical misadventure—she fainted two days after the procedure and wound up in the emergency room due to dehydration.

That's not uncommon, says Leo Galland, MD, founder and director of the Foundation for Integrated Medicine in New York City. The incident points to a troubling gap in colonoscopy communication—patients are told how to prepare for this procedure but often not what they should do afterward. *Dr. Galland's advice...*

•**Drink eight to 16 ounces of fruit juice right after the procedure.** Ask if the health facility will have juice. If not, bring your own. Any beverage will help with dehydration, but fruit juice also wards off hypoglycemia—low blood sugar. Drink another 48 ounces of fluid during the day and 64 ounces the day after.

•**Eat a light snack as soon as you feel able.** Bring a sandwich or an energy bar with you to the health facility, too. Avoid foods with high fat content—fats are difficult to digest.

•**Take a probiotic supplement.** Take one just before your first meal following the procedure and twice a day for the next 10 days at the start of a meal. Consuming probiotics can reduce bowel irritation and promote good overall digestive health. Try a few different ones well before your colonoscopy to find one that seems to aid your digestion.

Watch Out for Your Doctor's Smartphone: Infection and "Distracted Doctoring" Are Dangers

Peter J. Papadakos, MD, director of critical care medicine at the University of Rochester Medical Center and professor of anesthesiology, neurology, surgery and neurosurgery at the University of Rochester, both in Rochester, New York. Dr. Papadakos was one of the first experts to identify the potential for distraction from smartphones and to popularize the term "distracted doctoring."

If you're like most people, you love your smartphone, tablet or laptop. Doctors, nurses and other medical personnel are no different. But when they use these devices in the workplace, does that help or hurt your medical care?

It's true that smartphones, tablets and laptops allow doctors to quickly look up the newest drug information and case studies. But there are dangerous downsides for the patient when medical staff has constant access to this type of technology.

A NEW DANGER

Nearly 90% of all doctors currently use smartphones or tablets while at work. *The most significant potential dangers to patients include…*

•**Bacterial contamination.** Even though there are many nonsterile surfaces in a health-care setting, cell phones are of particular concern because they are typically handled so often. When the cell phones of orthopedic surgeons in the operating room were tested, a whopping 83% of the phones had infection-causing bacteria on them, according to a study published in *The Journal of Bone & Joint Surgery*.

Self-defense: When admitted to a hospital, ask what the guidelines are for disinfecting electronic devices, particularly any that are brought into and handled in an operating room. Some hospitals now have ultraviolet (UV) sterilizing devices that are 99.9% effective at decontaminating objects in 10 seconds.

If your doctor is holding a cell phone or other personal device, ask him/her if the device was cleaned before attending to you and make sure the doctor washes his hands as well.

Also: When visiting someone in the hospital, don't pull out your cell phone to show photos in an effort to cheer up the patient. Better yet, leave your cell phone at home or in the car. If you are a patient or visitor in the hospital and feel you need your phone, clean it regularly with sanitizing wipes (such as Wireless Wipes) or a UV sterilizing device for cell phones.

•**Interruptions to workflow and distractions.** Researchers at Oregon State University and the Oregon Health & Science University tested the impact of distractions on residents performing a simulated gallbladder surgery. When the surgeons were interrupted by a cell-phone ring, the sound of a dropped metal tray clanging or other distraction, 44% made serious errors that could have led to a fatality, including damage to organs and arteries.

Self-defense: To protect yourself from such forms of "distracted doctoring," ask your hospital whether it has a policy on the safe use of electronic devices throughout the hospital, and ask for a copy if it does. If electronic devices are allowed in the operating room, share your concerns with your surgical team.

At the University of Rochester Medical Center, we have a "Code of eConduct" to minimize the distractions of devices such as smartphones and tablets. Guidelines include that devices must be in "silent" mode (no ringing or vibrating) when in a patient's room and all personal business must be conducted only in break rooms and out of view of patients.

•**Addiction.** Just like everyone else, many doctors and other health-care professionals do not even realize how addicted they are to their smartphones and social media.

In a survey of more than 400 perfusionists (technicians who operate heart-lung bypass machines during heart surgery), more than half admitted that they had used a cell phone during heart bypass procedures to access e-mail, surf the Internet and use social networking sites.

While 78% of the technicians said that cell phones could potentially pose a safety risk to patients, when asked about speaking on the phone and texting, only 42% and 52% of them said that these, respectively, were always unsafe practices. Paradoxically, while 93% reported that they were not distracted by using their phones, 34% said that they had witnessed other perfusionists being distracted by their phones or texting during procedures.

To make health-care professionals more aware of a possible addiction to technology, my colleagues and I at the University of Rochester modi-fied a widely used screening survey for alcoholism to gauge people's addiction to their phones, texting and/or social media. To take the survey, see "Are You Addicted to Your Cell Phone?" below.

•**iPatient.** When doctors are fixated on the computerized record of a patient, what I call an "iPatient," they miss important information such as speech patterns and body language.

Self-defense: Politely ask your doctor to put the device away for a few minutes and listen to you.

ARE YOU ADDICTED TO YOUR CELL PHONE?

Researchers at the University of Rochester modi-fied the widely used CAGE survey for alcoholism by replacing the term "drink" with "personal electronic device" to help identify addiction to a smartphone or other devices.

1. Have you ever felt you needed to cut down on your personal electronic device use?

2. Have people annoyed you by criticizing your use of your personal electronic device?

3. Have you felt guilty about your overuse of your personal electronic device?

4. Do you reach for your personal electronic device first thing in the morning?

Two or more "yes" answers suggest an addiction. Recognizing that you have a problem is the first step to cutting down on excessive use of technology.

6

Big Corporations

Get the TV and Movies You Really Want...for a Great Price!

Ryan Downey, executive director, The Streaming Advisor, a website providing news, reviews and guidance related to online video content. TheStreamingAdvisor.com

Netflix and Amazon Prime Video are the big names, but they are far from the only options if you want to stream movies and TV shows to your television, computer or other digital devices. There are plenty of lesser known services that offer various combinations of old and new programming—and many do it for less than the $100 per year charged by Netflix and Amazon. You could combine a few of them to serve as a less expensive substitute for cable or satellite TV—or pick one or two as a supplement to cable or satellite. Many offer free trials, so there's no harm in trying them.

Eight attractive streaming services you may not know about...

•**Acorn TV** concentrates on British television shows and offers programs from Australia, New Zealand, Canada and Ireland as well. It has a particularly strong catalog of British mystery shows including popular series such as *Foyle's War*, *Mid-*

somer Murders and *Agatha Christie's Poirot*. There are plenty of lesser known shows worth watching, too, such as the award-winning Canadian police drama *19-2*...the Australian period drama *A Place to Call Home*...and the Acorn original British mystery series *Agatha Raisin*. All programs are free of ads.

Price: $4.99 per month or $49.99 per year. A seven-day free trial is available. Acorn.tv

•**CuriosityStream** is the streaming service for people who especially like intellectually stimulating television. There's a two-part series titled *The Secrets of Quantum Physics*...a David Attenborough documentary about bioluminescence called *Light on Earth*...a three-part series called *Deep Time History* about how civilization has been influenced by events that occurred long before humans ever walked on Earth...and hundreds of other thought-provoking shows. All programming is free of ads.

Price: $2.99 per month. A seven-day free trial is available. CuriosityStream.com

•**HBO** now offers access to the HBO network's original programming as well as the dozens of movies that HBO is playing in any given month—without having to subscribe to a premium package of cable- or satellite-TV service or even subscribe to cable or satellite at all. (If you do subscribe to the HBO network through a cable or satellite company, you likely can stream much of this programming at no additional charge through a video-on-demand service called HBO Go.) HBO Now provides more than just HBO's current programs, such as *Game of Thrones* and *Westworld*—subscribers also gain access to HBO's complete archive, including programs that it originally ran years earlier. You could watch the entire runs of the critically acclaimed series *The Sopranos* and *The Wire*, for example.

Price: $14.99 per month. A seven-day free trial is available. HBONow.com

•**History Vault** offers access to many of the documentaries and shows that have run on the History Channel over the years. Its emphasis is on the history-related content that the History Channel used to specialize in before it turned into yet another cable channel airing reality shows such as *Pawn Stars*. On History Vault, you'll find documentaries covering everything from Incan mummies to the space shuttle and from the Vikings to Vietnam.

Price: $4.99 per month or $49.99 per year. A seven-day free trial is available. HistoryVault.com

•**Hulu** is probably the best-known streaming service after Netflix and Amazon Prime Video, and it certainly provides an impressive amount of content. The service offers access to most of the shows currently airing on ABC, CBS, Fox and NBC (but not CW), with new episodes generally available the day after the first broadcast. Hulu also offers programming from dozens of cable networks (ranging from Comedy Central, Disney and MTV to CNN, Discovery and ESPN) as well as classic older series—Hulu offers every episode of *Seinfeld*, for example. And it has a number of original shows that are not available on cable or satellite or other streaming services, such as *11.22.63*, an action series featuring James Franco…and *The Handmaid's Tale,* an Emmy-winning drama. Hulu's movie selection is less impressive but not without some highlights—for example, recently more than a dozen James Bond flicks were available.

Price: $5.99 per month with commercials or $39.99 per month for a version with live streaming of network and sports channels. A 30-day free trial is available. Hulu.com

Smart: If you want to add CW to the lineup, its streaming service is available for free, with programs such as *Supergirl* and *Jane the Virgin* available one day after they originally air.

•**NewsOn** lets you stream local news broadcasts from stations across the US either live or up to 48 hours after they originally air. Broadcasts from more than 175 local TV stations in more than 110 US markets are available. You could use NewsOn to watch your own local news from anywhere in the world (assuming that you have Internet access)…or to watch the local news of a different part of the country—maybe you like to keep up with what's happening where you used to live or where your adult child recently moved, for example. These newscasts include commercial breaks just as they would if you were watching them over the air.

Price: Free. WatchNewsOn.com

•**Showtime** streaming service is the Showtime equivalent of HBO Now, described above. (If you subscribe to the Showtime network through a cable or satellite provider, you likely can stream its current and past movie and TV programming to other devices at no additional charge through a similar video-on-demand service called Showtime Anytime.) Current Showtime hits range from the spy thriller *Homeland* and the comedy-drama *Shameless* to the Wall Street drama *Billions* and the dramas *Masters of Sex* and *The Affair*. There are no ads.

Price: $10.99 per month. A 30-day free trial is available. Showtime.com

The "Zombie Debt" Collectors Are Coming to Get You

Gerri Detweiler, education director for Nav.com, a website that provides financial information for small-business owners. She has testified before Congress on consumer credit topics and is coauthor of the free e-Book *Debt Collection Answers*. DebtCollectionAnswers.com

Collection agencies often buy up delinquent loans and unpaid bills from many years ago and then demand payment from the debtors. But the "zombie debts" these collection agencies try to bring back to life often are so old that consumers have little memory of the bills and whether they were paid. The collection agencies also might add steep fees and penalties. Sometimes they target the wrong person, harassing someone who simply shares the real debtor's name.

If you receive a call from a collection agency about money that it says you owe from years ago…

•**Request a letter.** Say, "Please send me the details about this debt in writing. It is not convenient for me to discuss this right now." Collection agencies usually phone, but federal law requires that they provide details in writing within five days of your request. They also are barred from calling when it is inconvenient for the debtor, so saying "not convenient" should end the call.

Warning: Even if you know that the debt is yours, do not admit this fact and don't agree to make even a tiny partial payment. This could reset the clock on statute-of-limitations laws, making it possible for collectors to sue you over this debt (more on this below). And do not believe a debt collector who claims that you will face additional penalties if you don't immediately make at least partial payment—this often is an outright lie, and even if the collection agency does tack on an additional penalty, it almost certainly will agree to waive that penalty if you do eventually agree to pay the debt.

When you receive the letter, if you have any doubt at all about the validity or size of the debt, research it. Go through your old bank or credit card records and loan-payment receipts, etc., or contact the original biller to try to determine whether the debt is truly yours and whether you already have paid it. Try to confirm the size of the debt, too—collection agencies often tack on penalties and interest fees without disclosing that they have done so.

•**Next, try to determine whether the statute of limitations on the debt has expired.** These laws vary by state and type of debt, but in many cases, the collection agency cannot legally sue for repayment if the debt went into default more than four to six years earlier, though there are exceptions. If you live in a different state than you did when you originally incurred the debt, it might be

especially difficult to determine whether the statute of limitations has expired—in these cases, it is up to the courts to decide which state's laws apply. And in some cases, the original biller might have designated in a contract you signed that the laws of a different state would apply.

Of course, the fact that the statute of limitations may have expired so that you cannot legally be sued for repayment would not mean that you do not have a moral obligation to pay a debt you owe. But it does dramatically improve your negotiating position if you cannot determine whether you truly owe the money…or if the collection agency is trying to tack penalties and fees onto the bill.

Helpful: Entering the following into a search engine will produce details for many, though not all, states' statutes of limitations. Type the name of your state…"statute of limitations"…and "consumer debt."

•**Send the collection agency a certified letter explaining why the debt is not owed…or call and negotiate a payment.** If the debt is not yours or already has been paid, explain this in simple terms in your letter—for example, "This debt is not mine. You have the wrong person" or "My records indicate this debt was paid on February 8, 2010. I have enclosed a copy of the check." Be sure to include evidence that the debt is not yours (such as a different Social Security number than the one associated with the debt)…or that the debt has already been paid…or that the statute of limitations has expired. Also write, "Please do not contact me again." Save a copy of this letter. Once you have told a collection agency not to contact you, it is legally barred from doing so unless it needs to inform you that it is suing.

If the debt is valid, negotiate before paying anything. Collection agencies often reduce balances, including interest and fees, on old debts. If the statute of limitations on the debt has expired, you are in an especially powerful negotiating position—make it clear to the collection agency that you know about this expiration.

What to do: Insist on written confirmation that once you make the negotiated payment, the debt's balance will be listed as zero—and do not send any payment until you have received this confirmation. Since there is no clear-cut rule or law governing e-mail in an attempt to collect a debt, it is best to write a letter and send it by certified mail with return receipt.

•**If the collection agency sues you, show up in court to challenge it.** Collection agencies generally are required to sue in a court system that is geographically convenient for the debtor. And you do not necessarily need to hire a lawyer. Many consumers who show up in court to plead their case are successful in having the debt dismissed. If you do not show up, the judge might issue a "default judgment" in the collection agency's favor even if the debt is not legitimate.

Sports Channels Drive Up Cable Bills

Time.com

Sports channels are the main reason for high cable bills. More than $18 of an average $103/month cable bill goes to sports networks, such as ESPN and FoxSports. In areas where there are extra charges for seeing local sports teams, the monthly cost of sports is $20 to $25. Cable bills rose 39% from 2011 to 2015, eight times the rate of inflation, and the huge costs of sports programming are expected to drive bills even higher in coming years.

If you don't watch sports: Consider switching to a cable bundle that excludes sports channels or to on-demand streaming through sources such as Hulu, Netflix or Amazon Prime.

Avoid Getting a Credit Card Declined

Bill Hardekopf, CEO, LowCards.com, which helps consumers compare credit cards. He is coauthor of *The Credit Card Guidebook*. LowCards.com

In September 2014, President Barack Obama and First Lady Michelle Obama dined at *Estela*, a New York City restaurant. The meal went

well—until the president's credit card was declined. If the US president can have a card declined, it can happen to anyone, and occasionally it does, not just for a missed payment or breach of the credit limit but increasingly for reasons that have little to do with irresponsible card use. Having a charge declined can be mildly inconvenient…or it can cause a major disruption such as when you are traveling. *Here are potential causes and how to reduce the odds that they will result in a rejection…*

•**You make a purchase that does not fit your usual spending patterns.** Software is monitoring cardholder spending more closely than ever to prevent fraudulent charges by thieves. But it sometimes declines legitimate purchases. *Particularly likely to be declined are…*

•Purchases made in geographic areas—inside and outside the US—where the cardholder doesn't typically shop.

•Purchases larger than normal for the cardholder.

What to do: When possible, alert your card's issuer before making purchases that are unusual for you, and especially if you will be traveling outside the US. If a charge is declined and you suspect this could be the cause, try a different card or try to contact your card issuer on the spot to straighten things out.

•**Hotel and car-rental "holds" have pushed you over your credit limit.** Hotels and car-rental companies often place temporary "holds" on a portion of a customers' credit line to ensure that there will be enough credit available when the payment is processed. These holds can last for weeks and might be for hundreds of dollars more than the actual charge—the merchants want to protect themselves in case customers incur larger bills than expected. If you have several large holds in quick succession, it could push you over your card's credit limit even if you haven't spent more than that limit. (Gas stations often impose holds, too, but these tend to be more modest in size and duration.)

What to do: If you spend money on hotels and/or car rentals multiple times within about a month, spread these charges among several cards or use a card that has many thousands of dollars of additional credit limit available. Or contact the issuer of the card that you wish to use prior to making charges that are likely to involve holds. Explain the situation, and ask whether your credit limit can be increased.

• **Your credit limit has been slashed.** Issuers occasionally cut a credit limit even though the cardholder has never missed a payment or broken a rule. This tends to occur when the cardholder has recently applied for multiple new cards…or when something negative pops up on a credit report—even if the credit report listing is in error.

What to do: Read the notices that you receive from your credit card issuers, or at least skim them, for any mention of changes to your credit limit. Issuers must provide 45 days' written notice before reducing a credit limit.

Avoid Fees When You Close Your Bank Accounts

GoBankingRates.com

Banks often charge $15 to $30 to use a wire transfer or certified check. Instead, first set up a new account into which you will put your money. Then withdraw the funds from the old bank in cash if you are comfortable carrying that amount. If not, write a check on the old account—leaving enough to avoid possible fees and to handle a few days of expenses—and use that check as an initial deposit in the new account. If you are opening the new account online, you may be able to do a free electronic transfer. It is not instantaneous, like a wire transfer, but it takes only a few days to clear. Close your old account with a written letter of notice.

After closing an account: Watch for a confirmation letter from your old bank, and keep it for your records. Shred any checks and debit cards associated with the old account.

The Salmon Hoax

Karen Larson, former editor of *Bottom Line Personal*. Bottom LineInc.com

The Food and Drug Administration recently ruled that genetically engineered salmon can be sold in the US without any labels noting that its DNA has been altered. There is indeed strong scientific consensus that genetically modified foods are safe to consume. But safe or not, I believe I have a right to know what I'm eating. Label food for what it is, and let me decide for myself.

Thus I'm planning to buy my salmon at retailers such as Kroger, Safeway, Target, Trader Joe's and Whole Foods, which have announced that they will not stock the genetically modified fish.

But genetic modification isn't the only challenge for those of us who want to know what seafood we're consuming. When the nonprofit organization Oceana did DNA testing on the salmon sold in the US, it discovered that 43% of it wasn't what the seller claimed. Farmed Atlantic salmon often was sold as wild Pacific salmon. Oceana has found that other seafood has fishy labeling, too.

Here, advice from Oceana's Dr. Kimberly Warner…

• **Buy fish in supermarkets.** Oceana discovered that mislabeling is much less common in supermarkets—less than 20%—than in small markets, restaurants and especially sushi venues.

• **Eat fresh regional fish during its fishing season.** Misidentification is most common out of season, so lean toward buying regional seafood when you know it is in season.

Examples: Chesapeake blue crab is in season from April to December…Alaska wild salmon, in late spring through the fall.

• **Purchase whole fish when feasible.** Merchants are less likely to pass off one species as another when consumers can see the entire fish.

Moving Company Traps and Hidden Costs

Roundup of experts on moving, reported at GoBanking Rates.com.

Estimates made over the phone are likely to be inaccurate and may be scams—have movers visit your home, and get estimates from at least three companies. *Additional fees can raise costs*—for instance, packing and unpacking, temporary warehousing and specific-date delivery. *Movers that insist on a deposit* probably are scammers—upfront payments may disappear. *Cardboard boxes*—save by getting them for free from liquor stores and other retailers or look for giveaways on Craigslist. *Moving permits may be required* to park the moving van. Check the website of the city you're moving to. *Full-value coverage can be costly*, but it requires movers to pay replacement value for lost or damaged goods. *Hidden costs of renting a truck to move on your own*—these include gas, charges per mile driven, damage coverage and supplies such as furniture pads.

Beware Reverse-Mortgage Ads

Stacy Canan, assistant director of the Consumer Financial Protection Bureau's Office for Older Americans, Washington, DC. ConsumerFinance.gov

Reverse mortgages allow home owners age 62 and older to borrow against the value of their homes without any repayment being required until they move out, sell the home or die. Unfortunately, some companies that offer reverse mortgages put confusing, incomplete or inaccurate statements in their ads, making these already complex financial instruments even more difficult to understand...

•**Ads often refer to reverse mortgages as "government-backed" or "government-insured."** The ads might cite government agencies such as the Federal Housing Administration (FHA) or prominently feature US government symbols, creating the impression that reverse mortgages are a government program. In reality, reverse mortgages are offered by private companies, and consumers should proceed with great caution. The government's involvement is quite limited.

•**Ads often gloss over the fact that reverse mortgages are loans that charge interest and fees just like other loans.** Instead, these ads might make these mortgages seem like bank accounts—an asset you own that can be easily tapped. Some ads stress that reverse mortgages have no fixed monthly payments, fostering the impression that the home owner need not make any housing-related payments. In reality, the borrower must maintain the home in good repair and pay real estate taxes and insurance premiums.

•**Ads often refer to reverse mortgages as "tax-free."** This makes some consumers think that they won't have to pay property taxes. But "tax-free" just means income taxes are not due on money borrowed. That's not really much of a selling point—income taxes generally are not due on money received from other types of loans, either.

•**Ads often claim that "you can stay in your home as long as you want" or even that "you cannot lose your home."** In truth, you could lose your home if you fail to pay your property taxes or fail to comply with reverse-mortgage terms that might be buried in the contract's small print.

Hidden Reviews on Yelp

Michael Luca, PhD, associate professor of business administration at Harvard Business School, Boston. He completed an academic paper on consumer online reviews titled, "Fake It Till You Make It: Reputation, Competition, and Yelp Review Fraud." HBS.edu

More than 135 million consumers visit Yelp.com each month to look at customer reviews and star ratings that help them choose restaurants and other local businesses. But Yelp may be withholding some information that you need to make good choices.

Reason: Yelp uses automated software that sorts through millions of reviews and aggressively suppresses any it decides are fake. That's fine if it catches only the fake ones. The problem is that about 20% to 25% of all reviews are flagged as suspicious and removed, even though Yelp acknowledges that many of these may be authentic.

Yelp says that this vigilance is necessary to protect consumers. The company says it scans for measures of "quality, reliability and activity." Also, it says the filter can detect various inappropriate incentives—for instance, businesses that offer discounts to individuals if they leave a five-star rave on Yelp…or businesses that pay freelancers to malign their competition with one-star rants.

Yelp's controversial filtering has generated 2,000 Federal Trade Commission complaints from local businesses and spawned several lawsuits. Recently, however, a federal appeals court ruled that Yelp has a legal right to decide which reviews to feature on its site and how to present them.

To get the most complete picture…

•**Read the suppressed reviews yourself.** Yelp doesn't delete the reviews that it filters out—it hides them. They still are accessible by clicking the "not currently recommended" link at the bottom of each business's page.

•**Use common sense to decide which hidden reviews to ignore.** Fake reviews overwhelmingly tend toward the extreme. They often award a business one star or five stars without providing any good reasons why. Or they use over-the-top language such as "the best/worst ever."

Don't Pay for Storage! DIY Ways to Find Hidden Space in Your Home

Katie and Gene Hamilton are authors of 20 home-improvement books including *Fix It and Flip It* and creators of DIYorNot.com, an award-winning website about the cost of home improvements.

You can tap the hidden potential in your home with products and materials that make the most of the space. *Here are ways to find hidden areas in your house to solve your storage problems…*

•**Install a floor area in an unfinished attic for light storage.** An accessible attic with exposed floor joists has untapped potential—all it needs is flooring to create a usable destination for all your lightweight stuff.

Georgia-Pacific makes a tongue-and-groove particleboard flooring in four-by-eight-foot panels called Sturd-I-Floor (available at lumberyards and home centers) that is suitable for this purpose.

Most attic floors with at least two-by-six-floor joists will support light loads such as boxes of clothing and decorations, but consult a professional contractor if you want to store heavy objects such as furniture. Your local building department can be of help, too.

Nailing the flooring to the joists is a straightforward project. But getting the new flooring into the attic can be a challenge. In most attics, it's impossible to get full four-by-eight panels up there. If that's the case for you, cut the panels in half to make two-by-eight-foot panels. You may even have to cut these in half again to fit through a trapdoor.

Place the first panel on the joists, and nail it in place. Then use this panel as a base from which you can install the others. Be careful if you walk on the joists because putting your foot through the ceiling will cancel any potential saving that comes from doing it yourself and you could get hurt.

A contractor will charge you $473, which includes labor and materials, to lay an area of approximately 120 feet square. A handy home owner with carpentry tools and experience can do the job for $180* and pocket $293, a 62% savings. For more information, you can go to Buildgp.com/plywood-osb.

●**Expand outdoor storage under a raised deck with an under-deck ceiling.** The space under a second-floor deck can become useful storage space when it's protected from dripping rain and snow coming through the deck boards above. You can catch any runoff with an under-deck ceiling. The vinyl material is designed as a drainage system that attaches to the underside of a second-level deck and directs the water to a gutter system. This creates a ground-level outdoor room or useful space for storing bicycles and gardening equipment and other items.

A contractor will charge $2,430, which includes labor and materials, to install an under-deck ceiling below a 14-by-20-foot deck. A DIY home owner can purchase the materials for $1,900 and pocket a 22% savings. For more information, go to UnderDeck.com.

*The DIY cost of projects is based on national average cost data from major retailers and e-commerce websites with home-improvement products. The cost of hiring a professional is determined by averaging cost and data information in several construction books that are updated annually and used by contractors to prepare job bids.

7

Friends and Family

Exactly What to Say in Awkward Situations

Barbara Pachter, a business communication and etiquette consultant based in New Jersey. She is an instructor in the School of Business at Rutgers University and author of *The Communication Clinic: 99 Proven Cures for the Most Common Business Mistakes.* Pachter.com

A colleague criticizes you in front of your boss…an acquaintance asks you an overly personal question…a stranger cuts in front of you in line. The shock of unexpected and unpleasant situations such as these might make you say things that you later regret…or freeze up and say nothing at all, which can add to the awkwardness.

The best responses in these situations are both polite and powerful. Being polite reduces the odds that the already unpleasant situation will escalate, while being powerful shows that you stand up for yourself.

What to say in 10 common awkward situations…

•**Someone raises his/her voice while speaking with you.** Say, *"I want to talk about this but not this way."* Or "I want to help…but yelling won't help me help you. It will only make us both unproductive." Say this calmly but loudly enough to be heard.

Opening with the phrase "I want to help" (or "I hear you" if that better fits the situation) often begins to calm yellers—it lets them know that you are listening and potentially even on their side. Refusing to proceed with the discussion until this person lowers his voice sends the message that you will not allow yourself to be intimidated.

•**Someone cuts in front of you in line.** Say, *"Excuse me, I believe I was here first."* This response calls attention to the transgression without criticizing the transgressor, who may have cut ahead accidentally.

•**Someone says something thoughtless but not intentionally offensive to you.** Say something lighthearted that pokes gentle fun at the thoughtless statement. It can be tricky to get this just right—if your response is too hostile, you could develop a reputation for being touchy.

Example: A coworker says you're good with computers "for someone your age." You don't want to bite this coworker's head off—he probably was trying to pay you a compliment, and it just didn't come out right—but letting his comment linger without response could reinforce the impression that you are too old to be truly tech-savvy. You could respond with a smile and say, "Thank you! That's quite a compliment from someone your age."

If a good line doesn't pop immediately to mind, you could always smile and calmly repeat back the offending portion of the statement followed by "huh?"—such as "for someone my age, huh?" Saying this buys you a few extra moments to think of an effective lighthearted line, such as, "Looks can be deceiving." If you still can't, just leave it there, or just say, "Thank you."

•**There's something you want from someone.** Making requests often makes people feel uncomfortable, so they phrase the request in ways that seem undemanding. They might convert their requests into questions, asking, "Could I have…" or "Can you…" which gives the decision-making power to the other person. Or they might ask people to "try" to do whatever it is they are requesting. This softer approach can be appropriate at times, especially if you are talking up the ladder. But using a sentence that begins in a direct assertive way such as, "I would like…" or "I want to…"makes it very clear what you want and is more likely to produce the desired results. Listen to the difference—"Boss, I would like to be assigned to the ABC project" versus "Boss, can you assign me to the ABC project?" Both are polite, but the first version leaves no doubt about what you want and makes you seem confident—people are more likely to do things for people who appear certain about what they are asking.

•**A know-it-all is running his mouth.** Say calmly, "How do you know that to be true?" and/ or "What facts do you have to support your position?" If the know-it-all responds that he just feels it to be true or that "it's obvious," reply that "you are welcome to believe whatever you want, but if you expect me to believe it, you're going to need to produce facts to support what you say."

•**Someone asks about your income, your politics, your sex life or some other inappropriate subject.** Say, "I'm not comfortable discussing that," and then immediately take the conversation in a different direction before an awkward silence ensues. Saying, "I'm not comfortable…" is better than saying, "That's inappropriate," because it contains no accusation. Rather than taking someone to task

for a social faux pas, you are merely saying that your personal preference is to keep this private.

•**Someone criticizes something about you or your work in front of a group.** Say, "Why are you saying that?" or "Help me to understand what you mean by inadequate/wrong/incomplete…" You are requesting details about what this person thinks you got wrong. When you do this, do your best to make your tone and body language inquisitive, not defensive—don't cross your arms or raise your voice. Maybe this person is right and the criticism is deserved—if so, hearing the details will help you improve. Or maybe this person is wrong and/or intentionally trying to make you look bad in front of a group or a boss—if so, asking for details often will make this obvious. Whether the criticism is valid or not, asking for details sends the message that you are not defensive and that you are confident about your work.

•**Someone interrupts you.** Say, "Hold that thought…" and then continue with what you were saying. This acknowledges the person who wants to speak but leaves no doubt that you are not done speaking and have no intention of yielding until you are. You might have to raise your volume slightly and speak over the interrupter for a few seconds until he realizes you're not yielding.

Helpful: If the same person interrupts you frequently, pick a private moment to say, "You have useful things to say, but when I get cut off, I lose my train of thought. I'd appreciate it if you would let me get through what I'm saying before jumping in."

•**Someone accuses you of treating him rudely or unfairly—and he has a point.** Say, "You know what, you're right. It won't happen again." It's natural to become defensive in these situations, but even if you come up with a way to justify your misstep or misstatement, doing so will only escalate the awkward situation and damage the relationship. Admitting an error almost always dials down the tension—and despite what many people think, admitting mistakes shows strength, not weakness.

•**Someone pays you a compliment.** Say, "Thank you," or "Thank you. I appreciate your comments."

Receiving praise is an awkward situation for some people. They become embarrassed and feel an urge to downplay or deflect the positive things that are being said about them. Ignore this urge. Instead look the person in the eye, express sincere gratitude for the compliment and then stop talking before you spoil the moment.

The Sex-Starved Marriage

Michele Weiner-Davis, LCSW, founder of The Divorce Busting Center in Boulder, Colorado, which helps on-the-brink couples save their marriages. She is the best-selling author of several books including *Healing from Infidelity, The Sex-Starved Marriage* and *Divorce Busting*. DivorceBusting.com

It has been two months since Janet and Mark have had sex. They're hardly speaking to each other. If you asked Janet about this, she would say that their home has become a battle zone—they fight about every little thing. Janet goes out of her way to avoid Mark to protect herself from his wrath.

Mark tells a different story. His anger, he believes, is justified. He is fed up with Janet's lack of interest in their sexual relationship. "She never initiates sex. She recoils when I try to kiss or hug her. I'm tired of being rejected." To cope with his unhappiness, Mark spends longer hours at work and busies himself on his computer at night, deepening the chasm between them.

Both Mark and Janet think that the other one is to blame for the problems between them. They have hit an impasse.

The result: A sex-starved marriage. And sex-starved marriages are surprisingly common. In fact, in about one in three marriages, one spouse has a considerably larger sexual appetite than the other. This in and of itself is not a problem—it's how couples handle their differences that matters.

Here's what you need to know to fix a sex-starved marriage and make you both happier…

YEARNING FOR CONTACT

In a sex-starved marriage, one partner is longing for more touch—both sexual and nonsexual—and the other spouse isn't interested and doesn't understand why such a fuss is being made about sex. The less interested spouse thinks, *Is this just about having an orgasm? That's not such a big deal.* But the spouse yearning for more physical contact sees it differently. Being close physically is more than a physical release—it's about feeling wanted and connected emotionally.

When a misunderstanding of this magnitude happens and the less interested spouse continues to avoid sex, marriages start to unravel. Couples stop spending time together. They quit putting effort into the relationship. They become more like two distant roommates. Intimacy on all levels ends, which puts the marriage at risk for infidelity or divorce.

Typically, the spouse with the smaller sexual appetite controls the frequency of sex. If she/he (contrary to popular belief, men also can have low sexual desire) doesn't want it, it generally doesn't happen. This is not due to a desire to control the relationship—it just seems unthinkable to be sexual if one is not in the mood.

Furthermore, the lower-desire spouse has the expectation that the higher-desire spouse must accept the no-sex verdict and remain monogamous. The higher-desire spouse feels rejected, resentful and miserable.

How do two people with differing sexual appetites begin to bridge the desire gap? Regardless of where you stand on the sexual-desire spectrum, it's important to keep in mind that loving marriages are built on mutual care-taking. Don't wait for your spouse to change first. Be the catalyst for change in your marriage. *Here's how…*

IF YOU ARE THE LOWER-DESIRE SPOUSE

•**Just do it—and you may be surprised.** Over the years, countless clients in my counseling practice have said, "I wasn't in the mood to have sex when my spouse approached me, but once we got going, it felt really good. I had an orgasm, and my spouse's mood really improved afterward."

Why would that be? For many people, the human sexual response cycle consists of four stages that occur in a certain order—desire (out of the blue, you have a sexy thought)…arousal (you and your partner touch, and your body becomes aroused)…orgasm…and resolution (your body returns to its normal resting state).

But for millions of people, stages one and two actually are reversed. In other words, desire doesn't come until after arousal. These people must feel turned on physically before they realize that they actually desire sex. Therefore, being receptive to your partner's advances even from a neutral starting place—when you do not feel desire—makes sense because chances are that sex will be enjoyable for both of you.

●**Give a "gift."** Let's face it, there are times when people—even people with the typical desire/arousal pattern—simply don't feel like having sex. It's perfectly acceptable to decline your partner's offer from time to time. But when "no" substantially outweighs "yes," you are creating deep feelings of frustration and rejection—guaranteed.

What's the solution to an "I'm not really in the mood for sex" moment? Give a gift—a sexual gift—or to be more blunt about it, pleasure your spouse to orgasm if that's what he/she wants, even if you're not in the mood for the same. This is an act of love and caring and completely appropriate within a marriage.

IF YOU ARE THE HIGHER-DESIRE SPOUSE

●**Speak from your heart.** If you're feeling frustrated that your spouse hasn't understood your need to be close physically, chances are you've been irritable and angry. Anger is not an aphrodisiac—it pushes your spouse further away. Press your mental-reset button, and approach your spouse differently. Speak from your heart—express your vulnerability (yes, you are vulnerable, no matter how "tough" you are!) and your hurt.

Example: Instead of saying, "I'm angry that we haven't had sex in so long," it's better to say, "When we don't have sex for this long, I miss being close to you. I feel disconnected. It hurts my feelings that you don't seem interested in me sexually."

●**Rather than complain, ask for what you want.** Complaining, even when it's justified, leads to defensiveness. Instead, ask for what you want in a positive way.

Example: Instead of saying, "You never initiate sex," say, "I'd really love it if once in a while, you threw your arms around me and said, 'Do you want to make love?' That would make me feel great."

●**Figure out what turns your spouse on.** If buying sex toys or downloading X-rated videos has failed to entice your spouse to nurture your sexual relationship, there's probably a reason. Your spouse might need to feel courted by you first. You might be married to someone who feels more connected to you when you have meaningful conversations…spend enjoyable, uninterrupted time together other than having sex…are more affirming and complimentary…or when you participate in family activities together. This is how your partner feels loved—and the truth is, there are many people who want sexual intimacy only when they feel loved first.

If you're uncertain about your spouse's way of feeling cherished by you, ask. Say, "What can I do to make you feel loved?" Believe it or not, meeting your partner's needs, though different from your own, may be a turn-on for him/her. Try it.

6 Foods Proven to Make You Happy

Tonia Reinhard, MS, RD, a registered dietitian and professor at Wayne State University in Detroit. She is the program director for the Coordinated Program in Dietetics, course director of clinical nutrition at Wayne State University School of Medicine and past president of the Michigan Academy of Nutrition and Dietetics. She is author of *Superfoods: The Healthiest Foods on the Planet* and *Superjuicing: More Than 100 Nutritious Vegetable and Fruit Recipes.*

You can eat your way to a better mood! Certain foods and beverages have been proven to provide the raw materials that you need to feel sharper, more relaxed and just plain happier. *Best choices…*

HAPPY FOOD #1: **Chocolate.** Chocolate can make you feel good—to such an extent that 52% of women would choose chocolate over sex, according to one survey.

Chocolate contains chemical compounds known as polyphenols, which interact with neurotransmitters in the brain and reduce anxiety. An Australian study found that men and women who consumed the most chocolate polyphenols (in the form of a beverage) felt calmer and more content than those who consumed a placebo drink.

Chocolate also boosts serotonin, the same neurotransmitter affected by antidepressant medications. It triggers the release of dopamine and stimulates the "pleasure" parts of the brain.

Then there's the sensual side of chocolate—the intensity of the flavor and the melting sensation as it dissolves in your mouth. The satisfaction that people get from chocolate could be as helpful for happiness as its chemical composition.

Recommended amount: Aim for one ounce of dark chocolate a day. Most studies used dark chocolate with 70% cacao or more.

HAPPY FOOD #2: **Fish.** Fish has been called "brain food" because our brains have a high concentration of omega-3 fatty acids—and so does fish. These fatty acids have been linked to memory and other cognitive functions. In countries where people eat a lot of fish, depression occurs less often than in countries (such as the US) where people eat less.

The omega-3s in fish accumulate in the brain and increase "membrane fluidity," the ability of brain-cell membranes to absorb nutrients and transmit chemical signals.

A study in *Archives of General Psychiatry* looked at patients diagnosed with depression who hadn't responded well to antidepressants. Those who were given 1,000 mg of EPA (a type of omega-3 fatty acid) daily for three months had significant improvements, including less anxiety and better sleep.

Recommended amount: Try to have at least two or three fish meals a week. Cold-water fish—such as sardines, mackerel and salmon—have the highest levels of omega-3s. Or choose a supplement with 1,000 mg of EPA and DHA (another omega-3 fatty acid) in total.

HAPPY FOOD #3: **Dark green veggies.** Dark green vegetables such as spinach, asparagus, broccoli and Brussels sprouts are loaded with folate, a B-complex vitamin that plays a key role in regulating mood. A Harvard study found that up to 38% of adults with depression had low or borderline levels of folate. Boosting the folate levels of depressed patients improved their mood.

Dark green vegetables are particularly good, but all vegetables and fruits boost mood. Researchers asked 281 people to note their moods on different days. On the days when the participants consumed the most vegetables and fruits, they reported feeling happier and more energetic. Folate certainly plays a role, but self-satisfaction may have something to do with it as well. People feel good when they eat right and take care of themselves.

Recommended amount: The minimum you should have is five servings of vegetables and fruits a day.

Bonus: Middle-aged men who had 10 servings a day showed reduced blood pressure.

HAPPY FOOD #4: **Beans** (including soybeans). Beans are rich in tryptophan, an essential amino acid that is used by the body to produce serotonin, the neurotransmitter that affects feelings of calmness and relaxation.

Beans also are loaded with folate. Folate, as mentioned in the veggies section, plays a key role in regulating mood.

In addition, beans contain manganese, a trace element that helps prevent mood swings due to low blood sugar.

Recommended amount: For people not used to eating beans, start with one-quarter cup five days a week. Build up to one-half cup daily. This progression will help prevent gastrointestinal symptoms such as flatulence.

HAPPY FOOD #5: **Nuts.** Nuts are high in magnesium, a trace mineral involved in more than 300 processes in the body. People who don't get enough magnesium feel irritable, fatigued and susceptible to stress.

The elderly are more likely than young adults to be low in magnesium—because they don't eat enough magnesium-rich foods and/or because they tend to excrete more magnesium in their urine.

Also, many health problems can accelerate the depletion of magnesium from the body.

Examples: Gastrointestinal disorders (or bariatric surgery), kidney disease and sometimes diabetes.

Recommended amount: Aim for one ounce of nuts a day. Good choices include almonds, walnuts, cashews, hazelnuts and peanuts (the latter is technically a legume). If you don't like nuts, other high-magnesium foods include spinach, pumpkin seeds, fish, beans, whole grains and dairy.

HAPPY FOOD #6: **Coffee.** The caffeine in coffee, tea and other caffeinated beverages is a very beneficial compound. One study found that people with mild cognitive impairment were less likely to develop full-fledged Alzheimer's disease when they had the caffeine equivalent of about three cups of coffee a day.

Caffeine can temporarily improve your memory and performance on tests. It enhances coordination and other parameters of physical performance. When you feel energized, you feel happier. Also, people who feel good from caffeine may be more likely to engage in other happiness-promoting behaviors, such as seeing friends and exercising.

Recommended amount: The challenge is finding the "sweet spot"—just enough caffeine to boost mood but not so much that you get the shakes or start feeling anxious. For those who aren't overly sensitive to caffeine, one to three daily cups of coffee or tea are about right.

WHAT NOT TO EAT

Some people turn to food or drink for comfort when they're feeling down. *Here's what not to eat or drink when you've got the blues…*

•**Alcohol.** Alcohol is a depressant of the central nervous system. When you initially consume alcohol, it produces a euphoric effect and you become more animated and less inhibited. But as you continue drinking and more alcohol crosses the blood-brain barrier, the depressant effect predominates.

•**Baked goods.** When you eat high-sugar, high-fat carbs such as cookies, pastries and donuts, you tend to want more of them. The food gives you a temporary "good feeling," but the excess food intake that typically results causes drowsiness and often self-loathing.

How to Deal with Critical People

Mark Goulston, MD, founder and CEO of the Goulston Group, a consulting company in Santa Monica, California, that helps business owners think outside the box. A psychiatrist and an FBI and police hostage negotiation trainer, he has written numerous books including *Just Listen: Discover the Secret to Getting Through to Absolutely Anyone* and *Talking to Crazy: How to Deal with the Irrational and Impossible People in Your Life.* GoulstonGroup.com

Being criticized can bring out the worst in us. It's easy to become defensive…get drawn into an argument about who is right…and/or seethe quietly.

If you have a chronically critical person (or several) in your life, your first goal should be to stop repeated fights about the criticism and reach the point where you can have an actual discussion.

To do that, I recommend a counterintuitive response to criticism called assertive humility—taking responsibility instead of becoming defensive or counterattacking. This approach gives you a surprising amount of power and dignity in the face of criticism. Rather than criticizing the critic or trying to disprove his criticism, you offer an unsolicited apology.

How this works: When you are criticized, pause for a moment so that you do not react impulsively. Then say, "What you just said made me realize that I owe you an apology." The other person will be completely dumbfounded—it is likely that he/she has never received a spontaneous apology before.

Continue with, "I want to apologize for never making the effort to find out how you came to look at this issue the way you do. I was too busy reacting or trying to prove my point of view. That was disrespectful and counterproductive. If you are willing—and you don't have to be—I'd like to fix that right now by having you tell me how you came to think about this the way you do. I will do my best to listen and understand your point of view."

Adapt the language above using words that you would naturally use in conversation. It is important to keep your tone matter-of-fact and to have a genuine desire to understand. If you come across as phony or patronizing, the technique will backfire.

Turning a critical statement toward you into an apology from you is effective because the other person is expecting a defensive reaction from you. This disarms the person, and at that point, you have a much better chance of actually discussing the issue rather than just fighting.

Example: A husband feels that his wife has been criticizing him about everything. She says that he's not eating right, not exercising enough and has been moody and sullen. The husband offers an apology and an invitation for discussion, as described above. The wife is likely to feel stunned and might even look like a deer caught in headlights. She might respond by speaking constructively about her issues with her husband's behavior. But even if she doesn't, this gives her husband an opening to try to engage her in constructive conversation—possibly for the first time in a long time.

If apologizing seems like too big a leap for you, remind yourself that this is a technique—and ask yourself how much dealing with the critical person in the usual way is costing you in stress, anxiety and exhaustion. Being defensive or arguing with a chronic critic won't work because you won't win. Why not try an approach that has a better chance of working?

The Best Way to Accept an Apology

Harriet Lerner, PhD, a psychologist in private practice in Lawrence, Kansas, and the award-winning author of 12 books including *The Dance of Anger* and *Why Won't You Apologize? Healing Big Betrayals and Everyday Hurts.* HarrietLerner.com

When you're the hurt party, it's best to open your heart and graciously accept a sincere apology. Healing gets stalled if we refuse to accept the olive branch or if we use the other person's apology as a springboard to bring up more criticisms or rehash old grievances.

Wrong way to accept an apology: "I'm glad you apologized, but maybe next time you'll think about how much you hurt me when you say things like that."

Better way: "Thank you for the apology." There may be more you need to say on the subject, but save it for a future conversation when it won't cancel out the apology and make the other person think, What's the point?

"I Hate You": A 7-Step Plan for Getting Along with Adult Siblings

Cathy Jo Cress, MSW, a social worker specializing in issues involving families and aging. She is cofounder of CHN Consultants, an aging-services consulting firm based in Santa Cruz, California, and coauthor of *Mom Loves You Best: Forgiving and Forging Sibling Relationships.* CathyCress.com

It seems like siblings should be close friends. They probably understand each other in a deeper, more meaningful way than almost anyone else alive.

But many sibling relationships are badly strained. According to one survey, 35% of adults have either an apathetic or an outright hostile relationship with a brother or sister.

Damaged adult sibling relationships can be difficult to fix, but it can be done. *Here's how...*

1. Uncover your "I hate you" story. When adult siblings have very troubled relationships—not just short-term spats—the problem typically has roots in childhood. What anecdotes come to mind when you consider your childhood interactions with your sibling? Is there a story that you have relived and repeated over the years that casts you as the victim and your sibling as a scoundrel? This story might emphasize that your sibling bullied you...belittled you...or received preferential treatment from your parents. (Or, conversely, does your sibling tell such a story about you?) Or your "I hate you" story might have developed when you were both adults.

Write about this story during a relaxed, private moment. Write what happened and how it made you feel. As you write, consciously let go of any tension the story stirs up inside you. Take deep breaths…unclench your teeth and fists, and relax the muscles of your face…and touch your tongue to the roof of your mouth just behind your front teeth—this tends to make people feel calm.

2. Bring the story into present day. There is no way to change what happened between you and your sibling in the past, but you can change how those past events make you feel in the present. Discuss these feelings with someone you trust—that's better than allowing the feelings to continue to simmer silently inside you. Try to choose someone outside the family so that he/she doesn't get caught in the middle.

Also, do something that makes you feel calm whenever thoughts of or interactions with this sibling make you stressed or angry. This should begin to erode your mind's association between this sibling and the unpleasant feelings.

Potential calming activities include exercising…playing calming music…deep breathing…petting your pet…meditating…or writing in a journal.

3. Confront your family's hierarchical structure and unspoken inequalities. In many families the kids are not treated exactly the same.

Examples: Older siblings often are given additional responsibilities, while younger siblings are told they must do as the older ones say. And parents may become less strict with younger siblings. In past decades, boys often faced different expectations and received a larger share of the resources than girls. Write down the inequalities and hierarchies that prevailed in your family when you were growing up. (If these do not come quickly to mind, think about how household rules and responsibilities varied based on gender and birth order…and/or consult with siblings with whom you get along well.) Now consider what you have written—could these childhood hierarchies and inequalities be affecting the way you and your sibling interact with each other to this day?

4. Consider what made your sibling hurt you (or vice versa). Could the discord between you actually have been caused not by either of you, but by a family situation completely out of both of your control?

Example: Ted hated his elder brother, John, because John mistreated Ted when he babysat him after school as children. Ted's hatred festered well into adulthood—until he considered why John had mistreated him. His elder brother had been deeply unhappy because he did not want to be stuck home babysitting every afternoon. Once Ted realized this, he stopped seeing his brother as a monster and instead saw that they both were victims of the family's financial struggles—their parents had to work and couldn't afford a sitter.

5. Reflect upon how your sibling still wounds you (or vice versa). Does the sister who said mean things to you in childhood still say mean things today? Does the brother who ignored your opinions as a child still ignore what you say today? Make a list of the sibling's traits that have bothered you since childhood.

Now think about how you have grown and changed since childhood. You are not the same person you were when you were a child, so you do not have to let your sibling's words and actions wound you the way they once did.

Example: Your sister has always diminished your accomplishments, and this contributed to your feeling like a failure. Reflect on all that you have achieved in your life—you no longer are that child who needs to feel insecure about her worth. Remind yourself of this when your sister says something mean. Also list the ways in which your sibling has changed since childhood. It is easy to define people by their enduring traits, but everyone changes over time—which means that your sibling is capable of changing the behaviors that wound you.

6. Share what you have learned with your sibling. Invite your sibling to meet with you. Practice relaxation techniques before you get together. Then begin by expressing the positive feelings you still have for this sibling and explaining why you think fixing the relationship is worth the trouble.

Then explain that you have put a lot of thought into what's gone wrong between you and why you think the pattern can be overcome. Do this in a way that avoids placing blame.

Example: "You're my brother, and I love you. I want us to have a closer relationship, for our sake, for our kids' sakes, and so we can work together to take care of Mom if she ever needs our help. I've been putting a lot of thought into why we don't get along. I was younger, so Mom put you in charge. I think that made me resentful about having to do what you said…and maybe it made you resentful about having to take so much responsibility. But the situation wasn't your fault or mine, and we don't have to let it stand in the way of us getting along as adults."

Alternative: If your sibling harbors a deep well of anger toward you and tells you so, instead acknowledge your past mistakes and the legitimacy of the sibling's anger, then say that you would like to try to fix things if your sibling is ever interested in doing so. Understand that your sibling might not yet be ready.

7. Start building a new relationship. Add a new ending to your "I hate you" story so that it now includes how the two of you are overcoming your problems and becoming friends. Remind yourself of this ending whenever the old "I hate you" story comes to mind.

Discuss with your sibling that there inevitably will be setbacks along the way, but pledge to overcome these rather than allow the relationship to disintegrate.

Make a ritual of celebrating the rebirth of the relationship. Note the date when you agreed to patch things up, and call, write or get together to commemorate this date in future years.

Don't consider your efforts a failure if your sibling doesn't agree to rebuild the relationship. The main benefit of forgiveness is the peace that surrounds you when you move out of the past into the present…have used self-help to heal yourself…and turned off the endless spigot of your "I hate you" story. Forgiveness is about transforming yourself.

How to Influence Your Heirs from Beyond the Grave

Charles A. Redd, JD, a partner who handles estate- and trust-related issues for the St. Louis law office of Stinson Leonard Street. Stinson.com

Do you feel strongly that your granddaughter should attend the same college you did? Or that your wayward son should get married and have children, but only when he is at least 25 years old? Or that all of your children together should one day take over your family business?

And would you like to be able to compel these family members to heed your wishes even after you have died?

An estate-planning tool called an incentive trust could help you prod your heirs in a desired direction when you are no longer there to influence them. With an incentive trust, some or all of your assets are passed to the trust upon your death rather than directly to heirs. A trustee is empowered to distribute funds from the trust only if and when beneficiaries do whatever it is you have specified in the trust.

These trusts are not for everyone—some people consider it invasive to exert "dead hand" control over heirs, and others balk at their cost (expect to pay an attorney perhaps $2,500 to $5,000 to draft an incentive trust).

There are legal limits on what you can do with an incentive trust. And a poorly constructed trust could have unforeseen and unwanted consequences.

Still, there are times when this tool can be extremely useful…

POTENTIAL USES

Common uses of incentive trusts…

•**Encouraging education.** Your trust might pay college costs for your beneficiaries only if they earn specified degrees…and/or pursue specific majors.

Helpful: Consider placing limits on the number of years of education the trust will pay for so that you don't unintentionally encourage beneficiaries to become "career students." Some trusts require beneficiaries to maintain high grade-point averages. Do not set this GPA bar too high, or you might unintentionally discourage beneficiaries from choosing challenging majors.

•**Discouraging drug abuse.** If you leave assets to a beneficiary who has used illegal drugs, your gift might end up in the pocket of a drug dealer, and your beneficiary might end up in worse shape than ever. An incentive trust could provide this beneficiary with his inheritance in small amounts over time, with each distribution contingent on passing a drug test.

Helpful: Be specific, so that the beneficiary understands exactly what he cannot do if he hopes to receive the money. *Among the issues that you should think through before the trust is drafted…*

Does a single failed drug test mean all distributions cease, or can the beneficiary request a retest and/or get a second chance by entering rehab?

Are only illegal drugs banned, or will abuse of alcohol and/or prescription drugs block distributions, too?

What if the beneficiary uses marijuana in a state where it is legal?

Will there be surprise drug tests?

•**Rewarding hard work.** People who leave significant amounts to their heirs often fear that receiving this windfall will make their heirs slothful. An incentive trust could make distributions contingent on beneficiaries having full-time employment…or it could distribute assets by matching beneficiaries' earned income. This way, the more a beneficiary earns by his own work, the more he gets from your estate.

Helpful: If assets will be distributed only to beneficiaries who engage in full-time employment, explain precisely what that means. Do they have to work 40 hours per week, or is 32 sufficient? Is self-employment acceptable? What if a beneficiary is laid off from his job—do you really want to cut off his inheritance when he needs money most, or can his distributions continue for a while as long as he is actively seeking employment?

Also, if your trust will match earned income, understand that different beneficiaries could end up with very different inheritances. A beneficiary who goes into investment banking and earns a

bundle from his job will receive much more from your estate than the one who becomes a schoolteacher or firefighter or clergyman. If that's not a result you would like, you could cap the income match each year so that a high-earning beneficiary cannot quickly claim the lion's share of the assets.

Alternative: Some incentive trusts match the amount saved in retirement accounts rather than the amount earned, to emphasize thrift rather than earning power.

•**Rewarding specific life paths.** An incentive trust might provide a financial reward for taking over the family business…entering a specific profession…launching a business…devoting time or money to charitable causes…getting married…not getting married until a certain age…remaining married…having children…being a stay-at-home parent…or many other life choices.

Helpful: Consider whether there are potential loopholes in the wording of your trust that a beneficiary could exploit. For example, if you try to encourage entrepreneurship by providing financial backing when beneficiaries launch companies, a beneficiary might start numerous "paper" companies that do nothing real. If there is no obvious way to close all the loopholes, you could grant your trustee the power to rule whether beneficiaries are following the intent of the trust before making distributions.

Whatever behavior you try to encourage, think through how your trustee will confirm that beneficiaries have met the terms. For example, will beneficiaries be required to submit tax forms or provide some other evidence upon request?

LEGAL LIMITS

Your incentive trust could be challenged by a beneficiary and struck down in court if it encourages things that are "against public policy"—that is, things that harm the state or its citizens. *State laws vary, but in general, this includes…*

•**Religious restrictions.** A trust that encourages a beneficiary to leave a religion or adhere to a particular one is likely to be struck down if challenged.

•**Inhibiting marriage.** A trust that provides a financial incentive to leave a particular spouse is likely to be struck down if challenged. A trust that discourages marriage in general (or specific types, such as same-sex marriage) falls into a gray area—it would come down to a particular judge's ruling.

Speak with your estate-planning attorney about the limits that apply in your state of residence. If you move to a different state after having an incentive trust drafted, check with a lawyer there to see if anything needs to be changed.

Helpful: If you wish to include something in your incentive trust that is considered against public policy in your state but not in a different state, it might be possible to have your trust fall under that other state's jurisdiction.

CHOOSE THE RIGHT TRUSTEE

For the best chance of your incentive trust having the effect you envision, tell your estate-planning attorney that you wish to include precise instructions in the language…but that you also wish to include language granting your trustee the right to use his discretion and that the trustee's decisions should be final and binding. *This accomplishes the following…*

•**Allows the trustee to make commonsense rulings.** There might be situations where following the letter of the trust could have unintended and unfair consequences.

Example: Your trust provides financial incentives for heirs to have full-time employment, but one of your beneficiaries sustains a disabling injury and can no longer work. If your trustee has the right to use his own discretion, he could prevent this beneficiary from being disinherited.

•**Makes it very difficult for beneficiaries to successfully challenge the trust or trustee in court.** When a trust grants final decision-making authority to its trustee, it becomes almost impossible for beneficiaries to successfully argue that this trustee is not correctly implementing the trust's terms.

•**The key is selecting the right trustee.** This trustee must be intelligent enough to interpret your intent and have sufficient backbone to stand up to beneficiaries when necessary. The best solution is to name co-trustees. Select an individual you believe will act with wisdom and strength (and a successor trustee who will do the same if this trustee can no longer serve) plus a corporate trustee from a bank or trust company. Fees paid to a trustee vary widely depending on the state's fee schedules, the size and complexity of the trust, and conditions laid out in the trust.

Include language in the trust stating that funds will be distributed only when both trustees agree that the distribution is warranted. This way your individual trustee can handle mundane trust matters on his own…yet still deflect beneficiaries' anger by blaming the corporate trustee when a request for funds is rejected.

How to Get Grown Kids to Move Out

Kevin Leman, PhD, a psychologist based in Tucson, Arizona, who specializes in parenting, family and marriage issues. He is author of numerous books including *Making Children Mind Without Losing Yours* and *Planet Middle School: Helping Your Child Through the Peer Pressure, Awkward Moments & Emotional Drama.* DrLeman.com

For an increasing number of young adults, growing up no longer means moving out. About 23% of Americans between the ages of 25 and 34 are living with their parents or grandparents, compared with just 11% in 1980. Some have pressing reasons to live at home—perhaps they recently experienced a divorce or layoff and are in a period of turmoil. But many are simply choosing to live "at home."

This arrangement doesn't just complicate parents' lives…it prevents these young adults from truly launching their own lives. The kindest thing parents can do is not coddle these "kids" but nudge them out of the nest.

Here's how to respond if an adult child wants to move back in…and how to get an adult child currently living in your home out the door…

WHEN AN ADULT CHILD WANTS TO COME BACK

There's nothing wrong with letting an adult child live at home temporarily during times of turmoil. A child who has lost his/her job or his partner might need a safe place to lick his wounds. But it is in no one's interest for a parent's home to become a place where this adult child can hide from life. So when a child asks if he can return, say yes—but that you're concerned that he might not be happy if he does, because of the rules he would have to live by. *These rules might include…*

●**You must get a job.** If the child protests that he can't find anything better than flipping burgers, tell him he'll have to flip burgers. It's not enough for the child to promise to "look for work." This could mean nothing more than sending out a résumé every now and then. He must understand that living in your house will not help him escape or delay joining the workforce. Besides, working in an unpleasant or low-paying job could be the motivation he needs to go out and find something better.

●**You must contribute 25% of your take-home pay as rent.** This reinforces the message that living at home is not a free ride. The adult child also should be responsible for paying his personal expenses.

Helpful: If you do not need this rent money, set it aside in an interest-bearing account. If the adult child works hard to get his life on track, present the money to him when he moves out. This return of rent must come as a surprise, however—if the child expects it, that could undermine the message that he must pay his own way.

●**You will have to do housework.** List specific chores that he will have to do such as his laundry, clean his room, take out the garbage, etc.

Also: If this adult child has young children who will be moving in, too, and you have offered to help with child care, set limits. Perhaps you will provide child care one or two days a week or you will help when the adult child is working, but he should not expect you to babysit every evening while he goes out with friends.

You will have to abide by the house schedule. This might mean guests must be out by 10 pm… the TV volume must be turned way down (or off) by 11 pm…or that there's a midnight curfew.

●**You must deal with your own debts.** Do not get sucked into your adult child's financial problems. Not only could this cripple your retirement, it could cripple the adult child's sense of financial

responsibility. It's fine to offer guidance, but don't bail him out.

●**You must move out by a specific departure date.** This could be one month, three months or six months down the road—the timetable is up to you. The important part is that there is a deadline so the adult child doesn't start to see living at home as a permanent solution.

If these rules sound severe, they're meant to be. If living in your house is unrestrictive, the adult child will have less reason to move out and get on with his own life.

When you pitch all of this to your child, explain that you understand that it probably doesn't sound very appealing and that you won't be offended if he opts to get together with some friends and split a cheap apartment—no harm in floating this idea.

If the child still wants to move in, get a handshake agreement that he will abide by the terms you laid out. If he does, treat him with respect—don't joke about the bad job he has been forced to take or tell him he's made a mess of his life. Instead, commiserate by sharing stories about your struggles as a young adult—the child might not realize that you faced challenges early on, too. Offer advice when it is requested, but do not try to run his life—that will not foster the sense of responsibility you are trying to help him develop.

IF AN ADULT CHILD ALREADY IS LIVING IN YOUR HOME

If you failed to establish strict rules and a departure date before your adult child moved in, this child might now be showing little interest in moving out. If so, tell the child these five words—"I owe you an apology." This is more likely to get the child's attention than yet another admonition to get a job or an apartment.

When the child asks the reason for the apology, reply, "When we let you return home, we had the best of intentions, but in retrospect, it wasn't what was best for you. We should have had an agreement in place for how this would work, because without that, it clearly isn't working for anyone. We realize that you're not going to like this, but if you're going to continue staying here, this is what will be required..." then list rules and deadlines such as those described earlier.

HOW TO RAISE KIDS WHO RETURN ONLY FOR VISITS

Four ways to increase the odds that young children and teens will move out when they grow up...

•**Encourage without overpraising.** By all means tell your child "good job" when he works hard and accomplishes something—but do not consistently tell your child that he is the greatest thing in the world. Overpraised children can turn into adults with an inflated sense of self-worth. They might consider entry-level jobs beneath them and end up living at home when no one offers them a six-figure salary and corner office right out of school.

•**Assign children chores.** Kids raised in households where everyone pulls his weight tend to become adults who understand that they must work hard and take responsibility to achieve anything.

•**Let the child take the lead on college money matters.** College is supposed to prepare kids for adult life. Taking charge of college finances is a crucial part of that. Help your kids pay their tuition (or even pay for college outright) if you are in a financial position to do so—but insist that college kids take part-time or summer jobs to cover some costs. If college loans are needed, the child—not the parent—should take these out. Your role is to help the child understand loan terms and the dangers of going deeply into debt.

Tattoo Mania! If You Want to Get One...or Get Rid of One

Johanna S. Youner, DPM, a certified laser specialist and a member of the American Society for Laser Medicine and Surgery. She removes tattoos at Park Avenue Laser Treatment in New York City. She also is a podiatrist and cosmetic foot surgeon. ParkAvenueLaserTreatment.com

Tattoos have gone mainstream. One in five American adults has at least one tattoo (21%), which is up from the 14% who reported having a tattoo when asked the question in 2008. And 15% of all baby boomers have at least one tattoo. It's a fun way to bond with friends and family members.

Here's what you need to know if you want a tattoo—and what you need to know if you want to get rid of one...

GETTING A TATTOO

The vast majority of tattoo artists are scrupulous about cleanliness and using sterile instruments. You're unlikely to get an infection, but if any of the following symptoms develop after you get a tattoo, see your doctor...

•**Increased pain, swelling, redness, heat or tenderness around the tattoo site**

•**Red streaks extending from the area**

•**Any bad odor, drainage or pus**

•**Fever**

What's more likely to happen is that you will end up with a tattoo that you simply don't like.

To protect yourself...

•**Don't chase the trends.** If you're tempted to get the same tattoo that lots of other people in your social circle have, you might be out-of-date before you leave the parlor.

Example: The so-called "tramp stamp" (a lower-back tattoo) was popular among women more than a decade ago. It's considered passé today. Barbed wire around the bicep? It's been done (and overdone).

•**Think twice about names.** Reputable tattoo artists strongly discourage name tattoos. A tattoo, unlike love in many cases, really is forever—unless you're willing to pay big bucks to get it removed.

•**Plan for concealment.** Even if tattoos are acceptable in your social circle or place of employment, you're taking a chance if you get a tattoo where it can't be covered—the fingers, neck, etc.

•**Remember gravity.** The body that you have today isn't the one that you'll have in 10 or 20 years. A vibrant red rose that looks great on a 30-year-old abdomen might get a little (or a lot) wilted by the time you're 50. Tattoos age better on parts of the body that are less susceptible to changes—the shoulder, back, ankle, foot, wrist and hand.

●**Consider the pain.** Getting a tattoo is less painful on fleshy parts of the body, such as the upper arm or thigh. Tattooing hurts more when it is done on bony areas, such as the middle of the chest or top of the foot.

Caution: If you are taking a blood thinner such as *warfarin* or have a disorder that decreases clotting, talk with your doctor before you get a tattoo. Tattoo needles typically don't produce much blood, but if clotting is decreased, bleeding could be heavier or last longer, which also could affect how the tattoo turns out.

IF YOU CHANGE YOUR MIND

With today's lasers, it's possible to completely erase many tattoos. Look for a doctor trained in laser tattoo removal. It's fine if a technician operates the laser, as long as the facility is overseen by a physician. A tattoo parlor with a laser is not enough.

Certain colors are difficult to remove, so choose as few as possible. Yellow, pastel and fluorescent colors are the hardest to remove. Whites also are tricky. It's not always possible to completely remove these colors, although they often can be lightened. Black is the easiest color to remove.

What to expect…

The doctor will apply an anesthetic cream to the skin or ask you to apply it. When the laser is activated, you'll feel as though you're getting popped by a rubber band. Some people compare the sensation to being spattered with bacon grease.

A small, simple black tattoo can potentially be removed in a single session—but don't count on it. Most tattoos require multiple sessions—the national average is six to 10, with the sessions spaced about six weeks apart. With each treatment, the tattoo fades incrementally. You pay by the inch, usually about $100.

The first treatment hurts the most. Most people experience less discomfort during subsequent sessions. After each treatment, the area will be coated with an antibacterial ointment and bandaged. Your skin will feel slightly irritated for several days, and you'll have some residual redness for a week to 10 days.

Thinner skin, such as inside the wrist, has a tendency to scar. If you are a person who tends to scar

or get keloids (severely thickened scars), you probably will scar. People of color with good pigment in their skin may lose some of their pigment in addition to the tattoo ink. Having a lidocaine injection to numb the area increases the chances of scarring.

To Defuse a Family Feud…

Avidan Milevsky, PhD, associate professor of psychology, Kutztown University, Kutztown, Pennsylvania, quoted in *RealSimple.*

To help diminish a family feud when you are stuck in the middle…

Tell each family member involved something positive you have heard about him/her from the other. This can help break through the negative feelings they have. You also can let them know how much it would mean to you if they would at least agree to meet and try to talk.

How to Deal with Complainers, Whiners and Pessimists

Mark Goulston, MD, a psychiatrist and an FBI and police hostage negotiation trainer who has written numerous books, including *Just Listen: Discover the Secret to Getting Through to Absolutely Anyone* and *Talking to Crazy: How to Deal with the Irrational and Impossible People in Your Life.* MarkGoulston.com

Negativity is contagious. Even if you start off in a good mood, talking to a complainer or pessimist can turn a good day into a bad one.

That doesn't mean you shouldn't listen to other people's problems. Supporting each other through hard times is an important part of a good relationship. But talking through problems is different from the repetitive, unproductive negativity of chronic complainers. You know you are talking to a negative person when you feel tired during the conversation…you start feeling as powerless and victimized as he does…you notice yourself wanting to avoid the person because of the gloom that follows him/her around.

Most pessimists and whiners aren't trying to ruin your day. In fact, they often aren't aware of the negative effect they have on other people. After sharing their unhappiness, frustration or disenchantment with life, they feel temporary relief. They don't consider the possibility that the behavior bringing them such relief causes other people to feel worse.

They also may not be aware that by venting their gripes, they alienate others, further increasing their loneliness and dissatisfaction and increasing their sense of powerlessness.

To protect your emotional health, it's a good idea to minimize the time you spend with negative people. But if the complainer is someone you work with or is a friend or relative you care about, staying out of the person's path may not be practical or desirable.

Several simple tactics can keep a pessimist from wearing you out. Some techniques work better than others depending on the person, relationship and situation, so don't be afraid to experiment with different methods.

Important: Keep your tone matter of fact and pleasant. If your voice carries a hint of scolding, shaming or condescension, these strategies won't work.

How to keep a complainer from dragging you down…

QUIT PROBLEM-SOLVING

The chronic complainer doesn't want advice on how to improve his situation. He wants company in his downbeat view of the world. Even if he asks for your input, you are likely to wind up in a spiral where all your suggestions are rejected or lead to new complaints, and both of you will get progressively more annoyed.

Instead, ask in a friendly tone, "Are you looking for advice, or do you need to vent? If venting would be helpful, I can listen for five minutes. After that, I'll have to do something else or I will wind up in a bad mood—and that won't be good for either of us."

Another option is to let the person complain for a minute or two, then say in a friendly tone, "Gosh, what a drag. What are you going to do now?" If the person says he has no idea or asks what you think, say pleasantly, "Hey, my advice only works for me. It's your life, and I know you can figure this out. Keep me posted on how it goes."

DEFLECT

Practice a few quick, light or even playful phrases that you can choose from to change the subject from negative to positive. *Examples…*

●**"Wow, Mom, the doctor kept you waiting at the nursing home—sorry to hear it.** What did he say is causing the pain in your hip?"

●**"That does sound like something to complain about.** Tell me something that's going right. There's so much negativity in the world, it's starting to get to me, and some positive news would be a big help."

●**If you're in a group that's complaining:** "Hey, everybody, we're becoming a tad negative. Given the state of the world, we have more to be thankful for than upset about. Can we change the subject?"

EMPATHIZE

If you feel yourself being pulled into the other person's negative view, say in a compassionate tone, "You're doing a good job of helping me feel what it feels like to be you. I'm sorry you have to deal with all that."

For a person who probably doesn't receive many compliments and who feels alone in his unhappiness, this simple expression of empathy may provide the affirmation that he needs to let go of the negative topic for the time being.

ASK FOR CHANGE

If the relationship is in danger of deteriorating, a more active intervention may be needed. Use an approach I call assertive humility—clearly stating what you need by asking for help.

What to say: "I need your help. You're a special person to me, yet I find myself wanting to avoid you. The reason is that every time we talk, I feel unhappy during the conversation and for a while afterward. It seems to me that you focus more on the negative than the positive, and that's hard on me. Before I get to the point where I say something harsh or actively avoid you, I'd like to make a request. When we're together, I need to hear about at least one thing that's going right in your life. Would you be willing to try that?"

DEALING WITH TRULY TOXIC PEOPLE

The above techniques work well with garden-variety pessimists. With even stronger toxic negativity, you need to take a different approach.

The toxic person isn't looking for support but for control. He gains that control by throwing you off balance with upsetting, manipulative or irrational behavior.

You are dealing with a toxic person if he claims that his negative circumstances are your fault… goes beyond complaining to criticize or verbally attack you…twists your words so that you end up confused and frustrated.

Simple strategy: While the toxic person is ranting, look him in the eye neutrally and nonconfrontationally. When he's done, pause for two to four seconds—a little longer than is customary in conversation. *Then, in a matter-of-fact tone, say one of the following…*

•**"Do you want to run that by me again?"**

•**"Would you say that to me again in a quieter voice?"**

•**"Do you actually believe what you just said?"**

These responses work because they let the toxic person know that you are onto him and won't be provoked into an argument or outburst.

Rehearse these responses until you can keep your demeanor both pleasant and assertive when you speak. (For more on dealing with toxic people, read "8 Ways to Manage the Impossible Person in Your Life" at BottomLineInc.com/8-ways-to-man age-the-impossible-person-in-your-life.)

Living Fences: 10 Beautiful Plants to Create Privacy

Julie Moir Messervy, a landscape designer based in Saxtons River, Vermont. Her projects include the design of the Toronto Music Garden as well as many public and residential gardens across North America and beyond. She is author of *Home Outside: Creating the Landscape You Love* and creator of the Home Outside Palette landscape design app for iOS and Android. JMMDS.com

Are you considering trees or shrubs as a living fence on your property? Choosing a living fence over a conventional fence can be an excellent option. These planted perimeters look beautiful and can convey a feeling of peace.

Living fences can be less expensive, too—installing a wood privacy fence is likely to cost $20 to $30 per linear foot. Living fences can cost as little as $1 per linear foot. That's a savings of $1,450 on a 50-foot fence. And while many communities have rules restricting the construction of tall fences, restrictions governing the planting of trees and shrubs are rare.

On the downside, living fences may need pruning, watering, mulching and fertilizing. They also are less effective than traditional fences at keeping pets within the yard and other animals out. Indeed, deer might nibble windows into a living fence, though this can be overcome through smart plant selection.

The following plants can make wonderful living fences. But be sure to confirm with a local garden center that a specific plant is appropriate for your yard.

•**Privet can be an effective and extremely affordable living fence.** Confirm that the variety you select will grow to the desired height—some varieties of privet grow to only four feet, while others reach eight, 10 or beyond if not kept pruned. Prune once a year after the tiny flowers bloom in spring for a more informal hedge and again before late summer if you want a tighter, more formal look.

On the downside, some people find the scent of privet flowers unpleasant when they bloom, typically in late spring. And most varieties of privet are "deciduous"—that is, they lose their leaves in the winter—so a privet hedge might not provide full privacy year-round. Young one-to-two-foot-high privet plants often can be purchased for just $4 apiece and grow very quickly, typically adding two to three feet of height per year. Privet plants can be positioned as much as four feet apart to form a hedge (though two- or three-foot spacing will create a tighter hedge) for a total price as low as $1 per linear foot.

•**Yew grows into a tall, attractive and easy-to-prune hedge.** Unlike privet, it's an evergreen, so its privacy and beauty last year-round. Yew excels in the shade as well as in sun, making it a particularly good choice for sections of a lawn's perimeter that often are in the shadow of buildings or trees.

Yew is slow-growing, so if you purchase small plants, it could be many years before they give you full privacy. But slow-growing plants require infrequent pruning, done best in late winter or early spring. Young, small yew plants might sell for as little as $10 apiece, but you can easily spend $50 or more for more mature, larger plants. Space yews one to two feet apart to form an effective privacy hedge.

Note: Yew is a particular favorite of deer.

•**Pyracantha and holly are evergreen shrubs that provide more color than the typical privacy hedge.** They produce beautiful berries in the fall and winter, plus white flowers in the spring and early summer. Holly's berries typically are red, while pyracantha, also known as firethorn, feature a blaze of red, orange or yellow berries. Both of these shrubs are adaptable to a wide range of climates and growing conditions. But wear thick gloves while pruning them—some hollies have pointed leaves, and pyracantha has sharp thorns. Prices vary depending on plant size and variety, but expect to pay perhaps $20 to $30 for a young plant in a 2.25-gallon container. Position one plant every 18 to 30 inches to form a hedge.

•**Enkianthus features clumps of little hanging flowers that typically are white,** and it needs little to no trimming to stay in shape. It is well-suited for acid soils and shade, perfect for the understory of tall trees. Its fall foliage provides vivid orange and red colors. On the downside, it is slightly less dense than privet…and somewhat slower growing—it could take an extra year or two for enkianthus to provide full privacy. It also can be expensive—potentially $30 or more per plant. Enkianthus is deciduous, so do not expect full privacy in winter. Plant four to five feet apart.

•**Bamboo is a hearty, fast-growing type of grass that can form an elegant, effective living fence.** Some varieties can grow to 50 feet or more. It grows well in a wide variety of climates and is far more deer-resistant than the other plants on this list. Most varieties are not technically evergreen, but bamboo provides an effective privacy fence year-round because it never becomes sparse.

You're likely to encounter two basic types of bamboo in garden centers—clumping and running forms. The running form may look more attractive but is very difficult to contain. It's a good choice only in locations where it will not be able to spread, such as between two paved driveways or in a raised planter. Another way to contain it is to mow around its edges to keep the new shoots from developing. The clumping form grows in small hillocks and doesn't mass together to form a grove as running bamboo does, but it won't take over the surrounding land. Many varieties of bamboo appropriate for living fences sell for perhaps $30 to $60 for a three-gallon-container size. Expect to need one plant for every five to 10 linear feet.

•**Willows are fast-growing and attractive deciduous trees appropriate for a wide range of climates.** People don't normally think of willows as perimeter plants, but many varieties produce thick, drooping foliage that can form an effective living fence. Willow's foliage can have a silver, gold or lime green tint depending on the variety, but different varieties grow to different heights, so choose carefully. Willows tend to prefer moist soil, so they're good for sections of lawn that do not drain well.

Young willow trees might sell for $30 to $60 apiece. That might sound pricey, but you can plant willows five feet apart in a living fence, so you won't need as many of them to form a fence as you would many plants on this list.

•**Arborvitae, juniper and cedar are elegant, attractive evergreen trees** that can form effective privacy borders. Each is available in a range of varieties that generally do not require pruning. They are not as fast-growing as many other options on this list, however, and they can be fairly pricey—upward of $100 per plant if you purchase trees that already have reached four-to-six-feet in height. But if you're willing to wait a few years for privacy, small, young trees can cost $15 apiece. Plant three to 10 feet apart, depending on width at maturity.

NATURAL-LOOKING PLANT BORDERS

If the straight edges of a traditional border hedge strike you as too formal or artificial, selecting a shaggy plant such as willow is not your only option. *You also could…*

●**Incorporate more than one type of plant into your privacy hedge.** Using a variety of different plants will make your living fence appear more natural. It also means that you can choose plants well-suited to the varied conditions of your yard's perimeter—yew in shady spots, for example, or willows where soil drains poorly.

●**Build up to the living fence with plants of increasing height.** Plant the tall shrubs and trees listed here along the edge of the property, but also position shorter plants just to the inside of those tall plants. The resulting layered look will reduce the sense that the yard is surrounded by a wall.

●**Prune nonvertically.** Hedges such as privet and yew traditionally are pruned into vertical walls, but that's not the only option. You can prune border plants into more natural-seeming "mountain like" shapes that are thicker near their bases, for example.

Why You Don't Want the House in the Divorce…

Diane Pearson, CFP, CDFA, personal chief financial officer at Legend Financial Advisors, Inc., Pittsburgh. Legend Financial.com

Be very careful how you split up the possessions if you split up with your spouse. Accepting certain assets in a divorce settlement could leave you with a smaller slice of the total pie than you deserve. You can't necessarily depend on your divorce attorney to warn you about all these potential potholes, either—most divorce attorneys are experts on family law, not asset values. And your financial adviser may not understand divorce law.

Six types of assets that you may not want in a divorce settlement…

●**The family home.** Some people desperately want to keep their homes in a divorce. This may be where they raised their kids. It's where they know their neighbors. It's where they expected to grow old. It's only natural to want to maintain these emotional connections as a marriage crumbles—but taking the home in a divorce settlement usually is a big financial mistake.

Homes typically are worth hundreds of thousands of dollars. To keep this asset in a divorce, you probably would have to agree to let your partner keep the lion's share of the family's retirement savings and/or other investments. But while that investment portfolio is likely to increase significantly in value over the years and produce much needed retirement income, a home is more likely to stagnate in value and perhaps even be a financial sinkhole.

Don't be fooled by the recent real estate recovery—homes simply are not good investments. From 1890 through 2012, on average, home prices gained absolutely nothing in value after adjusting for inflation. Owning a home actually costs money—lots of it. In addition to mortgage payments, home owners must pay thousands of dollars each year in property taxes and insurance, maintenance and utility bills.

Most divorced people are much better served by agreeing to sell the family home during the divorce process. Buy or rent a smaller home, possibly an affordable condo or apartment, instead. (Or let your partner keep the house if he/she likes, while you get the lion's share of the savings.)

●**Tax-deferred retirement accounts.** When is $100,000 in savings not worth $100,000? When there's a big tax bill due. Unlike most other types of savings, assets held in tax-deferred accounts such as traditional IRAs or 401(k)s are taxed as income when the money is withdrawn. That means perhaps one-fifth to one-third or more of the savings might wind up in the government's pockets, not yours, depending on your federal and state income tax brackets.

Tax-deferred retirement savings may be illiquid, as well—you might face a 10% penalty if you withdraw any money from these accounts prior to age 59½.

In a divorce settlement, don't agree to take more than half of the tax-deferred assets, which eventually will be taxable, if that means your soon-to-be ex gets more than half of the Roth IRA savings, which typically won't be taxed, or more than half of the non-tax-advantaged savings.

Exception: You get more assets to make up for the future tax bite.

•**Investments that have gained a lot in value.** Which would you rather receive in your divorce settlement—$100,000 worth of a stock that has climbed steadily in value since you purchased it... or $100,000 worth of a stock that has lost money for your portfolio? Intuitively it might seem wise to take the stock that has done well, because it's more likely than the laggard to continue to increase in value. But that's the wrong choice, and doing that could leave you saddled with a big tax bill.

When you sell an investment that you have owned for more than one year, any increase in its value from its cost basis—what it cost you—is taxed at your long-term capital gains tax rate, which currently is 15% for most taxpayers. (Taxpayers in the 35% income tax bracket pay a steeper 20% rate when the new net investment income tax is included. Profits from the sale of assets held less than one year are taxed at a taxpayer's income tax rate.) On the other hand, selling an investment that has lost money can decrease your income tax bill.

Don't agree to take your portfolio's winning stocks in a divorce settlement while your former spouse takes the losers unless you receive a larger share of the total assets to make up for your future tax bill. *A few exceptions...*

Cost basis doesn't matter if an investment is held in a tax-advantaged retirement account. Whether or not they have gained value, investments held in tax-deferred accounts are taxed as ordinary income when withdrawn, while those held in Roth accounts typically are not taxed at all upon withdrawal.

Low cost basis isn't a problem if you intend to leave the asset to your heirs. In fact, it can be an ad-vantage to the family, because assets such as stocks that aren't held in tax-advantaged accounts generally receive a "step up in basis" upon your death. That means the capital gains up to that point are not taxed when the assets are later sold by your heirs.

You don't have to pay long-term capital gains taxes if your income is below a certain amount. As of 2018, single filers with taxable income of up to $38,600 fall into this category. These rules could change in future years.

•**Art, antiques and collectibles.** An appraiser typically is hired or a guidebook consulted during the divorce process to determine the value of any art, antiques and collectibles. Trouble is, the values these appraisers and guidebooks assign to these possessions often are much too high. The quoted amount is often what you would have to spend to buy a similar item in a shop, rather than the amount you would receive if you sold the one you have. Because of steep retail markups, these figures can be different.

Art, antiques and collectibles can be costly to insure. And if they eventually are sold for more than they initially cost, you might face a long-term capital gains tax of 20%.

If you don't want to give up your art, antiques or collectibles in a divorce, at least confirm that the appraiser or guidebook used will provide the amount your items would bring if you sold them, not their replacement or insurance value.

•**A small business (unless you know as much as or more than your spouse about the business and its finances).** Be very wary if your spouse suggests that you take the business in a divorce settlement if that spouse handles the finances. He/she might have good reason to believe that the company is worth less than its appraised value.

Example: Maybe your spouse knows that a key client is about to defect to a competitor.

•**Relatively new annuities.** Cashing out an annuity too soon (generally within five to 12 years of the date when it was purchased) could trigger a surrender fee of as much as 8% to 10%. Many annuities also have steep annual fees that can cut into their long-term value.

How to Defuse a Heated Conversation

Geoffrey Tumlin, CEO, Mouthpeace Consulting LLC, communications consultants, Austin, Texas, and author of *Stop Talking, Start Communicating.*

Here's what to do…don't fight back—retaliation only increases the intensity of the interaction…take a break and ask for a pause so that emotions can become calmer.…apologize for something—such as one part of the conversation or the escalation itself…give a relevant compliment about something the other person has said or suggested, as a reminder that there is an underlying positive relationship—it can be as simple as, "I hadn't thought of things that way"…and acknowledge that the other person has a positive intent, emotion or feeling and say that you appreciate his/her willingness to try to deal with a difficult issue.

Say No to Family and Friends…and Still Have Them Like You!

Daniel Post Senning, great-great-grandson of etiquette maven Emily Post and coauthor of *Emily Post's Etiquette*, 19th edition. He is cohost of the Awesome Etiquette podcast, which can be found through the Emily Post Institute's website. EmilyPost.com

Your friend asks for a loan. Your cousin asks for a business referral. Your neighbor asks you to donate to a charity. Your coworker asks for your help with a project that shouldn't really be your problem.

It can be uncomfortable to turn down unwanted requests from people close to you—it even can poison a relationship. Some people simply swallow hard and say yes to such requests to avoid these unpleasant consequences.

The trouble is, saying yes to unwanted requests can have unpleasant consequences all their own. It could cost you time or money that you really can't spare or mean that you must do things not in line with your beliefs. Saying yes could lead to similar requests being made in the future. And in the long run, it can damage relationships just as deeply as saying no.

Example: Loaning money to a friend could ruin the relationship if that friend doesn't pay you back.

Here's how to minimize the risk for hurt feelings or damaged relationships when you must reject a request. Keep in mind that the art of good etiquette is coming up with a response that is not hurtful and doesn't destroy your integrity.

TAKE A LITTLE TIME

A friend, relative or coworker could be especially insulted or embarrassed by a quick rejection—it sends the message that you didn't even consider the request worthy of consideration. Let the person know what your answer is likely to be, but ask for a few minutes, hours or days to consider the request. Stress that you need this time because of your positive feelings for the person making the request.

Examples: "I normally say no to requests such as these automatically, but because I consider you a very close friend, I'm going to give your request some thought." Or "I don't think there's any way I'm going to be able to do that, but out of respect to you, I'm going to mull it over. I'll let you know by tomorrow."

If an answer is needed very quickly, still take five to 10 seconds to mull it over before saying no. Use this time to come up with a way to let this person down gently—more on that below.

REJECT CLEARLY BUT KINDLY

People sometimes find it so hard to say no to friends that their nos accidentally come out as maybes or even yeses. When the time comes to give your answer, be clear from the outset that you are saying no.

Examples: Polite but unambiguous opening lines for rejections include, "I'm sorry, I have to say no" or "I just can't do it."

Remind yourself that the person wouldn't have asked if he/she didn't feel close to you—and follow up your clear rejection by expressing gratitude for that closeness. Say something along the lines of, "It means a lot to me that our relationship is close enough that you can come to me with this request. I'm really sorry I can't come through for you."

In truth, you probably are not grateful for the request—you actually might be upset with your friend for putting you in an awkward position. But expressing gratitude should help your friend get over any embarrassment that he/she might be feeling about the situation, which reduces the odds of long-term damage to the relationship.

Exception: If you reject a friend's request that you make a donation to a charity and/or sign a petition, there is no need to say anything to help this friend overcome embarrassment. People tend to feel good about themselves—not embarrassed—when they make requests on behalf of causes they believe in. Instead say something like, "It's wonderful that you're supporting a good cause…"

GIVE AN EXPLANATION

If possible, provide a brief explanation for the rejection—one that does not reflect negatively on the person making the request.

Among the options…

Explain that the request does not fit a system you have in place or rules you must follow. This makes the rejection seem less personal. *Examples…*

●**A friend asks you for a business reference.** You might say that your employer has a rule barring employees from providing references. (Many companies have this rule.)

●**A friend asks to stay with you for a month.** You might say that your condo board has a rule against guests staying that long.

●**A relative asks for a donation to charity.** You might say that you make all of your charitable donations to a small number of nonprofits whose administrative expenses you track closely.

●**A friend asks you to add him to your LinkedIn contacts.** You might say that you have a policy of adding only people with whom you have worked on multiple occasions.

●**Blame your own limits.** This sends the message that you truly would like to help but can't.

Examples: A friend asks for a loan. If you don't have room in your budget, say so. If you had a bad experience loaning to a friend before, say that.

●**Note that you already have done quite a bit to help.** This way you're not saying no, but rather that your yeses have reached their limit. *Example:* You are asked to chair a committee that you already have chaired two years in a row. You could mention the earlier service, then say, "It's time for me to let someone else have his turn."

BRAINSTORM
POTENTIAL ALTERNATIVES

Is there a way that you can say no but still provide some form of assistance that you do find palatable? If so, mention this. *Possibilities include…*

●**Offer your time, knowledge or network rather than your money or possessions.** *Examples:* A friend asks you to buy cookies to support her child's Girl Scout troop. You could say that you don't eat cookies (or that you already bought cookies from someone else's child), but you would be happy to ask people you know if they are interested. A friend asks to borrow your pickup truck to move a bulky item. You could say that you don't like to loan out your vehicle, but that if the trip is local, you would be willing to do the driving.

●**Offer to help find someone else who can help.** *Example:* A neighbor asks for your assistance with a median-strip beautification project. Perhaps you can provide an introduction to someone else in the neighborhood who enjoys gardening.

●**Offer to reevaluate the rejection in the future.** *Example:* A friend asks for a donation to his favorite charity. You say no, you already have made your donations for the year—but add that you will include this charity among the group of nonprofits you will consider in future years.

Even if your alternative is not accepted, making the offer sends the message that you do care.

How to Stay Close to Your Adult Kids

Scott Haltzman, MD, psychiatrist in private practice in Barrington, Rhode Island, and author of *The Secrets of Happy Families: Eight Keys to Building a Lifetime of Connection and Contentment.* DrScott.com

In our mobile modern society, many adult children live hundreds or thousands of miles from their parents. Even extended families whose members still live near one another face challenges, with ever-increasing demands on their time.

The good news: Parents can overcome these challenges and build strong relationships with their adult children no matter where they live. *Ways to make that happen...*

SHOW RESPECT

Adult children want one thing from their parents above all else—respect. The more you provide, the greater the odds that your children will want to remain close with you.

It also is important not to criticize your grown children when it seems as if they have failed. Criticism will only drive them away from you.

Helpful: If you catch yourself being critical, make at least five positive comments or actions before the end of your call or visit. Research has shown that a positive-to-negative interaction ratio of five-to-one or better can help maintain closeness in our relationships with our children (and our own spouses, too).

Warning: Never make family traditions seem like requirements. If you hold it against your son that he spent Thanksgiving with his in-laws, the holiday could become a source of anxiety, driving your family apart, rather than a tradition that holds you together.

DON'T GIVE ADVICE

Resist the urge to give advice, even when it is requested. Receiving guidance from a parent can make adults feel like helpless children again. They tend to rebel against this unpleasant feeling by pulling away from the parent—even if they asked for advice.

If your adult child requests your advice, say, "I'm happy to help you sort through the pros and cons, but it's your decision to make, and I know you'll make the right choice."

Provide direct advice only if the adult child is about to make a massive and potentially irreversible misstep, such as investing in a scam or buying an older home without an inspection.

BEFRIEND YOUR CHILD'S SPOUSE

Search for ways to support and praise your sons- and daughters-in-law—even if you don't really care for them. It's your relationship with your children and grandchildren that will suffer the most if you don't get along with your kids' spouses.

Warning: The fact that your child criticizes his/her spouse to you does not mean that you are free to criticize that spouse, too. What you take as serious criticisms might just be your child venting normal marital frustrations. He actually might love and respect this partner very deeply. If so, your criticisms might damage your relationship with your child.

DON'T INTRUDE

Select noninvasive communication methods. Frequent phone calls or drop-in visits from parents can seem overbearing to adult children. *Better options...*

•**E-mail and social-networking websites.** Modern technology lets families keep in touch without interfering with one another's schedules. You can write as much as you like in an e-mail message or on a Facebook page—and your kids can read it whenever they like.

Don't Let E-Mail Embarrass You

Keith Bradford, author of *Life Hacks.*

If you are writing an e-mail about a sensitive subject, be sure to add the recipient's e-mail address after you are done composing your message. This will ensure that if you accidentally hit "send" while writing, you won't send off an unfinished—and potentially embarrassing—e-mail.

8 Ways to Manage an Impossible Person in Your Life

Mark Goulston, MD, founder and CEO of the Goulston Group, a consulting company that helps business owners think outside the box. A psychiatrist and an FBI and police hostage negotiation trainer, he has written numerous books including *Just Listen: Discover the Secret to Getting Through to Absolutely Anyone* and *Talking to Crazy: How to Deal with the Irrational and Impossible People in Your Life*. MarkGoulston.com

Most people have to deal regularly with at least one irrational person—someone who routinely acts unreasonably. Whether that person is a raging boss, suspicious neighbor or an emotionally erratic teen, it's hard not to get dragged into feeling crazy ourselves.

The usual way we tend to deal with other people's irrationality is to try to get them to see reason. We use logic to convince them of the wrongness of their points of view. But this strategy just makes things worse. Instead of accepting our logic, the other person acts even more irrational, and the situation escalates until both people are acting crazy. This scenario is frustrating, stressful and unproductive.

Trying to argue an irrational person into rationality is pointless because from that person's point of view, his/her behavior is rational. He is in the grip of thinking patterns with roots in the past. His behavior is a response to a perceived threat, and your appeals to reason come across as scolding, condescending and threatening, causing him to cling even harder to the behavior that he views as protecting him from that threat.

Also, the chronically irrational person is more comfortable with extreme behavior than the rest of us. This makes it easy for him to escalate an encounter until the other person loses control.

A better way to deal with crazy-making behavior is the counterintuitive way—lean in to it. Instead of trying to talk the other person out of his world view, empathize with him and act as though that view is real—which it is to that person at that moment. This approach allows him to see you as an ally, not a threat. Though effective, this strategy is difficult. It requires you to stay calm and composed.

You need to manage the irrationality that the other person triggers in you. *What to do…*

●**Recognize the pattern.** Most chronically irrational people have a preferred way of operating and over time will drive you into wanting to do something irrational that you'll likely regret. Examples: Bullying…acting ice-cold…making wild accusations…bursting into tears.

When you can identify someone's habitual brand of irrationality, you are less likely to be blindsided. Instead of reacting automatically, you can be prepared with a calm response.

●**Practice poise.** When confronted with irrationality, repeat to yourself, over and over, This is an opportunity for poise.

Think of poise as a mental muscle that gets stronger the more you use it. To strengthen your capacity for poise, practice every day with less extreme challenges. At the beginning of each day, ask yourself, What are likely to be the most challenging situations I will deal with today? Make a commitment to demonstrate poise in those situations. Keep in mind that poise is worth developing not just because it makes you more effective with irrational people—it earns you respect from people in all areas of your life and improves your self-respect as well.

●**Remember your mentors.** A good way to access poise under pressure is to call to mind someone who has always cared about you and believed in you. This inner mentor can be living or dead.

Picture that person saying to you, *This is your opportunity for poise. Take advantage of it. You aren't going to shoot from the hip. You can handle this.*

Practice this daily. Picturing one or more inner mentors is comforting and also inspires gratitude. Gratitude acts like a shock absorber and cushions you against your angry reactions to others.

●**Assume innocence.** Adopt the view that other people are not setting out to make your life miserable—they are simply struggling to deal with their own problems, however clumsily. Imagine that nothing is going right in the difficult person's life, and remind yourself that his behavior is not really about you—it is his way of displacing his own fear and frustration.

•**Use the "3 strikes and you're calm" technique.** If an encounter escalates and you are about to lose control, this technique will help you regain composure. It is simple enough to remember even under intense stress.

Step 1: **Think of the first thing you want to say or do in response to the irrational person—which is usually to defend yourself—**and don't do it. Take a breath and exhale.

Step 2: **Think of the second thing you want to say or do—often getting even or giving an ultimatum—and don't do that either.** Take a breath and exhale.

Step 3: **Think of the third thing you want to say or do—which probably has to do with finding a solution.** At this point, you have shifted from irrational to rational. Take a breath and exhale.

•**Downshift the discussion.** Once you are poised and calm, say in a quiet, matter-of-fact voice, "Whoa, hold on for a second—what was that about?"

Instead of "whoa," you can say "gee" or "gosh." The key is to use a nonconfrontational tone and to ask with genuine curiosity. You are signaling to the other person that you recognize something is upsetting him and that you are willing to learn more about his world. This usually de-escalates the conversation.

If the other person is still on the attack, remain calm and say, "Whoa, and that too—what was that about?" He may continue to vent, but probably not at you. If you keep demonstrating poise, he will realize that his wild talk isn't working, and you can guide the discussion in a more positive direction.

•**Deepen the conversation with the FUD tool.** FUD stands for Frustrated, Upset and Disappointed. These words invite the person to calm down by talking about the concerns underneath his seemingly irrational behavior.

Start by saying, "You sound frustrated about something. What's that about?" Listen with the intent to understand and empathize—not to talk him out of what he is experiencing. After he has talked about his frustration, say, "I can understand that. You also sound upset. What are you upset about?"

Most individuals who have a hostile or agitated tone will own up to feeling frustrated because that seems less accusatory than telling them they're angry. Then after that, having them talk about what they're upset about helps them to further get things off their chests.

Finally, say, "You sound disappointed. What are you disappointed with?" The word disappointed has an almost magically calming effect. Even irrational people focus on the what when asked about being disappointed.

•**Use "mind's eye" language.** After the person has vented, say, "Going forward, in your mind's eye, what can we do to make this better for you?"

This phrasing often helps to shift the person from mindless venting to a positive focus on the future.

Sometimes a person's problems are so ingrained that he can't make the shift. Even then, you can be proud of your own calm response.

8

Big Government

Best Ways for Couples to Boost Their Social Security Income

Michael Kitces, CFP, director of planning research for Pinnacle Advisory Group, Inc., a wealth-management firm based in Columbia, Maryland. He is publisher of the financial-planning blog *Nerd's Eye View*. Kitces.com

Since Congress voted in 2015 to end two Social Security loopholes, many married couples have been searching for other strategies to maximize their benefits.

Best option for most couples: The spouse with the higher earnings history postpones claiming benefits, while the spouse with the lower earnings history starts collecting benefits as early as age 62. Your level of Social Security benefits depends, in part, on your earnings history and the age at which you start collecting benefits. Postponing the start of the higher earner's benefits increases the size of that spouse's future monthly benefits by 6% to 8% for each year of postponement, up to age 70. (There is no advantage to postponing the start of benefits past 70.)

Whether it pays to do this depends in part on how long the higher earner expects to live, making the choice difficult. But keep in mind that by postponing the start of the higher earner's benefits, you also can increase the amount that the spouse with the lower earnings history ends up receiving—that's because of "survivor benefits." When one spouse dies, the surviving spouse can, in effect, opt to claim the deceased partner's benefits. Because of that option, delaying the start of the higher earner's benefits until age 70 typically will produce the highest total benefits for a married couple if either spouse lives to at least 83. Based on actuarial tables, it's likely that for the typical married couple, if both reach age 65, at least one will live past 90. (Be aware that benefits claimed before full retirement age are subject to a Social Security earnings test, which could reduce or even eliminate benefits if the lower earner still is working and earning $15,720 or more.)

Example: Say a husband is entitled to monthly benefits of $2,000 if he starts collecting at age 62… or around $3,500 if he waits until age 70.* And say he decides to start collecting at age 70 and dies at 80, so he receives just $420,000 in total benefits, less than the $432,000 he would have received if he had started his benefits at age 62. But his wife lives to 90, so the combined benefits they receive from

*Social Security amounts cited in this article are based on current levels. Actual benefits may increase each year based on a measure of inflation.

his account, including her survivor benefits, total $840,000—much more (a difference of $168,000) than the $672,000 they would have received if he had started at age 62.

Meanwhile, the wife started collecting Social Security benefits at age 62 based on her own earnings history and kept collecting those benefits until she switched to survivor benefits. That way, the couple receives at least some benefits while waiting for the higher earner to start collecting at age 70. (Of course, if the wife had not earned much at all, these benefits might be very small. If her benefits are much less than half the husband's benefits, it might make sense for the husband to start collecting before age 70—more on that below.)

Possible alternative when the lower earner has an extremely low earnings history or no earnings history: Rather than waiting until age 70, the higher earner starts collecting benefits when the lower earner reaches "full" retirement age. One downside to waiting until age 70 to claim benefits, as the husband in the previous example did, is that under the new rules, the wife in the example could not claim spousal benefits based on the husband's earnings unless the husband is collecting his benefits. (Under the old rules, the husband could file for benefits to allow his wife to claim spousal benefits, and then he could immediately suspend his own benefits, allowing his eventual monthly benefits to continue to increase in size.)

The new barrier to claiming spousal benefits is not a major problem if the wife has a significant earnings history of her own, but for couples where one spouse earned virtually all the income, it could mean that the low-earning spouse loses out on substantial benefits for many years. And be aware that although most Social Security benefits increase in size for each month you wait to claim them up to age 70, spousal benefits stop increasing once the spouse reaches what the government refers to as "full" retirement age, which is 66 for people born between 1943 and 1954.

That means it might make sense for the higher earner to start collecting his benefits when the low earner reaches full retirement age so that the low earner can start collecting spousal benefits at that point.

Example: Say the husband is the higher earner and is eligible to start collecting monthly benefits of $2,500 when he reaches full retirement age of 66…or $3,300 if he waits until age 70. Say his wife, who is the same age, did not have significant earned income during her working years. The husband chooses to start collecting his benefits at age 66…the wife starts collecting spousal benefits at age 66…and both live to 80. The couple receives a combined $630,000 versus just $594,000 if they had waited until age 70 to start collecting benefits.

However, in some cases, it might make more sense for the high earner to wait, possibly until age 70, even though that means the low earner sacrifices some spousal benefits. The correct choice depends on such factors as whether the couple has enough assets to tide them over and their expectations about their life spans. (If the high earner is at least four years older than the low earner, this is a nonissue—by the time the low earner reaches full retirement age, the high earner will have started his benefits anyway.)

Example: Say the wife in the example above lives to 90 rather than 80. As a result, the couple would have been better off waiting until age 70 to start collecting benefits, which would have meant the couple earned a total of $990,000 versus a total of $930,000 if the husband started at age 66.

Find Out What's Coming in the Mail

NBCNews.com

You can find out what mail you will be getting with a new, free US Postal Service offer called Informed Delivery. The service gives a daily digital preview of your mail. Each morning you get an e-mail with images of the mail that will be delivered later in the day.

Information: InformedDelivery.USPS.com.

There Could Be Lead in Your Water, Too

Robert D. Morris, MD, PhD, an environmental epidemiologist based in Seattle and former professor at Tufts University School of Medicine, Boston. He is author of *The Blue Death*. EHTrust.org

Residents of Flint, Michigan, are not the only ones who could have dangerously high lead levels in their municipal drinking water. A water utility does not officially have a lead problem unless at least 10% of homes tested have problems. That means thousands of households could be exposed to lead poisoning even in areas where the water is "safe." Lead poisoning can cause behavioral and developmental issues in children, as well as high blood pressure and kidney disease in adults.

Lead is not easy for water utilities to monitor and control because it is not present when water leaves treatment facilities. It gets into water from the pipes in homes and under yards. Older homes face the greatest risks.

Prior to 1920, when local municipalities began to prohibit the use of lead pipes, they were routinely used to connect homes to the water main under the street. The EPA did not ban their use nationally until 1986. A private well installed before 1986 also may have pipes and fixtures that contain lead.

If you are uncertain whether your home is connected to the water main by a lead pipe, check the home inspector's report conducted when you bought the property—if there's a lead pipe, this should be noted. Or find where your water supply enters your home—if this pipe is dull gray and can be easily scratched with a sharp knife, it's probably lead. Or have a licensed plumber check for you ($45 to $150).

What to do: Install a water filter on your kitchen faucet or below your sink. Expect to pay $200 to $400 for an under-sink unit, plus a few hundred more to have it professionally installed. Faucet-mounted filters cost less than $100 and are easy to install but tend to slow water flow and don't fit every faucet. If you do not have a filter, run your tap for one to two minutes in the morning before using it (lead leaches into water as it sits in the pipes), and do not drink hot water from the tap (hot water absorbs more lead).

Not all water filters remove lead, so check the packaging or the manufacturer's website. Or use the independent-testing company NSF's online search tool to find lead-reduction filters (Info.NSF.org/certified/dwtu).

Your Dollars Could Be Worth More Than Face Value

Dave Undis, currency collector who runs the website Cool SerialNumbers.com.

US paper currency with an unusual serial number often is worth much more than face value, we hear from collector Dave Undis. The recent redesign of the $100 bill has spurred interest in currency denominations. Collectors, many of whom trade on eBay.com and LynKnight.com, often pay thousands of dollars, depending on the serial number and condition of the bills.

Examples of values above face value for denominations from $1 to $100: Serial numbers up to 100, such as 00000001, are the most sought after, $50 to $10,000…"solids" such as 77777777, $100 to $1,000…"ladders" such as 12345678, $150 to $1,500…and "radars," which read the same both ways, such as 31688613, $5 to $100.

9

College Costs

Paying Off a Student Loan? Avoid These Costly Mistakes

Mark Kantrowitz, former publisher and vice president of strategy for Cappex.com, which helps match students with colleges and scholarships.

The cost of college has skyrocketed in recent decades, and so has the burden of student loans. More than 40 million Americans now owe a total of about $1.3 trillion in student-loan debt. Repaying those loans is especially challenging when borrowers make loan-repayment mistakes—some that even the government is duping them into!

MISTAKE: **Assuming the Department of Education's new RePAYE program is the best plan for you.** RePAYE (Revised Pay As You Earn) allows borrowers who have modest incomes to repay certain government-subsidized student loans at slower-than-normal rates. That can sound very appealing to cash-strapped grads. But the government actually offers four different "income-driven repayment plans," and for most borrowers RePAYE is not the best. It does not cap monthly payments, so while required payments can be appealingly low for recent grads earning entry-level wages, the payments might skyrocket in future years. RePAYE also gives some borrowers an unwelcome

wedding present—a spouse's earnings must be included in income calculations, which can trigger a sudden spike in repayment requirements. (A cynic might even argue that the government is pushing RePAYE not because it saves borrowers money, but because it will net the government more money.)

Better: The older income-driven repayment plan known as Pay-As-You-Earn repayment (PAYE) is always the best option if you are eligible. Unlike RePAYE, PAYE caps monthly payment requirements and lets borrowers exclude spousal income if separate tax returns are filed. Under certain circumstances, PAYE forgives debt sooner than RePAYE, too. Consider RePAYE—and Income-Based Repayment (IBR), a third program—only if you do not qualify for PAYE.

Choosing between RePAYE and IBR is less clearcut—IBR requires borrowers to devote a higher percentage of their discretionary income to loan repayment...but like PAYE, it caps required payments and provides a way around the marriage penalty. (The fourth income-based repayment plan—Income-Contingent Repayment—is never the best option.)

If your total student-loan debt is less than your annual income, skip income-based repayment—these programs won't benefit you unless you work in the public sector. (Full-time public sector employees typically should sign up for IBR even if they have substantial incomes, because special rules might allow them to have any remaining debt completely wiped away in as little as 10 years.)

MISTAKE: **Consolidating student loans into a single larger loan just to make repayment a little easier or interest rates a little lower.** Private lenders make student-loan consolidation and refinancing sound appealing, advertising that it will lower interest rates and monthly payments and simplify borrowers' lives. (The federal government has a Direct Consolidation Loan program as well.)

But for most borrowers, consolidation has more downside than upside. It means borrowers cannot pay off their highest-rate loans first. And replacing federally subsidized student loans with a private consolidation loan often costs borrowers advantageous loan terms.

Example: Federal student loans often let borrowers defer repayment if they enroll in graduate school…reduce repayments if they have modest incomes…or stop making payments entirely if they become permanently disabled. Private loans generally are far less flexible.

It is almost never a good idea to refinance federally subsidized student loans, particularly if they are fixed-rate loans. It could be worth consolidating and refinancing private student loans if this leads to significantly lower interest rates. In that case, wait at least two to three years after graduation to refinance—recent grads' credit scores usually are too low to qualify for attractive private loan rates.

In contrast, it might make sense to refinance a Parent PLUS loan with a private lender if the interest rate savings are significant—at least two percentage points is a good rule of thumb. Parent PLUS loans lack many consumer protections provided by federal student loans, so the downside of refinancing is limited.

MISTAKE: **Skipping auto-debit.** Many borrowers are hesitant to have their student-loan payments automatically withdrawn from their bank accounts each month because they fear that it gives the lender too much control over their money. But you can cancel auto-debit to regain control at any time. And meanwhile, not only is auto-debit a great way to avoid late or missed payments, but many lenders will lower student-loan interest rates by 0.25 to 0.5 percentage points if you use auto-debit.

MISTAKE: **Paying off the smallest loans first rather than highest interest rate loans.** There's a loan-repayment technique called the "snowball strategy" that advocates paying off the lowest-balance student loans first. The idea is that paying off these small loans in full as quickly as possible will give borrowers a sense of accomplishment that will help them pay off their larger loans sooner.

Better: If you can afford to make more than the minimum payments on your loans, target your loans with the highest interest rates first, not your smallest loans. The faster you pay off high-rate loans, the less you will pay overall.

Example: Say you have a $10,000 student loan with a 4.5% interest rate and $100 minimum monthly payment…a $50,000 loan with a 7.9% rate and a $200 minimum monthly payment…and you can afford to make $200 in additional payments each month. If you used that extra money to pay off the small, low-rate loan rather than the large, high-rate one, you would end up making more than $4,300 in unnecessary interest payments.

MISTAKE: **Failing to tell lenders how extra payments should be applied.** Making payments greater than the minimum required amount is a great way to reduce the overall cost of this debt. But when borrowers try to do this, their lenders often do not apply the extra money in the manner that is most beneficial to these borrowers.

Examples: If the borrower has two loans with the lender, his/her excess payment might be applied to the loan that has a lower interest rate. Or if the borrower sends in an extra check, that payment might be treated as an early payment of the following month's required payment rather than as an additional payment. In that case, the lender might not charge the borrower for the following month's required payment, and as a result, the balance of the loan would not be paid off any quicker.

Better: Include a cover letter with any extra payment (or payment in excess of the minimum required amount) clearly stating, "This is an extra payment to be applied to [a particular loan number] to reduce the principal balance of that loan." If you make an extra payment electronically through a lender's website, there typically is a way to identify specifically how the money should be applied, such as clicking on a particular loan number. If it isn't obvious, call the lender and ask how to proceed.

MISTAKE: **Paying off student loans at the expense of employer-matched contributions to retirement plans.** In general, it is better to pay down student loans than to invest your money. The one big exception is if your employer offers matching on certain retirement plan contributions. It's like free money.

Better: Contribute the full amount matched by your employer before making any college loan payments above the minimum.

COSIGNING MISTAKES PARENTS MAKE

MISTAKE: **Agreeing to cosign a student loan if you intend to refinance your mortgage (or take out any other loan).** Lenders will treat the student loan as if it were your own debt. That might inflate your debt-to-income ratio enough that you will not qualify for better interest rates until the student loan is paid off.

MISTAKE: **Letting cosigned loans languish when students do not keep up the payments.** Those late or missed payments will devastate the parent cosigner's credit scores.

Mistake: **Making payments for the student if your goal is to be released as a cosigner.** Many student loans offer cosigners a path toward being removed from the loan—if the student proves he can make the payments himself. But if the cosigner makes even one loan payment on the student's behalf, the lender will take it as a sign that the student was unable to make that payment himself and deny the cosigner's release request.

Better: Give the money to the student, and let the student make the payment.

You Might Be Able to Sue Your College

Roundup of experts on the proposed new federal rules, reported at MarketWatch.com.

Colleges are easier to sue under rules proposed by the US Department of Education. Students who were misled about job opportunities after college, loan repayment rates and graduation rates may be eligible to have federal student loans forgiven…and colleges that receive federal financial-aid funding won't be able to require students to sign arbitration agreements.

Free College Tuition

Roundup of experts on special college programs reported at CNBC.com.

A free year of college tuition is being offered by some schools to get students to graduate. Only 52.8% of students who started at four-year private nonprofit colleges in 2007 graduated in four years (latest data available). And only 33.5% graduated in four years from four-year public colleges. To boost graduation rates, the University of Evansville guarantees graduation in four years or the fifth year is tuition-free. The University of Rochester offers students a fifth year tuition-free to pursue academic interests outside their majors. Lehigh University (tuition: $52,480) and Carnegie Mellon (tuition: $54,244) allow some successful students a free year of tuition to pursue further academic interests. Clark University lets students earn a bachelor's and a master's degree in five years, with the fifth year tuition-free. Eligibility requirements for the programs are strict and vary widely.

Get Cash Back for College

Mark Kantrowitz, former publisher and vice president of strategy for Cappex.com, which helps match students with colleges and scholarships. He also serves on the editorial board of *Journal of Student Financial Aid.* Cappex.com

Paying for your purchases with credit cards could earn you money for a child's college education. It even might help pay down student loans after graduation. *Here's how…*

•**Fidelity Rewards Visa Signature card.** This no-fee credit card gives you 2% cash back on all purchases, and you can have Fidelity automatically shift the money to a 529 college savings plan, which includes various mutual fund investments that you can choose plus tax-free investment growth and possible tax deductions in some states.

Those 2% rewards can add up.

Example: If you spend $25,000 a year with the credit card for 20 years and the investments you select for your 529 plan earn a 7% annual return, that's nearly $22,000 for college.

Grandparents also can take advantage of the Fidelity card for college savings, but there's a twist. If you want to save on behalf of a grandchild, it's best to call the number on the back of the card and ask to always have your rewards pushed directly into the Fidelity 529 account previously opened by the parents. (Grandparents can open 529 accounts, but grandparent-controlled 529 accounts receive less favorable treatment from college financial-aid offices than parent-controlled accounts.) For details, visit FidelityRewards.com.

•**Register your credit cards and store loyalty cards with Upromise.** This free program offered by student-loan issuer Sallie Mae enables students and their family members to earn cash for college by spending at any of the thousands of participating merchants and restaurants. *You can…*

•Earn up to 10% back on online purchases made from hundreds of merchants.* To do this, simply navigate to the online merchant's website through a link on the Upromise site.

*Features are subject to change.

Examples: Earn 3% cash back at Amazon.com …5% back at WalMart.com.

•Earn 2.5% cash back on meals at more than 10,000 participating restaurants. Simply pay using a credit card that has been registered on the Upromise website.

•Qualify for cash back on certain purchases at many supermarket and pharmacy chains. Earning this money takes a bit more effort—you not only have to register your store loyalty cards with Upromise, you have to activate the offers that interest you online before shopping.

•Cash earned through Upromise is automatically deposited into a college savings plan, such as a 529 or Sallie Mae "Upromise GoalSaver Account."

Alternatively, this money can be automatically transferred to a loan issuer to pay down a college loan…or you can request it in the form of a check.

•You also can sign up for the Upromise MasterCard. It offers 1% cash back on most purchases and as much as 5% back on purchases made at Upromise partners—on top of the rewards program described above. (UPromise.com)

Get Paid to Move After College

Fortune.com

Some states and municipalities are offering college graduates cash to help pay back student loans if the graduates move there. In Kansas, graduates can get tax breaks and up to $15,000 in student-loan repayments in 77 counties through the Rural Opportunity Zones program. In Niagara Falls, New York, $3,492 a year is available for two years to a small number of graduates. Chattanooga, Tennessee, has an incentive program that financially assists computer-software developers who relocate there. Detroit has a similar program, paying chosen applicants to move to the city.

Check local chambers of commerce and government agencies to find out about programs elsewhere.

10

Tech Frustrations

No More Weak Wi-Fi

Dong Ngo, a former editor at CNET, the consumer-electronics website that attracts more than 10 million visitors a month, and head of CNET's San Francisco testing labs. CNET.com

Your Netflix movie freezes. Your video chat breaks up. Or you simply can't post your latest cat video onto Facebook.

The culprit: Your weak Wi-Fi signal.

Having a strong home Wi-Fi signal is especially important at a time when the number of Wi-Fi–enabled devices that use the Internet in our homes is growing, whether they are being used to stream videos or connect to devices such as thermostats or security systems.

Good news: A new type of Wi-Fi system is available—a "home mesh network" that overcomes many drawbacks of the old-style routers that most of us have in our homes.

Because Wi-Fi signals degrade quickly over distance and are easily disrupted by walls and other obstacles, homes often wind up with dead zones. With a home mesh network, you can virtually eliminate this problem by drawing upon a fleet of smaller devices spread around the house that sync with one another. They even can work effectively in outdoor living areas such as a deck, a porch or around a backyard pool.

HOW THEY WORK

A home mesh network consists of a kit that includes a router base plus one or more remote extenders. You manage the network through a free iOS (Apple) or Android app on your smartphone or tablet, and some routers also allow you to use a laptop or a desktop computer. These starter kits use the latest Wi-Fi technology to support high-speed Internet, and they typically provide strong coverage throughout homes of up to 4,500 square feet or possibly even more. If a starter kit doesn't adequately cover your home, additional remote transmitters may be necessary to get a strong signal everywhere.

Setup typically takes less than 15 minutes, and in some cases, you are guided through the setup by the app. You connect the base transmitter to your Internet modem via an Ethernet cable just as you do with a traditional router. The additional transmitters connect to electrical sockets elsewhere in the house. In some systems, the app instructs you on the optimal areas to position the transmitters.

THE BEST DEVICES

A home mesh network costs more than a traditional router—$200 to $400 for the starter kit and another $100 to $250 per transmitter if you need additional transmitters. *All four of the following home mesh networks are fairly easy to set up, but there are differences in design, performance and features that will make each brand appeal to certain users...*

Best for performance: Netgear Orbi. This is the first Wi-Fi system that won't incur any loss of signal. When other systems extend a Wi-Fi signal, about 50% of the signal is lost because the system uses a single band to both receive and rebroadcast the signal. The Orbi eliminates this problem by using a separate dedicated band for extending the coverage. Its Wi-Fi speeds are faster than the Eero and Luma described below. The Orbi system includes a $399 kit of two devices—one router and one satellite extender—that can cover 4,000 square feet. Additional satellite units cost $249 each. You can use up to three satellites in an Orbi system to cover up to 8,000 square feet.

Drawbacks: If your home is larger than 4,000 square feet, Orbi can be very pricey...and the app does not help with setup. Netgear.com

Best for ease of use: Eero, from the first company to start selling home mesh networks when it launched about a year ago. The device has hundreds of thousands of users and has earned high praise. In contrast, most other home mesh networks just started shipping in the past few months, so it is hard to tell how reliable they are. Eero also is the only system that automatically installs network software updates so that you never have to go to a website or an app and download and install updates yourself.

Eero transmitters have an Apple-like design—sleek, palm-size devices with a glossy white finish. There is no visible antenna, and they can lie flat on a shelf or table, powered by a cord plugged into an electrical outlet.

Drawback: Eero—a starter kit, including two extenders—costs $399. Additional transmitters cost $149 each. Eero is not the fastest mesh network listed here, but that won't be a deterrent for many households because it's enough to handle multiple computers streaming video and surfing

the Internet at the same time with no slowdowns. Eero.com

Best if you want added security features: Luma, a start-up backed by Amazon.com, offers a home mesh network that is less expensive than Eero's but that has similar download-speed capacity. A starter kit, including two extenders, costs about $199, and additional transmitters cost about $85. Luma's extensive security features include the ability to scan connected devices for malware and built-in parental controls. GetLuma.com

Least expensive starter kit, widest coverage and impressive speed: Amplifi HD offers maximum download speeds up to 10% to 20% greater than Eero and Luma, and it claims to cover areas up to 20,000 square feet with only a starter kit, although this can vary depending on the layout of your home and the thickness of the walls. The kit's two remote transmitters are plugged directly into electrical sockets (no cords attached). The starter kit is $340. Two less expensive Amplifi kits also offer great range, but they use an older, slower Wi-Fi technology that is probably no better than your old Wi-Fi router.

Drawbacks: Amplifi HD has remote transmitters with 10-inch-long, paddle-shaped antennas that consumers may find cumbersome-looking plugged into their walls. Amplifi.com

A SIMPLER, CHEAPER ALTERNATIVE

You don't necessarily have to buy a home mesh network to improve the strength and speed of your Wi-Fi signal. If you have a small-to-midsize home, you might just want to replace your current Wi-Fi router with a more advanced one-unit router. If your current router is more than two years old, it's probably not delivering the best possible performance. Newer routers typically have more powerful internal radio equipment designed to improve range, and they have the latest Wi-Fi technology, known as 802.11ac, which is many times faster than the old standard, 802.11n.

Important: Your computer or laptop should be equipped with 802.11ac technology for a new router to make a difference in Wi-Fi speed. If you're unsure, check with customer support for your machine.

Recommended: The Asus RT-AC88U one-unit provides powerful hardware, easy set-up and excellent range.

Cost: $240. Asus.com

Carrier Cellphone Trap

Logan Abbott president of the independent cell-phone comparison site MyRatePlan.com, which was launched in 1999, San Diego.

Beware: Cell-phone–carrier transition trap. More than 25 million consumers switched carriers last year, up 20% from five years ago, thanks to the rise of no-contract carriers reimbursing switching costs. But you will be charged for any unused days from the last month of your old carrier's billing cycle, which could be costly if you switch several weeks before the final cycle ends.

What to do: Wait until a few days before your old cycle ends to start your new service.

Any Smartphone or Laptop Can Catch Fire

Susan McKelvey, communications manager with the National Fire Protection Association (NFPA). The NFPA is a nonprofit organization based in Quincy, Massachusetts, that has been working to eliminate fire deaths since 1896. NFPA.org

---

The popular Samsung Galaxy Note 7 smartphone was recalled in late 2016 after dozens of users' phones burst into flames. But while that smartphone was particularly prone to fires because of design and manufacturing defects, any smartphone that contains a lithium ion battery could overheat and catch fire—and virtually all smartphones contain this type of battery. There

have been several reported cases of iPhones catching fire, for example.

And it isn't just smartphones that are at risk—lithium ion batteries have become extremely common and are used in everything from laptop computers and tablets to cameras and headphones.

Lithium ion batteries are statistically quite safe, and fires are rare—but they store a large amount of energy in a very small space, so the danger is real. *How you use and recharge devices that contain lithium ion batteries could have a significant impact on the fire risk…*

•**Do not rest a device with a lithium ion battery on a bed, couch, pillow or other textile as it charges.** These surfaces tend to reduce the device's ability to dissipate heat. Also, if the battery overheats, such things could catch fire.

•**If you need to replace a lithium ion battery or its charging cord, purchase the same brand battery or cord designed to be used with the device.** Batteries or chargers made by third-party companies might not work as well with your device.

•**Don't leave devices that contain lithium ion batteries in direct sunlight or in parked cars on hot days if it can be avoided.** This can contribute to battery overheating.

•**If you notice an odd odor coming from the device and/or it feels unusually hot to the touch, report it to the manufacturer**—or your cellular service provider if it's a phone—and ask for guidance before using or charging the device again.

•**If you see smoke or flames coming from the device, submerge it in water if you can do so without burning yourself.** If you can't safely move it, call 911.

Important: To eliminate the possibility of electric shock from household current if a device is charging, unplug it before submerging it.

You Can Escape Password Overload

Paul Wagenseil, senior editor specializing in technology security for *Tom's Guide*, which reviews new computer technology products and software, New York City. Toms Guide.com

What sort of password person are you? Are your passwords all easy-to-remember variations of the same basic theme, so you don't forget them? Or do you have many different passwords that you can't remember, so you list them in a notebook or perhaps on sticky notes plastered around your computer?

Neither way of managing your passwords is good enough if you care about online safety.

If you want to be safe from potentially disastrous ID theft or hacking, you need a better way to manage your passwords—a solution that makes it simple for you to use your passwords but very difficult for cyberthieves to guess them, steal them or trick you into disclosing them.

Solution: Password manager software. This type of secure, easy-to-use software allows you to automatically fill in your log-in "credentials" (typically a user name and password) at any site so that you don't have to remember them or look them up each time you visit the site.

HOW THEY WORK

There currently are more than a dozen password-manager products to choose from. With each, you download the software from the password manager's website to your computer and/or your mobile device such as a smartphone or tablet.

The software allows you to create the digital equivalent of a bank vault with your information heavily encrypted and stored in the cloud and/or on your hard drive. During the set-up process, the software automatically gathers all user names and passwords that you already have saved on your device and stores them in your vault...and, with some of the password managers, removes the information from your hard drive. It also captures and stores any additional user names, passwords and other personal information that you enter on various websites from then on.

You can set the password manager to always automatically activate itself...or you can activate it when you need it by clicking on a toolbar icon on your computer or an app on your smartphone and entering a single master password that you have previously created. Then, when you visit a password-protected website that you have logged into previously, the password manager automatically fills in your log-in information. It also can store and fill in other personal information such as your credit card numbers, mailing address and e-mail address, which is a more secure way to store that information than saving it on shopping sites, where it may be vulnerable to being stolen.

ARE THEY SAFE?

All communications between your device and the password manager—and the information stored by the password manager—are heavily encrypted using standards that the US military uses for some of its information encryption.

In addition, password managers evaluate all of your passwords to see how vulnerable each might be to hackers. Then they suggest more complex substitutes for passwords that are not safe enough and, with some password managers, for passwords used on too many sites. Because you no longer have to worry about remembering any of your passwords or typing them in, you can use complex ones that are extremely difficult to crack such as Sk$ltyF>z%OyQ4h^ijI.

Using a single master password to protect all of your other passwords may sound unwise because if someone gets hold of the master password, you're completely vulnerable. However, for most people, it is easier to create, memorize and protect a single, complex password that you never write down or tell anyone about than it is to remember and keep track of numerous weak ones.

For a guide on how to create a strong password, go to TomsGuide.com, click the magnifying glass in the top-right corner and search for "Create Secure Passwords."

Of course, a password manager can't protect information that you have stored with Google, Yahoo,

Home Depot, your bank, your credit card issuer or any other company if a hacker is able to break into the company's user databases.

BEST PASSWORD MANAGERS

Password managers work with almost any computer, laptop, smartphone or tablet, and they support both the Windows and Mac operating systems on computers and the Android and Apple operating systems on mobile devices.

The three password managers below are among the best. The first two have a feature that allows you to automatically change weak or overused passwords on multiple sites to newly generated ones with the press of a button. Not every site allows third-party programs to do this, but even so, it can save a lot of time and help make your accounts more secure.

Best for people looking for a free version: **Last-Pass** is the most popular password manager, with more than seven million users in more than 100 countries. Although the premium version costs only $24 per year, most people will find the free version to be adequate. That's because LastPass recently began allowing users to open a single account and use the free version on all devices. LastPass.com

Best for people who want a very user-friendly program: **Dashlane** has more than three million users and offers the most intuitive interface and easiest-to-use software of all the password managers.

Downside: Its premium version is more expensive than most competitors at $60 annually. (Its free version manages up to 50 passwords.) The premium version enables you to sync passwords across multiple devices and also gives you priority access to customer service. Dashlane.com

Best for people who don't want to deal with remembering a password at all: **True Key,** offered by the technology giant Intel, lets you use facial recognition or fingerprints instead of a master password. It uses your webcam or smartphone camera to scan your face.

Cost for premium version: $20 a year, which lets you save up to 10,000 passwords…the free version lets you save only 15. TrueKey.com

Smartphones with Best Battery Life

ConsumerReports.org

Smartphones that have the best battery life are…

Motorola Droid Turbo…Motorola Droid Turbo 2 …Samsung Galaxy Note 4…Samsung Galaxy S5… Samsung Galaxy S6. These smartphones each boast 24 or more hours of talk time, except for the Samsung Galaxy S5, which gets about 20 hours of talk time. A bonus feature of the Samsung Galaxy Note 4 and Samsung Galaxy S5 is that they have removable batteries, so you can carry a spare battery if you expect to need extra power.

To get longer battery life from all smartphones: Set the screen brightness to Auto…lower the baseline brightness…set the screen to sleep after 15 to 30 seconds without activity…turn on airplane mode when you are in an area with no signal…reduce the frequency of updates for e-mail, social-network feeds and other apps to once per hour.

Protect Your Business from Bad Reviews

Stanley Coren, PhD, professor emeritus of psychology at University of British Columbia who has studied dog behavior in addition to human psychology. He is an instructor with the Vancouver Dog Obedience Training Club and author of several books about dogs, including *Do Dogs Dream? Nearly Everything Your Dog Wants You to Know.*

If you own a small business, you're probably very aware that disgruntled customers vent their displeasure on websites such as Yelp, Angie's List and TripAdvisor. *What to do…*

1. Respond—but not immediately. If you post a response immediately after reading an online consumer complaint about your business, your reply is more likely to be defensive or angry. This won't just annoy the complainer, it could scare away other potential customers. It's better to let your initial emotional reaction abate before responding.

2. When you do respond, acknowledge the validity of the complainer's feelings, even if your business was not at fault. This makes you seem like a calm, reasonable person who cares about his/her customers. It also lets the complainer know that he/she has been heard, which typically is what complainers want most.

Examples: "I'm sorry your experience with us did not go as you had hoped"…or (if the complaint is justified) "We messed up."

3. Offer a solution. If you will take a concrete step in response to a complaint or can offer something to the customer, note this. You might write, "I shared your message with my entire staff to make sure that everyone knows not to do this in the future"…or "Please call me. We stand by our work. I'll send a service tech out to fix this." *A few variations…*

If a negative review lacks specificity or the complainer seems unhinged, the solution you offer could be, "I'd appreciate it if you would contact me with additional details so that we can get to the bottom of this and try to make it right."

If you suspect the complainer is being dishonest, do not come right out and say this—you risk appearing childish if you get sucked into a he said/she said online spat. Instead, write something noncommittal such as, "That certainly is not the way we usually handle things here." Politely ask the complainer to supply dates and times or other details so that you can investigate the accusation.

4. Scan positive reviews for complaints. Sometimes business owners overlook rave reviews that include minor complaints, as in, "I love this company, but I do wish that it would change this one thing…" But it is particularly important to respond promptly to these "positive complaints." Unlike many complaints, these are posted by reasonable people who want to be loyal customers. Moreover, people who read this online review will put particular weight on its complaint because the person who wrote about it seems so evenhanded. Thank the reviewer for his praise, apologize for the problem, then offer a solution.

5. Solicit additional reviews to balance out the negative ones. The more positive reviews there are of your business on the site, the less one or two negative reviews will hurt you. Keep in mind, though, that research has shown that having a small number of bad reviews on your site among many good ones actually helps—when reviews are uniformly positive, readers tend not to trust that they are real.

7 E-Mail Secrets to Make Your Life Easier and Safer

Ryan A. Teeter, PhD, clinical assistant professor of accounting information systems at University of Pittsburgh and coauthor of *Google Apps for Dummies*. He developed training curriculum as a training specialist at Google. Ryan Teeter.com

Here are seven surprising things that can transform the way you use e-mail…

1. You might be able to cancel an e-mail after you have sent it. Have you ever pressed "Send" only to regret it a moment later, possibly because you included words of anger or other emotions in your message that you wish you hadn't shared…addressed it to the wrong person…or hadn't completed your message? With Gmail, the most popular e-mail service, there is an undo option that is easy to use.

What to do: Adjust your settings now, because there's a time limit of 30 seconds after you actually send a message. Go to your e-mail settings by clicking on the gear icon in the upper right of the in-box page. Click on "Settings," scroll down to "Undo Send," enable it and choose a cancellation period that can last from five to 30 seconds. Click "Save changes" at the bottom of the page. From then on, whenever you send an e-mail, you'll see a message at the top of your in-box with an undo option available for the length of time you selected.

**2. Quirky text and punctuation can trigger spam filters that may keep someone from receiv-

ing your e-mail. These include using more than one exclamation point (!!!)…putting a sentence in ALL CAPS…using unusual spellings of words such as speci@l…or using too many spam-associated "trigger" words, phrases and/or symbols.

Among those: Viagra…drugs…porn…guaranteed winner…prize…free…act now…limited time …$$$. Spam filters typically don't block e-mail with known addresses regardless of the content. If you suspect or discover that your e-mail did wind up in someone's spam folder, ask the recipient to add you to his/her e-mail program's contacts list or address book.

3. You can get a free temporary e-mail address in seconds without filling out a long form. This can be very useful when you want to enter a site that requires you to establish an account or join a mailing list but you don't want to provide your regular e-mail address. That way you don't leave yourself vulnerable to a deluge of unwanted messages. To get your temporary e-mail address, go to Mailinator.com, type in an address you choose or that the site suggests (for example, YourName@Mailinator.com), and that's it. There are no passwords. If you need to check e-mail, you just type in your address at the site. After a few hours, your address and your e-mail messages are automatically deleted.

Important: The site is designed for speed and convenience, not security. So don't use it to receive any e-mail with sensitive information.

4. You can use the e-mail program on a computer to send text messages to cell phones. This is handy if your phone is not charged, you're in an area with spotty cellular service or you just don't like typing on a tiny keyboard. The address you will send your message to will consist of the recipient's 10-digit mobile number (without hyphens or spaces), the "@" symbol, and the SMS gateway address of his/her cellular provider.

Example: If the recipient's provider is AT&T, you would send your e-mail to the person's number@txt.ATT.net. Addresses for the other major cellular providers: For Sprint, use @messaging.sprintpcs.com…Verizon, @vtext.com…T-Mobile,

@tmomail.net. For other SMS gateway addresses, go to EmailTextMessages.com.

5. E-mail providers such as Gmail and Yahoo Mail scan every word you write, and they sell the information to advertisers. Although no humans read the text, and your name and e-mail address are not identified, a software program searches for keywords and compiles data for sale. It's called contextual ad targeting. You have to agree to this practice to be able to use these e-mail services, but that policy is hidden in the small type. And if you reveal private information in your e-mails—for instance, that you plan to get divorced—you and other people who share your computer may see ads for such products or services as divorce attorneys in your browser. If these policies make you uncomfortable, try Microsoft Outlook or Apple Mail instead. Although they reserve the right to scan your e-mail, Microsoft does not target ads to you based on your e-mail content, and Apple doesn't make e-mail information available to third-party advertisers.

6. Even today, many e-mail services don't allow sending or receiving attachments larger than 10 megabytes (MB)—so it is hard to send high-quality photos or videos. Gmail and Yahoo allow sending files of up to 25 MB, but even that is restrictive when a single high-resolution photograph can surpass 50 MB. There are several ways to give your recipients access to larger files, however. None of them involves actually attaching the files and transferring them from your computer to the recipient's e-mail in-box. Instead, you upload the files to a remote server over the Internet. The recipient receives a link in your e-mail that he/she clicks to download the file from the remote server. *Here's how to do this…*

●**If you have Gmail, use Google Drive.** It's an online file-storage and file-sharing service available to anyone with a Google account. With Google Drive, you can send files as large as 15 GB, which is 15,000 MB. After you compose your Gmail message, instead of attaching a document, video or photo using the paper clip icon, click on the Google Drive icon next to the paper clip. You can select a file that already is in Google Drive or first upload the file straight from your computer to Google Drive. The recipient does not need Gmail to retrieve the file.

●**For Microsoft Outlook, use Microsoft One-Drive, which works similarly to Google Drive.** Learn how to do this at OneDrive.Live.com/about.

●**For Yahoo Mail and other e-mail services, use Dropbox.com.** It's a free online storage and file-sharing site that works with all major e-mail programs. It operates similarly to Google Drive, but it allows you to send the recipient a link to as large an attachment as you want.

Downside: You need to install Dropbox software on your computer, and you need to pay if you want more than 2 GB of storage. (However, 2 GB can accommodate many high-resolution photos.) It costs $9.99 per month for an additional 1,000 GB of storage.

7. You can back up all your online e-mail to your computer hard drive…and you should. What would happen if you signed into your e-mail account and all your old e-mails and attachments, including work documents, photos and video, had been deleted? Although the chance of this occurring is remote, it's possible—Gmail and Yahoo Mail, for example, have both suffered glitches on their servers that erased the contents of entire e-mail accounts. Fortunately, backing up e-mail is easy. *What to do…*

●**For Gmail,** go to Google's data download page (Takeout.Google.com/settings/takeout), log into your account and follow directions. You will receive a file in your Google Drive with the backed-up data that you can download to your hard drive or to any storage drive you attach to your computer.

●**For Microsoft Outlook,** use the Microsoft Personal Folders Backup tool, which you can download at bit.ly/1TeFOYf.

●**For Yahoo Mail,** download Yahoo backup software from Yahoo.googleapps--backup.com. Install and follow directions.

These Gadgets Are Always Listening

Kim Komando, host of *The Kim Komando Show*, a call-in talk radio show about consumer technology. Komando.com

Digital assistants such as Apple's Siri, Google Assistant and the device Amazon Echo are designed to respond when you speak to them. But to accomplish this, these high-tech helpers must monitor what you're saying, though digital assistants are not supposed to respond unless you say a particular phrase—"Hey, Siri" on the latest iPhones…"OK, Google"…or "Alexa" for Amazon Echo.

Some people find it a bit creepy that something is monitoring every word we say. And security experts have uncovered a sneaky trick that a hacker could in theory use to send commands to your phone if you use Siri or Google Assistant (though the hacker would have to get within 16 feet of your phone).

If you find it unsettling that a device might be eavesdropping, you can stop these digital assistants.

●**Siri.** To turn off Siri, enter the Settings menu of your Apple device. Select "General," then "Siri," then change the setting to off.

●**Amazon Echo.** To turn off Echo, simply press the microphone on/off button on the top of the device. The LED light will turn red. Echo will not listen until the button is pressed again, turning the light blue.

●**Google Assistant.** How you turn it off depends on the device…

On an Android device, select the "Google Settings" app (its icon is gray and contains a "g"). Choose "Search" under "Sources," then "Voice," followed by "OK Google Detection." If it currently says "On," tap it once to turn it off.

On an Apple device, select the Google app (its icon is either a blue box containing a "g" or a white circle containing a multicolored "G"). Touch your profile picture in the upper-left corner, then "Voice Search." If the box next to "OK Google" is checked, touch it once to turn it off.

Surprising Computer-Screen Cleaner

Lifehacker.com

Gently swipe a coffee filter over your computer and TV screens. The filter catches dust and cuts static (which attracts dust) without leaving behind fibers as a paper towel would.

The Friendly "Unfriend"

Carolyn Abram, author of *Facebook for Dummies*, reported by Karen Larson, former editor, *Bottom Line Personal.*

I recently unfriended a friend on Facebook. I didn't do it because I dislike her…I did it to save time. Whenever I logged into Facebook, my feed was dominated by her posts. So spur of the moment, I unfriended her and didn't think about it again. But I haven't heard from her in a long time—she used to call occasionally—and I wonder whether she knows that I unfriended her.

"No one is ever notified by Facebook that they have been unfriended," says Carolyn Abram, author of *Facebook for Dummies* and a former Facebook product manager. "But if they are attentive, there are ways they can tell."

My friend might have noticed that my name is no longer listed among her friends…that she is no longer receiving posts from me…or that a button labeled "Add Friend" now appears when she visits my Facebook page.

If she did find out that I unfriended her, it could easily explain why she hasn't been in contact. According to a 2013 survey by a researcher at University of Colorado at Denver, 40% of surveyed Facebook users say that they would avoid someone in real life who unfriended them on the site.

He notes that there are other ways to avoid people's Facebook posts that are less likely to cause offense. Just click the downward pointing arrow in the upper-right-hand corner of a post from this person, then…

•**Click "Unfollow…"** to remain Facebook friends with this person but not receive his or her posts, or…

•**Click "I don't want to see this"** to remove a particular post from your feed, then click "See less from…" to reduce, but not entirely eliminate, the number of posts you receive from this person.

Save Time…and Your Sanity: Remove Yourself from Social Media

Roundup of experts on social-media-site use, reported in *The New York Times.*

Removing yourself from social media can give you a lot more time to do other things. And it can eliminate the fear of missing out that drives many people to spend huge amounts of time at social-media sites. To get rid of entire profiles, use sites such as AccountKiller.com, Deseat.me and JustDelete.me—the sites give step-by-step instructions. Deleting Facebook, Twitter, LinkedIn and GooglePlus accounts will eliminate most of your online presence. But dating sites, blogs, Flickr, eBay, Amazon, Craigslist, PayPal and support forums may retain data even if you rarely use them. Also, sites may retain your data in an inactive version of your account—and you cannot stop others from posting about you.

Remember: Some social-media profiles may make sense to keep, such as a LinkedIn account if you are looking for a job..

Great Laptops for a Lot Less

Eric Grevstad, a contributing editor to *Computer Shopper.* He also contributes laptop reviews to *PC Mag* and other media outlets. ComputerShopper.com

A laptop computer can easily set you back $1,000 to $3,000 or more, but you don't need to spend that much. *Here are today's cost-effective alternatives to high-end laptops for three kinds of users…*

●**Basic home or business use.** *High-end option:* The Apple MacBook Air ($999) is a great-looking and powerful machine. With a 13.3-inch screen, 8 gigabytes (GB) of RAM (the memory used to run programs and applications) and a fast, reliable 128-GB solid-state drive for storage, the MacBook Air breezes through web browsing and basic business applications such as Microsoft Office.

Affordable alternative: At $300*, the Acer Swift 1 has a 13.3-inch, high-definition screen that not only is superior to the screen of most computers at its price point but also rivals the brightness and resolution of the screen of the MacBook Air. Acer no longer manufacturers the Swift 1, but you can find certified refurbished models on Amazon.com

The Swift 1 has half the memory and storage of the MacBook Air and a less powerful processing chip, meaning that it's less adept at running professional photo and video applications. But it's powerful enough to surf the web, handle basic productivity applications and stream videos. And while it has limited storage of 64 GB, you can easily store larger files on a removable memory card or in the cloud. And you'll have more than $600 in your pocket versus the Mac.

●**Photo and video work.** *High-end options:* The Apple MacBook Pro 15-inch ($2,399) and the Dell XPS 15 ($1,049) with an Intel Core i5 processor are media workhorses. Their processing power and graphics cards help them excel at memory-intensive activities such as video editing and the 3-D modeling done by artists and architects.

Affordable alternative: The Lenovo IdeaPad 320 15-inch ($699) has a full-HD screen and the same Intel Core i5 processor as the Dell XPS 15.

*Prices subject to change.

It's perfect for touching up family photos and putting together videos for friends and colleagues using software such as Movie Maker, which can be downloaded for free from the Microsoft store, and Adobe Photoshop Elements.

●**Gaming.** *High-end option:* The Alienware 17 ($2,024) has amazing power and configurability for hard-core video game players. At this price, it features a best-in-class graphics card that works in concert with a 17.3-inch, high-definition screen displaying images at 120-frames-per-second for extremely smooth game play.

Affordable alternative: The HP Omen 17t ($1,529) has a less powerful graphics card than the Alienware laptop and "only" a high-definition (1080p) 17.3-inch screen, but it features a similar processor, memory and storage options. In terms of performance, most gamers won't experience a noticeable difference between the two—except in their wallets.

Block That Call!

Edgar Dworsky, an attorney and founder of the consumer advocate websites ConsumerWorld.org and MousePrint.org. Formerly, he served as a consumer education consultant for the Federal Trade Commission and was a Massachusetts assistant attorney general.

S igning up for the federal government's Do Not Call Registry was supposed to protect us from unwanted telemarketing phone calls. But a lot of unwanted calls still sneak through, and it's only getting worse. Inexpensive international Internet-based calling allows telemarketers to evade US laws by contacting us from overseas. And certain callers, including pollsters, politicians and charities, are exempt from the National Do Not Call Registry restrictions.

You still should register your landline and cellphone numbers with the Do Not Call Registry (DoNotCall.gov) because it does reduce unwanted calls. *But here are four additional steps to further block these calls…*

1. Stop writing your phone numbers on forms and entering them into websites. Retailers, websites, charities and political organizations often ask for phone numbers, but that doesn't mean you have to provide them. An e-mail address should be sufficient when contact information is needed.

When a website won't let you proceed without entering a phone number, supply a fake one starting with "555" after the area code. (No real numbers start with 555.)

Exceptions: Do provide your real phone number(s) to doctors' offices, insurers, credit card providers and other organizations that might have a legitimate reason to contact you quickly.

2. Sign up for Nomorobo—if your telecom provider is eligible. Incoming calls to your phone number are routed not just to your phone but also to Nomorobo's computers. These computers very quickly determine whether the call is from an automatic dialer—a tool used by many of the worst telemarketers to call several numbers quickly—and hang up on the caller after the first ring if it is.

Nomorobo does allow legitimate automated phone calls through, such as reminders about doctor and other appointments.

Unfortunately, you can use Nomorobo only if your phone provider and/or cellular provider offers a service called "simultaneous ring," which allows calls to one phone number to ring at a second number as well.

Most Internet- or cable-based telecom providers offer Nomorobo, but many cellular and traditional landline providers currently do not—though that could change if Nomorobo continues to gain popularity. At Nomorobo.com, click "Get Started Now" to determine whether you can sign up.

3. Block calls from troublesome phone numbers. Some telecom providers allow their customers to block incoming calls from specific numbers, perhaps by entering a code immediately after receiving a call from someone you don't want to hear from again. Contact your provider(s) to see if such a feature is available to you.

Unfortunately, blocking individual phone numbers won't stop the most unethical telemarketers—they tend to use "spoofing" technology to make their calls appear to come from a different phone number each time.

Because of this limitation, it's usually worth blocking individual numbers only if your phone provider lets you do so for free.

Also: Some telemarketers block their own numbers so they don't appear on your caller ID at all. Some phone-service providers offer the option of blocking incoming calls from callers that have blocked numbers—ask your provider.

4. Ask legitimate organizations to "put me on your do-not-call list." Pollsters, politicians and companies that place unsolicited calls generally are required to maintain their own do-not-call lists. Ethical organizations comply with requests to be placed on these lists.

Exception: Prerecorded-message calls typically include instructions for opting out of future calls, usually by pressing a key on the phone's keypad. Do not follow these directions if the automated call is from an unknown or a potentially untrustworthy caller—doing so can lead to an increase in call frequency.

11

Travel Nightmares

12 Ways to Save on Rental Cars

Christopher Elliott, a consumer advocate who writes the "On Travel" column for *USA Today* and *"The Navigator"* column for the *Washington Post*. He is author of *How to Be the World's Smartest Traveler (and Save Time, Money and Hassle)*. Elliott.org

Don't let a car-rental company take you for a ride. Whether you think the daily rental rate you are quoted is a bargain or steep, even more tricky charges probably lurk down the road. And it's not just the infamous overpriced insurance that rental companies are known to push at the checkout counter.

Here are ways to find lower rates and reduce the odds of being victimized by sneaky rental-car charges…

FIND THE BEST RATES

Travel websites such as Expedia, Priceline, Kayak and Hotwire sometimes offer appealing rental rates and are worth checking. *But if you are willing to invest a bit more time, you could also…*

• **Try a travel agency.** Old-fashioned brick-and-mortar travel agencies often have access to special car-rental rates through the travel agent consortiums they belong to.

• **Search for deals at rental locations that aren't at an airport.** Airport-related taxes and fees can in-crease the cost of renting there by 10% to 25% or even more in some cases. You often come out ahead if you pick up your car at a lot that isn't right at the airport even after factoring in the cost of taking a cab or car share to this lot.

• **Shop early and late.** Is it better to search for car-rental deals long in advance of the trip…or just before the trip? Both. Many rental-car reservations can be canceled without penalty. Reserve the best deal you can find as soon as your travel plans are set, but continue shopping as the travel date approaches. If you find a lower price, book it, too.

If you like, you could call the rental-car company that provided the original price and say, "I'm calling to cancel my reservation because I found a lower price…but before I do, could you match it?" The company often will.

Warning: Confirm that any reservation you make can be canceled without penalty. "Prepaid" rates that are offered by car-rental companies and many third-party travel websites are nonrefundable.

• **Modify pick-up and drop-off times if your timing is somewhat flexible.** Adjusting these by just an hour or two when you search for car-rental rates online could significantly affect the prices you find.

GET ADDITIONAL DISCOUNTS

You don't have to search the entire Internet for rental-car special offers. *Just take a few minutes to…*

•**Search for car-rental coupon codes on Auto Slash.com.** It offers details about dozens of current car-rental coupon codes and other promotions. If you find an appealing offer, just enter its code on the rental company website when you make your reservation.

•**Check whether an organization you belong to offers rental-car savings.** AAA…AARP…USAA… and warehouse clubs BJ's and Costco have partnered with rental-car companies to provide deals.

Examples: You might save 5% to 30% off the "base" rate…receive free upgrades…or get certain fees waived.

•**Reserve a smaller car, then ask for a free upgrade.** If you would like a larger rental but don't need one, reserve a smaller, less expensive car and then politely ask for an upgrade at the counter. Rental company employees typically have lots of leeway when it comes to upgrades. This is particularly likely to work if you can point out that you rent from the company often…or that you are on your honeymoon or celebrating a special occasion such as a silver anniversary.

BEWARE OF ADD-ONS AND OVERCHARGES

Questionable rental-car company tactics are more common than ever. *Self-defense…*

•**Reject rental cars that have partially full gas tanks.** If you return a rental car with less gas than you started out with, the rental company likely will charge a very steep per-gallon rate for the difference.

The best option is to reject the gas prepay option and instead fill up the tank at a gas station right before returning the car. But if the car started out with less than a full tank, it will be difficult to refill it to precisely the right level.

To avoid this issue, insist that the car you rent starts with a full tank of gas. Then you simply can top it off before returning it.

Save the receipt from the gas station when you fill the tank, and take a photo of this receipt (in case you misplace the original) and a photo of the car's gas gauge when you return the car. Rental lots have

been known to bill customers for gas even though the customers refilled the tank properly.

•**Reject cars that have even small scratches or scuffs.** It's become distressingly common for car-rental firms to charge customers $400 to $499 for minor damage they did not cause.

Why $400 to $499? It's because many people have $500 auto insurance deductibles. The car-rental companies don't want insurance companies getting involved because insurers are aware of this scam and often won't play ball.

The traditional advice is to inspect rental cars very carefully and report any damage to the rental agent before driving away so that it is noted on the rental agreement.

If possible, demand a different car that has no damage. A car that has visible damage often also has other damage that is not easy to spot.

Whether or not you spot any damage, take numerous pictures of the car from every possible angle, inside and out, before you drive the car off the lot. Do so again when you return the car. An app called Record360 (for iOS and Android) can document precisely when and where these images were recorded, improving the strength of your case if you later need to prove that you returned the car in the same condition you got it.

•**Turn down rental company insurance.** The insurance offered by car-rental firms is massively overpriced—and you probably don't even need it. Most drivers already have rental-car coverage through their auto insurance…the credit card they use to rent the car…or both. (Contact your insurer and card issuer before your trip to confirm this, especially because there are exceptions and limits.)

If you do need rental-car coverage—or you prefer to leave no chance that potentially costly gaps might lurk in your coverage—purchase it through InsureMyRentalCar.com prior to your trip. It provides reliable coverage for a fraction of what rental firms charge. Prices start at just $5 per day or $17.50 per trip.

•**Reject the toll transponder, and avoid toll roads.** Rental-car companies often charge $4 or $5 per day for a toll transponder that pays tolls automatically—on top of the cost of the tolls that the renter incurs.

Renters might be given the option of paying for this transponder when they pick up the car…or the transponder—and its daily fee—might be automatically triggered if the car passes through an automated toll plaza during the trip.

The best option is to reject this transponder (if it is optional) and use a map app to avoid toll roads—especially toll roads that do not offer a cash-payment option. When that isn't practical, lean toward renting from Enterprise or Avis, which tend to at least be up front with transponder charges rather than try to trap customers with gotcha fees that show up later.

Another option is to bring your own transponder if you have one that will work on toll roads in the area you will be visiting—but there is a chance that a rental company transponder installed in the car could be triggered as well, leaving you to sort out a double-billing situation.

Similar: If you have your own portable GPS navigation unit (or a smartphone with a navigation app that you are comfortable using), bring it and reject the rental company's optional navigation unit. This may save you $4 or $5 per day.

•**Don't get stuck with an age surcharge.** You may know that young drivers (under age 25) usually are charged more for rental cars. But some rental companies in Europe now charge older drivers a surcharge or refuse to rent to them at all. And these companies often do not make these rules clear when people book reservations—older would-be customers are simply turned away when they try to pick up their rentals.

If you are age 70 or older and you intend to rent a car in Europe, contact the car-rental company, perhaps through its website, to ask whether any age limits or age-based surcharges will apply. This surcharge is most common in Bulgaria, Croatia, Greece, Hungary, Ireland and Portugal.

Best US Airline

Middle Seat's annual scorecard of US airlines' performance on seven different measures important to travelers, reported in *The Wall Street Journal*.

Best US airline for overall service: Alaska Airlines. It was tops in certain categories for on-time arrivals, avoiding extreme delays and complaints. Delta scored first on measures of canceled flights and involuntary bumping. Virgin America was tops for minimizing mishandled baggage. Alaska recently acquired Virgin America and is meshing the two carriers' systems.

7 Cruise Mistakes That Can Cost You Big

Dori Saltzman, senior editor with the travel website Cruise Critic, which offers cruise reviews and information. CruiseCritic.com

The simplicity of cruise vacations is part of their appeal. You choose a ship going where you want to go…and it is easy to imagine that the planning virtually is complete. Unlike with most journeys, there is no need to choose hotels, reserve rental cars or even find restaurants.

But novice cruisers still can stumble into mistakes that make their voyages less enjoyable—or more expensive—than they should have been. Experienced cruisers sometimes make mistakes, too, particularly when they book trips on cruise lines that they have not sailed with previously.

Seven cruise-planning mistakes…

MISTAKE: **Booking with the wrong cruise line.** Different cruise lines provide very different cruise experiences—even when they stop at the same ports. Perhaps most notably, some cruise lines strive to supply a high-energy environment for passengers…while others offer a more relaxing experience. Choose the wrong cruise line, and you could feel out of place. If you have not previously cruised on a particular line, speak to experienced cruisers about it…use search engines to find online reviews of it…and/or book through an experienced travel agent who can help you select an appropriate cruise line.

Examples: Carnival Cruise Line's party atmosphere attracts people who want to be social, let down their hair and be silly…Disney Cruise Lines attracts primarily families. On the other hand, Crystal, Oceania, Seabourn and Silversea offer a relaxed atmosphere and higher pricing that tends to draw cruisers age 45 and older.

Helpful: Any cruise that is three weeks or longer is likely to be dominated by retirees. Few younger people can spare that much time.

MISTAKE: Picking the wrong cabin. Do not select a cabin based only on its size, cost and the presence of a porthole or balcony. Also, pay careful attention to the cabin's location on the ship. Avoid cabins adjacent to elevator shafts, theaters, nightclubs, casinos or crew entrances, especially if you are a light sleeper. And don't just look for potentially noisy neighbors such as those on a map of the cabin's deck—also check the decks immediately above and below to make sure that the cabin is not under or over something that is likely to be loud. (Avoid cabins under pool decks, too—chairs scraping on these decks are a common source of annoyance for the occupants of cabins directly underneath.) Crew-only spaces such as staff storage rooms might not be labeled at all on ship maps, so be wary of rooms next to map "white spaces." Ideally a cabin should be surrounded by other cabins.

If you are prone to motion sickness, avoid cabins that are high on the ship and/or near the front or rear of the ship—that's where the nausea-inducing feeling of movement tends to be greatest. Cabins low and near midship will be much better for you.

MISTAKE: Failing to notice the downside of a special price. Read the fine print before snagging a cruise line special offer—special fares sometimes come with unexpected restrictions.

Examples: A special low fare might be nonrefundable…a special low-deposit requirement might mean that the deposit is nonrefundable…if the cruise line is running a special promotion, such

as "$100 in free onboard credit upon booking," this might not be included with certain discounted fares.

MISTAKE: Packing items that are not allowed. Many cruise lines impose severe restrictions on outside alcohol, such as allowing passengers to bring only one or two bottles of outside wine onboard and no outside beer or liquor. A few don't allow any outside alcohol at all.

The portable surge protectors that many travelers use to protect their laptops and other electronics usually are not allowed on cruise ships. Shipboard electrical systems work somewhat differently from electrical systems on land (in part because there is no easy way to "ground" an electrical system at sea). One consequence of this is that surge protectors can create a fire risk. Non-surge-protecting power strips and plug adaptors generally are permitted.

Electrical devices that heat up, such as travel irons and coffeepots, are almost always banned for safety reasons—though curling irons usually are allowed and most cabins come equipped with hair dryers. Read the packing rules on the cruise line's website for details. Cruise line employees do search bags, so don't assume that you can sneak things aboard. Confiscated items generally can be reclaimed after the cruise.

Helpful: Some ships have self-service launderettes where passengers can use irons and ironing boards—Carnival has these fleetwide, for example.

MISTAKE: Failing to prebook reservations for shore excursions and/or onboard spa treatments and specialty restaurants. These sometimes fill up, so it's worth investigating these options and booking as soon as the cruise line allows—often that's when you make your final cruise payment, long before the ship sets sail.

It typically is possible to cancel these reservations later without penalty, so there likely is little downside to making these early reservations. This can vary, however, so it is worth reading the fine print to learn cancellation rules.

MISTAKE: Cutting your arrival too close. If your flight is scheduled to arrive in the departure port city the same day that the cruise begins, any delay could cause you to miss your ship. A much safer plan is to fly in the day before your ship departs—particularly during winter, when weather-related flight delays are common. Flying in a day early means that you must pay for lodging the night before, but a night in a port city is not a bad thing—it just means that your vacation is one day longer. Some people think that if their airfare is part of the cruise package and the plane is late, the ship automatically will be held in port until their arrival. That's not so, but the cruise line typically will make arrangements to get you to the ship at the next port—always check the fine print before purchasing airfare from a cruise line.

Alternative: If you cannot fly in a day early, purchase travel insurance that will cover your losses if you miss your ship's departure.

MISTAKE: **Waiting for last-minute deals.** In decades past, the best way to get big cruise discounts was to wait until a few weeks before departure dates and snap up remaining cabins for a fraction of their original price. But cruise lines have become much more aggressive about offering appealing deals earlier, so fewer cabins remain as departure dates near…and the cabins that do remain often are unappealing. If you are willing to be extremely patient and flexible, you still can find some attractive last-minute cruise deals from time to time. But for most travelers, the downside of waiting outweighs the upside. To find attractive prices, start to monitor prices on cruises of interest starting up to a year before the departure date. Buy when you see a special offer significantly below the usual rate. Locking in a cruise sooner also gives you time to shop for a good deal on airfare into and out of port cities.

Travel Stress Reducer

Clark.com, a website that gives free advice on consumer issues.

When you travel, do you find yourself worrying that you left the stove on? Or the AC or the iron, etc.? Before you leave, use your smartphone to take a photo of the item you worry about. A glance at the photo will relieve your mind!

For a More Comfortable Airline Seat…

Roundup of experts on airline seating, reported at Market Watch.com.

Choose airlines that generally offer more legroom, such as JetBlue, with 32 to 34 inches in most planes—compared with 30 to 32 inches for most domestic airlines and only 28 inches on Spirit. Know which planes have the most space—Airbus planes generally are roomier than Boeing's, but for specific flights, go to SeatGuru.com to check. Avoid regional jets, which generally have tighter seating. Ask the gate agent if the bulkhead seat is available—you may be allowed to move into it for free. Consider paying for a roomier seat if your flight will last more than four hours.

Hotel Thermostats Trick You

Tim Leffel, editor of *Hotel Scoop.* He is a veteran travel writer based in Tampa, who has reviewed hotels on five continents and is author of *Make Your Travel Dollars Worth a Fortune: The Contrarian Traveler's Guide to Getting More for Less.* Hotel-Scoop.com

Adjusting a hotel wall thermostat might have little or no effect on the room's temperature. That's because it is increasingly common for these thermostats to allow guests to change temperatures by only a few degrees one way or the other—or not at all. In some cases, the thermostat even might give guests the impression that they are adjusting the temperature, but the number the guests set on the screen does not actually alter the room temperature.

And the latest hotel thermostats have not only temperature sensors but also motion sensors, so even if the thermostat temperature is adjustable, it might switch into power-saving mode when its motion sensor thinks the room is unoccupied, which could happen at night when you are asleep. That means you could wake up in the middle of the night drenched in sweat or freezing cold.

What to do: Enter the make (and model name and number, if displayed) of the thermostat into a search engine, along with the term "bypass" or "hack," to discover step-by-step directions posted by travelers who have figured out ways to gain control over many common hotel thermostats.

Example: With certain Inncom-brand thermostats commonly used in hotels, you should hold down the "display" button while pressing the "off" button, followed by the up arrow and then release the "display" button. This accesses "VIP" mode, which allows you to set the temperature above or below the hotel's normal limits.

Insider trick: If you cannot override a hotel thermostat and its motion detector sets it to uncomfortable temperatures as you sleep, buy a helium-filled Mylar balloon and let it float around the room as you sleep. The balloon likely will drift on the air currents created by the heating/cooling system, which should be enough movement to convince the thermostat motion sensor that someone is present.

This strategy is not especially useful on your first night in a hotel—by the time you discover that the motion sensor is problematic, it likely will be too late to get a balloon. But it can be helpful when staying at a hotel for multiple nights or returning to a hotel where you have encountered motion sensor problems in the past.

Recent Carry-On Restrictions

George Hobica, founder of AirfareWatchdog.com, an airfare alert and listings website.

Amerircan Airlines and United are offering "basic class" discount fares that prohibit the use of overhead bins. Your carry-on must fit under the seat in front of you…if it doesn't, you must check it for a fee.

Maximum dimensions for under-the-seat carry-ons: American, 18 x 14 x 8 inches…United, 17 x 10 x 9 inches.

What to do: Use a duffel or gym bag, which is easy to squeeze into place.

5 Ways to Get Through Airport Security Faster

George Hobica, founder of AirfareWatchdog.com, which reports on airfare bargains. He previously was a travel writer for *Travel + Leisure*, *National Geographic Traveler* and other magazines.

The average wait time at Los Angeles International Airport security checkpoints is 40 minutes, according to the airport-delay monitoring app MiFlight. Waits longer than three hours have occurred at Chicago's O'Hare…Miami International Airport…and New York City's John F. Kennedy International Airport. It's not unheard of for travelers to spend more time getting though airport security at US airports than they do in the air. It even has become common to miss flights because of extensive security delays.

Enrolling in the "PreCheck" expedited security program administered by the Transportation Security Administration (TSA) was supposed to allow travelers to sidestep these delays—but the PreCheck program has had problems of its own.

Travelers who sign up for PreCheck and fly on participating airlines get to use special security lines where several time-consuming steps are not required—they do not have to remove their shoes and belts…or take their electronic devices out of their luggage, for example.

In theory, that should make PreCheck security lines a big time-saver. In practice, PreCheck has experienced a huge surge in popularity in the past year, and a growing glut of PreCheck travelers means that its lines sometimes take longer than standard airport-security lines.

What's more, these days it can take upward of one month just to get the in-person interview that is required by the PreCheck application process. Travelers must pay an $85 five-year membership fee and pass a security vetting process to participate in PreCheck (TSA.gov/precheck).

Fortunately, PreCheck is not the only way to get though airport security faster. *Potentially better options include…*

•**Global Entry,** a government program that lets preapproved travelers speed through customs and immigration checkpoints in more than 59 US and international airports. And if you are a Global Entry member, you also qualify to use PreCheck security lines. To take advantage of PreCheck if you are a Global Entry member, enter your Global Entry membership number (which is in the upper-left corner on the back of your Global Entry "Trusted Traveler" card) into the "Known Traveler Number" field when you book flights on participating airlines—or enter it on your frequent-flier profile with the airline.

As noted above, those PreCheck lines are not always as quick as they should be, but Global Entry membership truly does reduce delays at customs and immigration. And it outdoes PreCheck in another way—the Global Entry interview-and-approval process often is weeks quicker than the PreCheck process, though this does vary by location. (Go to CBP.gov, then select "Global Entry" from the "Travel" menu.)

Cost: Global Entry has a $100 application fee. That's only $15 more than the application fee for PreCheck alone, so Global Entry is the better deal. After approval, renewal is not required for five years, so the annual cost is just $20.

You even can avoid this expense by charging Global Entry's application fee to a credit card that provides a statement credit to cover it. Predictably, these tend to be cards that have high annual fees, however, including The Platinum Card from American Express ($550 annual fee, AmericanExpress.com)…and Citi Prestige and Citi AAdvantage Executive World Elite MasterCard (both with a $450 annual fee, Citi.com).

•**Clear, a private security-screening alternative to the government-run PreCheck and Global Entry programs.** Clear features high-tech, automated biometric authentication—that is, fingerprint or retinal scanners—and usually is much faster than all other airport security options. Often there is virtually no Clear line at all…except when those high-tech biometric scanners go down, which does happen on occasion (ClearMe.com).

Clear currently is available in more than 20 airports—Atlanta…Austin…Baltimore…Dallas/Ft. Worth…Denver…Detroit…Houston's George Bush and William Hobby airports…Las Vegas…Los Angeles…Miami …Minneapolis…New York's JFK, LaGuardia and Westchester county airports…Orlando…Salt Lake City…San Antonio…San Francisco…San Jose…Seattle…Washington's Dulles and Ronald Reagan National airports. Clear is also available in a number of major league sports stadiums, where it enables you to avoid the sometimes lengthy security checkpoint lines.

Because of the cost, most people will find that it's worth enrolling in Clear only if they frequently use at least one of the currently served airports or, perhaps, if they have season tickets with a team that plays in a stadium that offers Clear.

Cost: $179 per year, or $79 to $99 per year for Delta SkyMiles members. Up to three family members 18 and over can be added for $50 each. Family members under 18 can use Clear for free when traveling with a Clear member.

Other possible ways to avoid long security lines…

•**Paying airlines for expedited security occasionally is possible.** JetBlue and United offer passengers the option of paying a modest fee for onetime access to a special security line in some airports. (Travelers who have elite status in an airline's frequent-flier program and/or who are flying business or first class often qualify for access to a special security line without paying an added fee.)

This option typically is offered at the airport check-in kiosk or desk when available.

Strategy: Check the length of security lines before checking in to a JetBlue or United flight.

Pay the extra fee if the lines look longer than is acceptable to you.

Cost: JetBlue's Even More Speed starts at $10... United's Premier Access starts at $15. (Some other airlines offer VIP airport services that include significantly expedited security, such as the American Airlines Five Star Service program. But these programs tend to cost hundreds of dollars per flight and often are available to only first-class passengers.)

•**Investigate alternative security checkpoints.** Many large airports have multiple security checkpoints—and one might have significantly shorter lines than another.

Ask an airport or Transportation Security Administration employee whether there is another security checkpoint where the lines tend to be shorter. It might be a long walk to get to the other checkpoint, but even so, this can be a time-saver.

Helpful: Apps including GateGuru (iOS, Android and Windows. GateGuru.com) and MiFlight (iOS, GoMiFlight.com) can help you locate alternate security checkpoints and sometimes provide user-generated wait-time estimates.

Sell Your Nonrefundable Hotel Reservation

Pauline Frommer, editorial director of the Frommer Guides and cohost of *The Travel Show* radio program, New York City. Frommers.com

You can sell your nonrefundable hotel reservation—or buy someone else's. Two services—RoomerTravel.com and Cancelon.com—allow you to list your reservation for resale. The online sites handle the actual transaction, contact the hotel or booking agency to transfer the name on your reservation and guarantee that you'll be paid.

Caveats: To get a buyer, you may have to offer a price much lower than what you paid. And the fee for sellers is 15% of the selling price at Roomer Travel and 10% at Cancelon.

Little-Known Ways to Save at Hotels

Experts on travel, reported at GoBankingRates.com.

Book 30 days in advance...and if that is not possible, good rates often are offered seven to 10 days in advance of a stay. If you can wait until the last minute, try booking on the day you want to stay—only 60% of rooms are occupied on most nights, so hotels may cut rates drastically at the last minute. Also, you can book a room and get any price drops refunded to you by booking through Tingo.com.

More ideas: Stay on a Sunday, the day with the lowest room rates...visit tourist locations midweek, not on weekends...go to major business areas on weekends, after business travelers have left...book during shoulder season, between high-cost high season and off-peak times when weather tends to be poor...stay in the suburbs rather than in major cities...check on local events before booking—rates may rise when big events occur.

New Multicity Airfare Trap

George Hobica, founder of AirfareWatchDog.com.

New rules from American, Delta and United often make it much more expensive to book a multicity trip. Previously the booking tools on the airline websites would display the cheapest available fare for each leg of a journey whether you were booking a simple round-trip or a multicity trip—that is, from City A to City B and then from City B to City C before returning to City A. Now the lowest fares often are not offered for each leg, which can result in massive price increases for the overall multicity trip.

Example: When I recently tried to book a trip on American from Los Angeles to New York to Sarasota, Florida, and then back to LA, the lowest price for an economy-class seat was around $2,200. If American's booking tool had quoted me that airline's lowest available fare for each leg, the total would have been less than $600.

What to do: Before booking a multi-city ticket, use airline booking tools to search separately for one-way fares on each leg. Buying several one-way tickets separately will often be cheaper than booking the entire trip as a single unit. That reflects the fact that in recent years, the major airlines have dramatically reduced the cost of many one-way tickets to compete with the low one-way fares offered by discount airlines. Buying separate one-way tickets also lets you travel on multiple airlines, increasing your savings if different carriers have the lowest fares on different legs.

Alternatively, you could book multi-city itineraries through a third-party travel website such as Kayak.com, which does a good job of combining one-way trips to complete an itinerary. But if you use a third-party site, also check Southwest.com—Southwest Airlines does not offer its flights through any third-party sites.

Helpful: Sometimes it's possible to save money by searching for one-way fares before booking simple round-trip tickets, too. The lowest round-trip fare for a weekend trip from San Antonio to Chicago recently was $400…but one-way tickets were available on two different airlines for $109 apiece.

Get Bumped on Purpose!

Scott Keyes, founder of Scott's Cheap Flights, an e-mail subscription service that searches for airfare bargains, Fort Collins, Colorado. He is author of *How to Fly for Free: Practical Tips the Airlines Don't Want You to Know.* ScottsCheapFlights.com

For the passenger who was dragged off a United Airlines flight in April 2017, getting bumped was a nightmare. But for travelers who have the flexibility to switch flights at the last minute, getting bumped purposely can be desirable. And if you are able to do it over and over, it can be quite lucrative—even more so if you know the best strategies to become a frequent bumpee…

VOLUNTARY VS. INVOLUNTARY BUMPINGS

When airlines need to free up seats, usually because they have overbooked a flight, they offer to bump passengers in exchange for rewards and a seat on a later flight.

To become an expert at being bumped, first you need to know the rules, which differ depending on several factors, including whether you are bumped voluntarily or involuntarily.

If it's voluntary, which is most often the case, the airline usually offers a voucher that can be used to pay for a future flight.

Typically, the gate agent will announce that the airline is willing to give a travel voucher worth perhaps $150 to $250. Sometimes airlines, including Delta and United, ask passengers if they would be willing to be bumped when they initially check in for an overbooked flight.

If not enough passengers accept an initial offer, the value of the travel vouchers will increase—$500 to $1,000 is not uncommon. United recently said it would start offering up to $10,000 if that's what it takes to get someone to give up a seat voluntarily—though in practice, the airline is unlikely to need to offer anywhere close to that amount.

If it's involuntary, FAA rules now require the airline to pay the passenger twice the value of the one-way ticket, up to $675, if the new flight is scheduled to get the passenger to the destination between one and two hours after the original arrival time (one to four hours on international flights)…or four times the value, up to $1,350, if it's more than two hours past the original arrival time (four hours on international flights). Involuntarily bumped travelers have the right to demand this payment in the form of a check or cash rather than a voucher.

Exceptions: The airline does not have to pay if it puts an involuntarily bumped passenger on a different flight that reaches the destination within one hour of the original arrival time…if the passenger is bumped because the airline substituted a smaller plane for the flight…or in certain other situations. Rules also differ on flights departing from foreign airports.

Involuntary bumpings have become rare, however—out of approximately 475,000 passengers bumped last year, only about 40,000 were involuntary, and that figure is likely to fall in the wake of the United incident.

Helpful: Consider what the travel vouchers are truly worth. If you travel on the airline frequently, its vouchers might be almost as valuable to you as cash. Unlike frequent-flier miles, there generally are no restrictions on when these vouchers can be redeemed. But if you do not fly much and/or this airline does not offer many routes you often travel, the vouchers might not be worth the trouble—particularly because these vouchers often expire in 12 months if not used.

PLAYING THE BUMP GAME

Here's how to get the most from getting bumped…

•**Check the "seat map" before heading to the airport for a flight.** If there are no available seats shown for a flight on the airline website a few hours prior to departure, there's a good chance the flight is overbooked. If you are interested in getting bumped, get to the gate at least 45 to 60 minutes before departure time to ensure that you're there when the gate agent requests volunteers.

•**Position yourself as close as possible to the gate agent.** If there are more volunteers than the airline needs, the first ones to reach the agent usually are the ones who get bumped.

•**Do not check luggage unless necessary.** Travel only with carry-on bags if getting bumped is your goal. Otherwise your checked luggage might take the flight you miss and end up lost…or the gate agent might choose a different volunteer to avoid having to redirect your luggage.

•**Evaluate how desperate the airline is.** Often the gate agent will announce how many volunteers are needed. As a rule of thumb, if five or more volunteers are needed, there's a good chance the airline will have to increase its initial offer to find enough volunteers, so the smart strategy might be to decline the initial offer. If only one or two volunteers are needed, the opening offer might be the only one. Exceptions: The airline might have to increase its offer to find even one or two takers if the flight is the last of the day to its destination…or if it's the last day before a holiday or a major event such as the Super Bowl.

•**Instead of saying, "I accept," say, "What's my new route and arrival time if I accept?"** There's no way to know whether the offer is worth taking until you find out how much of your time you will lose. Also: If the delay will be lengthy, confirm that the airline will provide vouchers for any meals you need to eat in the airport and/or the hotel room you will need for an overnight stay.

•**If the airline needs multiple volunteers, ask for its final offer.** Rather than accept the initial offer, tell the gate agent that you are willing to give up your seat as long as you receive the same compensation as the next-to-final passenger to accept, which is likely to be a better offer. Gate agents often will agree to this.

•**Ask for upgrades and other perks.** In addition to a travel voucher, the gate agent might be willing to give you a first-class seat on a later flight if one is available…a more direct route with shorter or fewer layovers…and/or airport lounge passes. Such things generally are at the gate agent's discretion, so ask politely.

•**Ask for compensation if you get "unbumped" back onto your original flight.** This is rare, but sometimes a volunteer ends up back on the original flight after the airline discovers that it does not need to bump as many travelers as it first thought. Not only does the unbumped passenger not get the promised travel voucher, he/she often doesn't get the original seat, either—and may end up in an undesirable middle seat. And because unbumped passengers usually are the last to board packed flights, there often is no room in the overhead compartments for their carry-on bags.

What to do: Politely request some compensation, such as a voucher or lounge passes that you can use on a future layover (though they probably are much less than you would have received if successfully bumped). If you don't get anything, later go to the airline's website and send a politely worded e-mail to the airline's executives requesting some sort of compensation. The airlines are so worried about bad press these days that there's a good chance you will be offered something.

Ultralow Fares to Europe

Kiplinger.com

Inexpensive travel to Europe is possible on Norwegian Air and Iceland's Wow Air, which offer ultralow fares to Europe from US cities including Boston and Los Angeles. These are no-frills carriers flying limited schedules and charging for all amenities.

Example: One recent nonstop Norwegian Air flight from Los Angeles to London was priced at $546 round-trip, but cost $708 when checked baggage, a seat reservation and meals were included. However, that compares with a typical carrier's nonstop LA-to-London charge of $928 recently, so the no-frills flight could still save $220.

Prices vary widely and change constantly—always shop around.

The World's Smartest Traveler Busts Myths About Flying

Christopher Elliott, author of the *Washington Post* travel section's "Navigator" column and cofounder of *Travelers United,* which advocates for travelers' rights. He is author of *How to Be the World's Smartest Traveler.* Elliott.org

Some of the things people think they know about airline travel are not really true. Widely followed strategies for finding affordable airfares turn out not to save money…while widely held beliefs about avoiding airport delays turn out not to save time. *The truth about six air travel myths…*

MYTH: **Stopovers save travelers money.** Conventional wisdom holds that travelers pay significantly less for connecting flights than for nonstop flights. This might be true on certain routes, but in general, stopovers save air travelers far less than they likely expect. A recent study of more than 57 million tickets sold in 2014 found that nonstop flights, when available, cost only $1.03 more, on average, than connecting flights between the same airports.

What to do: When you use an airfare website to search for flights, do a search specifically for nonstop flights in addition to a search for lowest-priced flights—almost any fare-finder website will let you do this. Even if nonstop flights do cost more, you often will discover that the price difference is small enough that it's worth paying this premium to avoid the delays, inconveniences and potential complications involved in making a stopover.

MYTH: **Booking tickets early usually will save you money.** Actually, history suggests that ticket prices are as likely to fall as they are to climb during the months leading up to the flight—and if you buy a ticket many months before a flight, you essentially are giving the airline an interest-free loan. Besides, the earlier you book your ticket, the greater the odds your travel plans will change, which might mean that you must pay a hefty fee to change your flight.

What to do: It is reasonable to book a ticket months in advance if your travel plans are very unlikely to change and you spot a fare that is well below normal for the route. In general, there is no great savings to be had by booking months early. Do try to buy tickets at least seven and preferably 14 days before the travel date—fares tend to trend upward in the week or two before departure, sometimes significantly.

Exception: It occasionally is possible to obtain great last-minute deals by buying tickets a week or less before flight time, but you cannot depend on this, so it is advisable only if your travel plans are very flexible.

MYTH: **Summer air travel is more reliable than winter air travel because bad weather is less likely to interfere.** Surprisingly, flight delays and cancellations due to weather are more common in summer than winter. Winter blizzards get lots of media attention, but summer thunderstorms and tropical storms are much more common and just as capable of wreaking havoc on airline schedules. Airlines are not required to compensate travelers whose flights are delayed or canceled because of bad weather.

What to do: Monitor weather reports and watch for flight status updates if you have an upcoming flight—or are picking someone up from the airport—even if it's summer. Websites and apps such as FlightAware make it easy to monitor flight status (FlightAware.com, the app is free for Android or iOS).

MYTH: Every flight is packed these days, and the lines are almost always endless in the airport. Yes, airports and planes generally have been crowded—but there still are flights with plenty of open seats and times when the lines are not very long.

What to do: If you want to avoid the crowds, choose flights that depart before 8 am or after 11 pm. Even the largest, busiest airports and most heavily traveled routes tend to be fairly quiet during these hours.

Joining the TSA Pre-Check program can help you speed through airport security checkpoints. This lets you skip the normal airport security line in favor of a special line that tends to move much faster. The Pre-Check program generally makes sense only for fairly frequent fliers, however—there is an $85 application fee, and the application process itself takes time (TSA.gov/tsa-precheck).

Best Hotel for Rewards

Switchfly Hotel Reward Payback Survey.

Best hotel chain for rewards: Marriott. The Marriott Rewards program returns an average of 9.4% on each dollar spent on hotel rooms when rewards were redeemed for a later stay (that's $47 for every $500 spent). Hilton Honors returns 8.9%… IHG Rewards, which includes InterContinental and Holiday Inn, returns 8.6%. But Starwood's loyalty program, which includes Sheraton, Westin and other brands, pays back an average of only 6.1%.

Cruising Solo? How to Save Up to 75%!

Dori Saltzman, an editor with *Cruise Critic*, which offers cruise reviews and information. CruiseCritic.com

Solo travelers can now save 25% to 75% on cruises. In the past, solo passengers had to pay for a double cabin…or agree to share a cabin with a stranger to avoid the "single supplement." Now cruise lines sometimes don't charge the entire or possibly even any of the single supplement…and many new ships offer single-occupancy cabins.

Examples: Royal Caribbean International's Quantum of the Seas…Norwegian Cruise Line's Norwegian Escape.

5 Things Casinos Don't Want You to Know: Yes, You Can Improve Your Odds!

Steve Bourie, who has published the *American Casino Guide* annually since 1992. He has more than 70 gambling videos available online at YouTube.com. He also has a free American Casino Guide app for iPhones, iPads and Android devices. AmericanCasinoGuide.com

The odds are stacked against you when you gamble in casinos—the house has an edge on almost every bet. But there are ways that even novice gamblers can greatly improve their odds of winning—or at least reduce the amount they lose. The key is to choose the right games…the right bets…and the right casinos.

Five secrets the casinos don't want you to know…

TABLE GAMES

•**Casinos are making it harder than ever to win at blackjack.** Hitting a blackjack—that is, getting dealt a two-card opening hand that adds up to 21—traditionally pays the player 3:2 ("three to two"), which is $15 on a $10 bet. But in the past five years or so, many casinos have quietly lowered this payout to 6:5, or just $12 on a $10 bet, greatly reducing players' odds of coming out ahead—even if they play blackjack very well.

Look for a placard at the table that explains the game's payouts. If you don't see this or cannot understand it, ask the dealer, "Is this a 6:5 or 3:2 blackjack game?" If the answer is 6:5, don't play.

Sometimes the only 3:2 blackjack tables in a casino have fairly steep minimum bets—often $20 or higher. If you cannot find a 3:2 table with stakes you feel comfortable with, play a different game.

•**Baccarat is a good table game for novice gamblers.** Many casino goers think of baccarat as a game for high rollers and experienced gamblers. Not so. It requires no skill…many casinos have "mini-baccarat" tables with affordable $5 minimums…and the odds are among the best you'll find in the casino—the house edge is just a little over 1% on each of the two primary bets you can make.

To play mini-baccarat, simply place a bet on either the player or the banker—the dealer will do the rest. (You also can bet on a tie, but the odds against you are much higher if you do.)

The player and the banker hands are marked on the table, and each will be dealt two cards (or sometimes three, for complicated reasons that you don't need to understand to play). Face cards and 10s are worth 0, aces are worth 1 and other cards are worth the number shown. These values are added up after the cards are dealt, and the hand that has the total closest to 9 wins.

Examples: A hand consisting of a 2 and a 6 produces a score of 8. A king and a 4 would create a score of 4 because face cards are worth 0. A 7 and an 8 would result in a score of 5—the cards add up to 15, but only the final digit of this figure matters.

•**Full tables are good for gamblers.** More players at a table slows down the game and results in fewer hands played per hour. That gives you more time to think.

A slower pace of play also can increase the odds that you will be offered free meals and hotel rooms. Casinos award these perks based in part on how much time a gambler spends at the tables. If the pace of play is slow, you can spend more time at the tables without putting additional money at risk.

Helpful: You typically will receive perks only if you join the casino's players club. Players clubs are free to join. Ask a casino employee how to sign up before you begin gambling.

VIDEO POKER AND SLOTS

•**Seemingly identical video poker machines can have significantly different odds.** A row of video poker machines that all look the same might actually differ in an important way—they might pay different returns for certain winning hands. Compare the "pay tables"—usually displayed on their screens—before playing.

Example: With "Jacks or Better" video poker—a game where players receive a payout if their final hand is a pair of jacks or better—check the payout for full houses and flushes. The best Jacks-or-Better machines pay nine coins for each coin bet if you make a full house and six for a flush. But many others pay only eight coins for a full house and five for a flush—some even less. This reduces your expected return on each hand from 99.5% of the amount you bet to 97.3% or less.

Helpful: Always play five coins per hand at video poker. This will earn you a big bonus if you hit a royal flush.

There are many different varieties of video poker, but Jacks or Better is a good choice for novice gamblers because it is very common and relatively easy to understand.

•**Max bets usually are bad bets on slot machines.** If you make the max bet on a penny slot machine, for example, you might be gambling $3 a spin. If you're going to bet that much, you're better off playing on a $1 slot machine—higher-denomination slots inevitably offer substantially better odds.

Example: On the Las Vegas strip, penny slots return an average of 88% of the money bet on each spin, while dollar slots return an average of 93%.

The best amount to bet when you play slots is the minimum amount that qualifies for any bonuses or progressive jackpots offered by the machine. Or better yet, don't play the slots at all—they offer among the worst odds in the casino.

CASINOS WITH THE BEST ODDS

Where you gamble in Las Vegas can significantly affect your chances of winning. Casinos on the Las Vegas Strip use glitz and prestige to attract out-of-town gamblers. Some casinos in less touristy parts of town, such as North Las Vegas and the Boulder Strip along the Boulder Highway, instead try to attract locals and other savvy gamblers by offering more favorable odds than their better-known competitors.

•**From July 2016 through June 2017,** the 25-cent slot machines returned, on average, 96.56% of each bet on the Boulder Strip and 96.45% in North Las Vegas…but just 89.97% on the Vegas Strip and 94.41% downtown.

•**You can find blackjack tables with a $5 minimum bet on the Boulder Strip and in North Las Vegas,** while the minimum bet at blackjack tables in tourist-oriented casinos is rarely below $10.

Examples: The Boyd properties, including Sam's Town on the Boulder Strip (SamsTownLV.com) and The Orleans west of the Strip across Route 15 (OrleansCasino.com), offer some of the best odds for gamblers and free shuttle buses to and from the Strip. The Station casinos, such as Boulder Station on the Boulder Strip (Boulder Station.SCLV.com), are good choices as well.

Other cities: In Atlantic City, the Borgata has the highest slot-machine returns plus high-paying low-denomination video poker machines (TheBorgata.com). In Reno, Nevada, the Peppermill offers appealing video poker machine returns (PeppermillReno.com), while the Alamo Travel Center, a truck stop just outside of town, offers very gambler-friendly, low-limit blackjack rules (TheAlamo.com). In Biloxi, Mississippi, IP offers some of the area's best video poker machines and craps table odds (IP Biloxi.com), while Treasure Bay offers favorable blackjack rules (TreasureBay.com).

How to Cope with Lost Luggage

WiseBread.com

How to cope with lost luggage: Report the loss immediately—there usually is a counter for this near the baggage carousels. Bring your baggage ticket to be used for a search. Go to the airline's website, and click on the lost-luggage section if you have not heard anything in 24 hours. Continue to follow up if necessary—by calling customer service if the website is not enough. Keep your claim updated—for instance, if you are traveling and change hotels, be sure the airline knows. Ask the airline how much essential spending is covered, and use the coverage to buy new travel basics such as clothing, shampoo and deodorant—keep all receipts for submission later. Be prepared to negotiate if your luggage is not found—the airline will not immediately make its best offer. Complain on social media if the airline drags its feet about reimbursement or makes the whole process harder than it already is—this can sometimes get the airline to speed up the process.

12

Retail Rip-Offs

Secrets Restaurants Don't Want You to Know

Darron Cardosa, who has more than 25 years of experience waiting tables in the New York City area. He is author of *The Bitchy Waiter: Tales, Tips & Trials from a Life in Food Service.* TheBitchyWaiter.com

E ating out means trusting strangers to prepare and handle your food. Usually that trust is well-placed—but at times, the hectic pace and financial pressures facing restaurants result in corners being cut in ways that could jeopardize your enjoyment of the meal…or even jeopardize your health. *We asked a veteran waiter to share what restaurants don't want you to know…*

FOOD QUALITY AND SAFETY

•**Seafood stew, soup and pasta "specials" often feature fish that's too old to serve any other way.** Restaurants do not like to throw away expensive ingredients. When seafood is no longer fresh enough to serve on its own, it might be chopped up and served in a stew, soup or pasta dish, where sauces and other bold flavors can be used to hide its age. This can happen with meat and poultry, too, but it's most common with seafood, which has an especially short shelf life.

Tip from the waiter: It's generally OK to order a seafood stew, soup or pasta dish if it is on the regular menu. But when these are listed as specials, the odds are high that the restaurant is trying to sell past-its-prime seafood.

•**Restaurant menus rarely are cleaned.** Responsible restaurants take cleanliness very seriously. Almost everything in the kitchen and dining room is cleaned regularly—except the menus. At most restaurants, menus are rarely, if ever, wiped down, even though they are handled by many people and occasionally dropped on the floor.

Tip from the waiter: Wash your hands after you've ordered and handed your menu back to the waiter.

•**Complimentary bread or chips might have been served to other tables before yours.** A Mexican restaurant in Michigan recently received negative press when it was caught taking chips and salsa that were not consumed at one table and serving them to a second table. That restaurant is far from alone—it is not uncommon for uneaten slices of complimentary bread to find their way onto multiple tables rather than get thrown away. And even restaurants that hold themselves to a very high standard usually send out the butter packages that accompany bread to table after table until they are used.

Tip from the waiter: It might be worth skipping complimentary premeal items such as bread and chips unless the restaurant has an open area where you can watch these items being prepared specifically for you.

●**The week following an extended power failure might be the wrong time to eat out.** Cash-strapped restaurants often cannot afford to throw away everything that was in their fridges and freezers after power outages, so ingredients may no longer be as fresh as they should be.

Tip from the waiter: If you want to eat out following a long power failure, choose a restaurant in a neighboring area that did not lose its power.

●**You might not want to eat your leftovers if you saw how they were put into to-go containers.** This task might be delegated to a busboy who has little training in hygienic food handling…or it might be done by a harried server who uses the same spoon to transfer multiple customers' partially eaten meals.

Tip from the waiter: Ask your server to bring to-go containers to your table, and then transfer your leftovers yourself.

●**Your dessert might not be fresh even if the menu says desserts are "made fresh in house every day."** Typically this means that one or two of the dessert options are made fresh each day, while others remain from earlier days.

Tip from the waiter: Before choosing a dessert, ask your server which desserts were made that day. Be leery of any dessert that features "chocolate crumble" or "chocolate crunchies" sprinkled on top. That chocolate topping might have been made by breaking apart stale chocolate cake, cookies or brownies that didn't sell in their original form.

BILLING AND SERVICE

●**Billing mistakes are common—and rarely spotted.** Servers are responsible for multiple tables at the same time—and billing mistakes are inevitable. But patrons rarely catch the mistakes, in part because roughly half of all restaurant customers do not bother to check their bills at all.

Tip from the waiter: If you do not want to take the time to check your bill closely, at least do a quick count to confirm that there are not more drinks, appetizers or entrées listed than you ordered. If at lunch, also make sure that you were charged lunch prices and not dinner prices for entrées, a particularly common billing error.

●**The last tables seated often receive less-than-stellar service—but you can be treated better.** If you walk into a restaurant shortly before its closing time, there's a good chance that both your server and the kitchen staff will be more focused on getting you out the door than on providing an enjoyable meal.

Tip from the waiter: Say something that sends a message to your server that you understand time is an issue, such as, "Don't worry, we won't order dessert"…and/or, "What can the kitchen prepare quickly?" This shows respect for the restaurant employees' priorities, greatly increasing the odds that they will show you respect in the form of a quality dining experience.

BEVERAGES

●**Wine sold by the glass could come from a bottle that has been open for days.** It even could come from a bottle that was originally ordered by another patron but rejected because that customer didn't like it.

Tip from the waiter: Order wine by the bottle, not by the glass, when possible. If you want only a single glass, boost the odds that it was opened recently by choosing something that's likely to be ordered often, such as the "house wine."

●**Your regular coffee actually might be decaf if closing time is near.** The regular coffeepot often is one of the first things emptied and cleaned by the restaurant staff at the end of the day. If you order a regular coffee after this has occurred, there's a good chance that you'll be given decaf with no mention of the substitution. (The reverse—receiving regular after ordering decaf—is much less common in well-run restaurants because the staff would not want to risk giving caffeine to a customer who, for example, has a heart condition.)

Tip from the waiter: If you really need a cup of regular coffee after a restaurant meal that concludes late in the evening—for example, if you're feeling drowsy and need to drive home—explain that to your waiter. He may be able to have a cup of regular coffee made for you. Or order cappuccino, which is typically made in an espresso machine one cup at a time.

●**Your water might not be as pure as you are told.** Some restaurants serve only filtered water… and some patrons pay extra for bottled water. But if there is ice in the water, that ice is almost certainly made from unfiltered tap water. Restaurant ice makers rarely have filters.

Tip from the waiter: If water purity is important to you, skip the ice.

●**Drink garnishes sometimes are germy or old.** That lemon or lime slice in your drink might have been cut hours earlier and then left to sit in an open, unrefrigerated container where numerous restaurant employees pick out pieces with their bare hands. Restaurants may have policies requiring the use of tongs for grabbing these garnishes, but rushed servers and bartenders frequently skip that.

Tip from the waiter: Tell your server to "hold the lemon" when you order a drink.

Save Money at Popular Restaurants

WiseBread.com

Restaurant substitutions that save you money or give you more for what you spend…

At McDonald's, instead of a Big Mac, order a McDouble with no ketchup—but with lettuce, onion, pickles and secret sauce. It is essentially the same sandwich as a Big Mac except for the extra bread in the middle, but average cost is only $1.39 rather than $3.99. At Chipotle, order a half order of two kinds of meat instead of a single meat, and both bean types instead of pinto or black beans alone—this typically ends up being larger. At Starbucks,

ask for half ice in your iced coffee to get more coffee, and skip its bottled water. The free ice water it offers is triple-filtered.

The Extra-Virgin Olive Oil Hoax

Larry Olmsted, author of *Real Food, Fake Food: Why You Don't Know What You're Eating & What You Can Do About It.* Based in Hartland, Vermont, he also writes the "Great American Bites" column for *USA Today.* RealFoodFakeFood.com

The "extra-virgin olive oil" in your kitchen is probably not extra-virgin at all. To qualify as extra-virgin, olive oil is supposed to be subjected to minimal processing and be made exclusively from fresh, high-quality olives. But a highly publicized research report from the Olive Center at University of California, Davis, found that 69% of the olive oil sold as "extra-virgin" in the US does not meet those standards. The flavor of these fakes typically falls well short of the real thing. Also, a diluted or heavily processed olive oil might not provide the same cancer- and heart disease–fighting benefits of a true extra-virgin olive oil.

Producers get away with selling fake extra-virgin olive oil because the US government does little to enforce olive oil standards…and because most Americans have never tasted a true high-quality, extra-virgin olive oil, which makes it difficult to spot fakes.

What to do: Buy from trustworthy brands, such as California Olive Ranch (about $12 for a 500-ml bottle, CaliforniaOliveRanch.com)…Cobram Estate (from $12.99 for a 375-ml bottle, Cobram Estate.com)…Whole Foods' 365 Everyday Value brand (from $5.99 for a 500-ml bottle)…and Oro Bailén (often $20 or more for a 500-ml bottle, OroBailen.com).

Or buy from an importer or a distributor of high-quality olive oils, such as Oliviers & Co. (Oliviers AndCo.com) and Zingerman's (Zingermans.com). Alternately, you could join the Fresh-Pressed Olive Oil Club and receive three bottles of stellar olive oil four times a year ($99 per quarter for three 250-ml bottles, FreshPressedOliveOil.com).

Other good bets include any US-produced olive oil that has the "COOC" seal of the California Olive Oil Council on its label...or any Italian olive oil that says "100% Qualità Italiana." Extra-virgin olive oil produced in Australia is a reasonable choice, too—Australia enforces the world's strictest extra-virgin olive oil standards.

Note: To read research results from the University of California, Davis, go to OliveCenter.UC-Davis.edu and click on "Research" and then "Our Reports."

Fresher Eggs

Clark.com

You can find out when eggs were packed in a carton by looking at the Julian date number, located near the best-by date. The number is between 1, meaning January 1, and 365, meaning December 31. Eggs may have been laid up to 30 days before being packed.

Missing $$

Money.com

People spend 8% more at restaurants when the menu omits the word "dollar" or the $ symbol. The word or symbol reminds customers they are spending money and triggers negative feelings linked to paying.

Pay Less to See the Latest Movies

Kiplinger's Personal Finance.

MoviePass.com charges $9.95 a month to see three movies at any major theater chain. Go-

FoBo.com offers free tickets in major cities for selected screenings before release dates to build films' word-of-mouth buzz before they open.

The Pink Tax Rip-Off

Clark Howard, founder of Clark.com and host of *The Clark Howard Show*, a syndicated radio program, reported by **Karen Larson**, former editor, *Bottom Line Personal.*

A recent report by New York City's Department of Consumer Affairs found that products designed for women cost 7% more on average than virtually identical products marketed to men. This pricing gap is greatest with personal-care products—women's deodorant, shampoo and conditioner tend to cost around 50% more than men's.

One solution: Skip the women's versions, when possible, and buy men's products instead.

We asked consumer expert Clark Howard, founder of Clark.com and host of radio's syndicated *The Clark Howard Show,* to share some other examples of how women and men can both save...

• **Clothes and shoes tend to be much cheaper in the children's section.** And if you're a man or woman of less-than-average stature, there's a good chance that the largest children's sizes will fit you just fine. Walmart stocks especially large kid's clothing.

• **Battery prices can vary depending on where you pick them up in a big-box store.** Batteries often are stocked near the toy department...in the electronics department...and by the cash registers. It is difficult to predict where they will be cheapest, but batteries shelved in checkout aisles often are priciest.

• **Prescription medications can be 50% cheaper per dose if you buy higher-dosage pills.** If you or your child is prescribed a low-dosage pill, ask your doctor if he can prescribe a higher dosage that can be split, then use a pill splitter to cut each pill in half. (*Caution:* Not all types of pills can be split safely.) With over-the-counter medications, dollar stores and deep discounters generally charge less than pharmacies.

Save Money on a Gym Membership

Roundup of experts on gym memberships, reported at Cosmopolitan.com.

Compare gym prices close to home and work. Request the best possible rate—check whether the gym is running any online promotions, and ask whether further discounts will be offered later in the month. Even if there are no discounts provided, you can request one if you are a student, teacher or civil servant…or can explain why you are on a tight budget and would appreciate some help. Find out if there are off-peak rates available if you use the gym at less crowded times. Sign up for free trials at all gyms you are considering. If you intend to use only specific equipment—just the treadmills, for example—ask if you can get a lower price. If you have the money to pay for a full year up-front, offer to do so in return for a discount. Consider joining with others—many gyms offer group discounts. Find out if your employer or insurance plan has negotiated discounted rates at specific gyms.

For a Better Deal on a Diamond Ring…

Josh Holland, spokesperson, BlueNile.com, online diamond seller, quoted in *USA Today.*

Look for stones just below benchmarks for weight, color and clarity.

Example: A 0.95-carat stone costs much less than a one-carat stone of the same quality. Focus on cut rather than size—diamonds with more sparkle, caused by the way they are cut, look larger. Negotiate price—local jewelers have plenty of room to reduce prices…national chains have less, but because their salespeople work on commission, they will be motivated to make a deal if they can. Visit multiple stores, from large chains to local shops, to compare offerings. If using credit to buy a ring, try

to get store financing with 0% interest instead of using higher-cost credit card debt.

Here's to Free Refills!

DailyFinance.com

Taco Bell gives free refills on fountain drinks when you are inside—drive-through customers are not eligible for free refills. Chipotle allows unlimited refills of fountain drinks. Starbucks gives free refills on brewed hot or iced coffee or tea in the store to loyalty-club members (available at participating stores only). Five Guys gives unlimited refills at the Coca-Cola Freestyle Soda Fountain, which now has more than 100 possible combinations. Casual sit-down restaurants such as TGI Fridays, Friendly's, Olive Garden, Chili's and Fuddruckers typically offer free refills on fountain drinks and sometimes other beverages—but the policies vary by individual restaurant and franchise, so ask.

The Imported-Beer Hoax

Randy Mosher, author of *Tasting Beer: An Insider's Guide to the World's Greatest Drink.* He teaches beer-related classes at Siebel Institute of Technology in Chicago. RandyMosher.com

Beck's is among the most popular German beers in America. Or it would be, if it really were German. While Beck's labels proclaim "originated in Bremen, Germany," and "brewed under the German Purity Law of 1516," the beer sold in the US actually has been brewed in St. Louis for the past several years. (Anheuser-Busch InBev, which owns Beck's, recently settled a class action and agreed to make the fact that the beer is made in America more visible on the label. Beck's drinkers who feel duped may be eligible for a refund of as much as $50.)

Beck's is by no means the only "imported" beer that isn't really imported. If you drink Foster's Lager (marketing slogan: "Foster's: Australian for beer")… Bass Ale ("the original English pale ale")…Kirin

Ichiban ("Japan's Prime Brew")...Red Stripe ("The Taste of Jamaica")...or George Killian's Irish Red in the US, you are drinking a US-brewed beer.

There is nothing wrong with drinking American beer, but it is a breach of trust for breweries to market domestically produced beers in a way that implies they are imported. Differences in the barley, water or other ingredients used to brew these beers in the US might mean that they don't taste quite the same here as they do abroad.

The good news is, there's so much good distinctive beer being made by small and midsize American brewers these days that drinkers in search of something different and better can easily find it without resorting to fake imports—or real imports.

Example: If you have been drinking Beck's, try Firestone Walker Brewing Pivo Pils...or Victory Brewing Company Prima Pils. Both are brewed by midsize American breweries in the style of Czech and German pilsners such as Beck's. They cost more than Beck's, but they also have a lot more flavor—and they're not pretending to be something they're not.

Phony Egyptian Cotton Sheets

Jordon Lea, chairman and co-owner of Eastern Trading Company, a cotton merchandising firm in Greenville, South Carolina. He is past president and a board member of the International Cotton Association.

Your very soft—and expensive—sheets and pillowcases may not be made of what you think they're made of. That's because a major scandal is rocking the world of "Egyptian cotton." After an investigation, the Target retail chain declared that 750,000 Fieldcrest-brand Egyptian cotton sheets and sheet sets it offered from August 2014 through July 2016 contained no Egyptian cotton, and the chain offered refunds. Walmart stopped selling sheets from the same provider, Welspun India, that it had sold under the brands Better Homes & Gardens and Canopy. Other stores (and consumers) may have been duped, too.

Egyptian extralong staple (ELS) cotton is renowned for its softness and durability. The extremely fine but strong fibers of the cotton benefit from the long growing season in a desert climate.

Without laboratory testing, even experts can't easily distinguish between ELS cotton from Egypt and the world's other premium cotton, Pima ELS, which is grown in the deserts of Arizona and California as well as in Australia and Peru. Because Egyptian cotton is so much rarer—representing just 7% of global ELS production—it carries added cachet. The Cotton Egypt Association, which licenses and certifies suppliers, estimates that 90% of products labeled "Egyptian cotton" are fakes.

What to do...

●**Don't assume that if it says Egyptian cotton, it's 100% Egyptian cotton.** It's more likely a blend of different cottons, perhaps including Pima ELS cotton or Upland cotton, a very common, coarser variety that is used for jeans, tablecloths and underwear. As a rule of thumb, authentic Egyptian cotton products command premium prices.

Example: You should expect to pay at least $200 for 100% Egyptian cotton sheet sets in full size but less for partial Egyptian cotton.

●**Buy products with the 100% Supima label as an alternative.** Supima is a licensed trademark used to promote and market textile and apparel products made with the highest-quality American Pima ELS cotton. It's the equal of Egyptian cotton in feel and durability but often commands a lower price because supplies are more plentiful. The growers and supply chains that produce Supima cotton are closely monitored in the US to ensure the integrity of the product.

Better Online Shopping

InternetRetailer.com reporting on a year-long price-comparison study by Wells Fargo Securities LLC and price-tracking firm 360pi.

Walmart and Target can be lower-price alternatives to Amazon.com when shopping online. Both had generally lower prices in the categories of clothing and shoes, electronics, housewares, health and cosmetics. Walmart's prices were 10% lower than Amazon's, and Target's were 5% lower, excluding shipping costs and taxes. As when buying at physical stores, it pays to shop around.

Amazon Savings Tricks

David Pogue, technology critic for Yahoo Finance. He spent 13 years as the personal technology columnist for *The New York Times* and is author of *Pogue's Basics: Money—Essential Tips and Shortcuts (That No One Bothers to Tell You).* DavidPogue.com

More than 300 million customers shop at Amazon.com, including more than 60 million who belong to Amazon Prime, which provides benefits ranging from free two-day shipping to streaming video content and unlimited photo storage. *Yet many of those customers are unaware of some of the best ways to save the most at the site...*

•**Share a Prime membership.** Amazon's rules allow any two adults to share a single $119 annual membership and get nearly all Prime benefits.

One catch: The two of you also must share access to the same credit/debit cards for use on the site, so share only with someone you trust.

•**Share a digital library.** If you and a friend or family member each has a separate Prime membership, you can link the two accounts and share any Kindle e-books, audiobooks and apps that you have purchased. As with shared Prime membership, you also must share access to credit/debit cards.

•**Complain your way to extra months of Prime membership.** If you are a Prime member and an item that you ordered doesn't reach you by its expected delivery date or the wrong item is shipped or you have any other problem with an Amazon purchase, politely complain about this to an Amazon. com customer service rep. There's a good chance that the rep will extend your Prime membership for an additional month or two to keep you happy. (To reach customer service, call 888-280-4331.)

•**"Clip" Amazon coupons.** Most Amazon users don't realize that there are digital coupons available on the site. These are comparable to those found in newspapers or on Coupons.com, but they can be redeemed at Amazon.com. Simply Google "Amazon Coupons." Click the "Clip Coupon" button for any coupons you might want to use. The savings will be applied when you put the appropriate product in your Amazon shopping cart and make your purchase.

Recent examples: $10 off an Oral-B Pro 1000 rechargeable electric toothbrush...$2 off a package of 18 rolls of Charmin Sensitive Toilet Paper.

•**Sign up for the Amazon Prime Rewards Visa Signature credit card or Prime Store Card.** Prime members receive 5% back when they use either of these cards to make Amazon.com purchases. The cards have no annual fee beyond the usual Prime membership fee.

•**Take advantage of Amazon Warehouse Deals.** When an Amazon customer opens a product but then returns it or when a product's packaging is damaged, Amazon.com sells the item at a big discount through its "warehouse." Savings range from 25% to 75% off the usual price. To reach Amazon's warehouse, simply Google "Amazon" and "Warehouse."

Similar: Amazon Outlet offers clearance, overstock and slightly imperfect new items at discounts that range from 20% to 80%. Google "Amazon" and "Outlet."

•**Use CamelCamelCamel.com** to decide when to buy on Amazon.com. Third-party website CamelCamelCamel lets you view the price history of any item Amazon stocks so that you can make your purchase when the fluctuating price is relatively low. Or choose a target price for an item, and have CamelCamelCamel send you an e-mail if and when the price drops to that level or below.

13

Car Troubles

Save $1,000s on a Used Car: Big Bargains on Demos, Fleet Cars and Rental Cars

Ron Montoya, senior consumer advice editor at Edmunds. com, a leading provider of automotive information. He is based in Santa Monica, California. Edmunds.com

Not every used automobile has been owned by an individual. Some are "demos," which dealerships have used for test-drives and other purposes… "program" vehicles, which have been used by the manufacturer in various settings such as trade shows…"fleet" vehicles, which have been owned by municipalities or corporations and used by employees…or rental vehicles. These sometimes are priced hundreds or even thousands of dollars below vehicles of a similar model, age and mileage. But are they great bargains…or no better than a standard used car? *Here's what you need to know…*

DEMO AND PROGRAM VEHICLES

Demos usually are from the current model year. They have been driven by employees of the auto dealership…have been taken on test-drives…and/ or have been loaned to customers while their own vehicles were being worked on by the dealer's service department.

Program vehicles might have been put on display at trade shows, driven by one of the automaker's employees or test-driven by journalists writing reviews. Unlike the other vehicles covered in this article, demos and program vehicles usually are classified as new cars, not used cars. Autos are legally considered new until someone takes out a title on them, something that dealerships and manufacturers rarely do with demos and program vehicles.

Buying a demo or program vehicle likely will shorten your warranty coverage compared with buying a truly new car. Ask the salesperson to tell you the "in-service" date. This will serve as the vehicle's warranty start date—which is likely many months earlier than the date you purchase the auto, reducing your warranty coverage. The miles already on the odometer will cut into your warranty, too. Demo/program vehicle warranties do not reset when the car is purchased.

But demos and program vehicles still can be smart buys. They tend to have extremely low mileage (potentially a few thousand miles or less)…may include attractive options packages…and, for the most part, have been driven responsibly and were well-maintained. When dealership employees drive demos, for example, they tend to baby them because they know that any damage or serious wear would detract from their value. Salespeople often are in vehicles during customer test-drives, which tends to discourage irresponsible test-driving.

If you can find a manufacturer-certified used car of similar age and mileage, it might sell for a lower price than a comparable demo/program car—but it might not be possible to find the used car that you want with just a few thousand miles on the odometer. Privately owned cars rarely are resold that soon.

What to do: If you consider buying a demo or program car, confirm that you really are getting a good deal. Sometimes a salesperson will present a demo or program vehicle as though the price is a steal when the price actually is similar to what a buyer could have negotiated on a 100%-new vehicle. Use a car-shopping website such as Edmunds.com (where I am employed) to compare the price you are being offered to what other buyers actually are paying for the new vehicle. (Remember to include the value of any options packages.) Also, use this or another car-shopping site to research the fair purchase price of this make and model as a low-mileage used car, and make a counteroffer based on this figure. A demo or program car might legally be new, but it is reasonable to argue that it really is more like a low-mileage used car despite its legal status. The dealership is unlikely to come down to this used price because it probably can find a buyer willing to pay more, but because of the mileage, it should be willing to offer you a significantly better deal than you would get on a similar 100% new vehicle.

Ask what the dealership charges for an extended warranty on the vehicle as well, and then use this in your negotiation. If one year of the demo's warranty already is used up, for example, and it would cost you an average of $300 per year to extend the warranty, point this out and ask to have the price reduced to compensate. If you are asked to sign any disclosures about the vehicle, read this paperwork carefully—occasionally dealerships disclose precisely how a demo or program vehicle was used because its use was atypical or extreme. You probably don't want to buy a program car, for example, that was used to teach people how to drive aggressively on a track.

Where to find them: Ask in person whether a dealership has a demo or program version of the car you are shopping for.

FORMER RENTAL CARS

Car-rental companies often sell vehicles when they are one to four years old and have 25,000 to 50,000 miles on their odometers. Most—though not all—rental cars are base or midlevel models with few options. Are they a smart buy? Only if you are comfortable with the fact that your car has been driven by hundreds of different people, at least some of whom probably treated it poorly.

On the plus side, major rental companies generally maintain their cars well, and they often sell them for hundreds less than you likely would pay for similar individual-owned cars at a used-car lot. These days, many rental-car companies also make used-car buying simple—you can view the cars for sale in your area on their websites along with their no-haggle prices. If your priority is a low-pressure, no-haggle used-car buying experience, this could be the way to go. Some rental agencies provide limited warranty protection in addition to any remaining manufacturer warranty. Enterprise and Hertz, for example, provide 12-month, 12,000-mile limited powertrain warranties.

What to do: Check whether the rental company will let you rent the car for a few days before you commit to buying it. This usually is allowed, and it's a great way to weed out problem vehicles. (Besides driving the car to see how it performs and feels, take the car to an independent mechanic for a once-over during this extended test-drive.) Most major rental firms will waive the resulting rental charges if you decide to buy the car.

Where to find them: Check on the major rental firms' websites.

FLEET VEHICLES

Governments and companies sometimes sell cars that they owned for employee use.

Are they a smart buy? Potentially—if the price is attractive and you choose carefully. Overall, fleet vehicles tend to be in no worse shape than similar used cars that were in private hands. They even might be a bit better because they usually are professionally maintained on a regular schedule.

Fleet cars are more likely than rental cars to have been driven responsibly. The employees who drive fleet vehicles know that getting a ticket or getting into an accident in their employer's car could have negative career ramifications. There are exceptions, however—former police cars and taxi cabs often are driven very hard, for example. Some delivery vehicles have endured hard miles as well.

What to do: Before buying a fleet vehicle, ferret out details about how it was driven and who drove it. If it is a nice sedan that was used to ferry around clients, it probably was driven conservatively…but if it's a pickup truck that was used to carry heavy loads or pull a trailer, it has had a tougher life than the average privately owned used pickup.

Request a copy of the vehicle's service records—most companies keep meticulous fleet records. Check these to confirm that maintenance was handled on a regular basis and that the vehicle had no major accidents or recurring problems.

Where to find them: Former fleet vehicles are sold in the same places that other used vehicles are sold—on used-car lots, through classified ads or Craigslist.com, etc. But when a fleet vehicle is sold on a used-car lot, it might not be possible to obtain that vehicle's service history…and you might not learn that it was in a fleet unless you obtain a vehicle history report from a service such as CarFax. Some fleet vehicles are sold at auctions—but these auctions are best avoided if you are not an auto expert (or cannot bring an expert with you). Bidders often are not even allowed to test-drive vehicles before bidding on them.

Apps to Help You Avoid Speeding Tickets

USA Today.

For iOS devices, the Speed Cameras & Traffic app lets you see the speed limit for whatever road you are traveling on, plus alerts you to upcoming speed cameras and radar traps. For Android, try CamSam Plus, $0.99.

Premium Rises Even If It's Not Your Fault!

Douglas Heller, an insurance consultant for Consumer Federation of America, conducted a study of auto-insurance premiums. ConsumerFed.org

Your auto insurance premium is likely to rise after an accident even if you were not at fault. After a driver had just one accident in which another driver was at fault, Allstate, Farmers, Geico and Progressive raised annual premiums by an average of $176 (10%). Among the five major auto insurers studied in 10 big US cities, only State Farm did not penalize innocent drivers. In California and Oklahoma, consumer laws prohibit such premium hikes.

How to Beat the Traffic on Long Weekends

Study by AAA, reported in USA Today.

The Friday before Memorial Day has had less traffic than the Thursday before the holiday, according to a five-year study of the Washington, DC, area.

Reason: So many people try to leave early to beat the expected Friday rush that Friday has become less crowded.

Best Times to Buy a New Car

Roundup of experts on car sales, reported at Kiplinger.com.

In the market for a new car? *Here are the best times to buy…*

End of the year, especially right before New Year's Day, if you want the previous year's model—although choices likely will be limited. Labor Day, when dealer lots still have many old models just as new ones are coming in. After a major model redesign if you like the old model and the redesign is more for appearance than functionality. End of the day at the end of the month—salespeople need to meet quotas and even may sell a few cars at a loss if it boosts total sales so that they get a special bonus. Black Friday—some dealers offer special discounts because many people are in the mood to make purchases on the day after Thanksgiving.

Avoid Fad Colors

Eric Ibara, director of residual value, Kelley Blue Book, quoted in *USA Today*.

Black, white and silver vehicles are worth more at resale than ones in trendy colors—especially if the fad color has been discontinued by the time the car is sold.

Also: Light-colored vehicles, such as white and silver, are less likely to show scratches.

Cheaper Cars That Are Expensive to Insure

Laura Adams, senior insurance analyst, insuranceQuotes.com, where you can see the full survey it commissioned on insurance rates.

Small sedans are the most expensive vehicles to insure relative to their prices. A recent national survey found that the worst deals in car insurance, based on likely damage, injuries and theft rates, were on the Ford Focus…Toyota Corolla…Hyundai Elantra…Honda Civic…and Chevrolet Cruze sedans. The best insurance values were SUVs or trucks—Ford Explorer and Chevrolet Equinox

SUVs…and GMC Sierra, Chevrolet Silverado and Dodge Ram 1500 trucks.

Consider all long-term costs when choosing a vehicle.

6 Things Car Dealers Don't Want You to Know

Karl Brauer, executive publisher at *Kelley Blue Book*, which provides information about new and used cars. He has more than 15 years of experience as an automotive journalist and was the first Web-based journalist to be named to the jury of the prestigious North American Car and Truck of the Year award. KBB.com

Today's car shoppers are harder to trick. Many know to refuse overpriced add-ons such as rust-proofing and fabric protection. They even may know they can get price quotes from multiple dealerships online and detailed information on dealer costs, rebates and financing.

But that doesn't mean customers—even those who think they have learned many of the standard tricks—can withstand all the tactics that a car salesperson can throw at them. That's especially true when they face some new twists on the classic sales techniques.

Of course, not all salespeople are out to trick you, but here are the things that a car salesperson might say that could signal he/she intends to try to get you to pay more than you should…

• **"I'm selling it to you for just $300 over cost.** Look up the invoice price yourself—you'll see I can't go any lower." Salespeople know shoppers have become used to looking up the so-called "invoice price" of a new vehicle online. So rather than try to hide this information, they sometimes encourage buyers to look up invoice prices…and encourage them to believe that these prices are what dealers actually pay for cars. They aren't. Invoice prices are sometimes referred to as "dealer cost," but in fact, automakers typically use "dealer holdbacks" and "dealer incentives" that reduce the amount dealerships pay to hundreds of dollars below invoice price—sometimes thousands.

What to do: Do not let a salesperson convince you that you are getting an incredible deal just because the price you are paying is fairly close to the invoice price. A better sign you're getting a good deal is if you are paying less than the typical buyer in your area paid for the same vehicle. Several major car-shopping websites provide this information, including my company's site, KBB.com.

• **"You have to decide today."** Car buyers can easily get quotes online from multiple dealerships, even dealerships hundreds of miles away. That gives salespeople more incentive to convince shoppers to buy the first time they set foot on a dealership lot—if they walk away, there's a strong chance they'll buy somewhere else. To encourage a quick purchase, a salesperson might claim a price is available only today...that supplies of a model are very limited...or that the dealership has only one vehicle with the desired colors and options and that another buyer is interested in it, too.

What to do: Ignore these classic high-pressure tactics. Buyers who move slowly and shop around almost always get better deals than those who rush. Any "today only" price you are offered is likely to be offered in the future, too.

Exception: It is possible that a "today only" price is available only today if it is the last day of a month and the dealership needs to make some final, quick sales to meet its quota and earn a bonus from the manufacturer. Even so, do not rush to buy unless you have researched the prices other buyers have paid for this vehicle and you are confident you are being offered a competitive price.

• **"We're a different kind of dealership—we offer no-haggle pricing."** No-haggle pricing, also called "guaranteed pricing," has been tried on and off for decades and is becoming increasingly common as dealerships try to attract buyers who dread the difficult, protracted negotiation process. It sounds sensible—almost everything we buy has a fixed price, so why not cars?

Trouble is, at many dealerships, the no-haggle guaranteed price is guaranteed to not be a very good deal. In fact, it often is not much different from the opening price the salesperson would have offered to a buyer who did negotiate. Choosing the no-haggle option just might mean you don't get to make a counteroffer.

What to do: Use a car-shopping website to check how the no-haggle price that you are offered compares with the price the typical buyer in your area is paying for the car. (You even can do this right at the dealership using your smartphone, tablet or laptop.) While some no-haggle prices are fair, in many cases you can save perhaps up to $500—potentially much more on a high-end vehicle—by haggling just a little at a no-haggle dealership.

Exception: If you buy a car from Tesla, the luxury electric-car maker, there is a fixed price and no haggling.

• **"Bad news—you didn't qualify for that interest rate."** Unscrupulous salespeople sometimes offer an attractive deal...then make up an excuse for changing the terms when the deal is nearly finalized. Even smart buyers often fall for this—the buyer has invested so much time and mental energy in the purchase by this point that it would be psychologically difficult to walk away.

Increasing the interest rate charged for an auto loan is perhaps the most common way to do this. The dealership claims the buyer did not qualify for the low interest rate originally quoted. This lets the dealership pretend it's the buyer's fault that the original deal fell through—he/she didn't have a good enough credit rating.

What to do: Have a financing offer in place from a credit union, bank or some other third-party lender before you shop for a car. If the dealership tries to charge a steeper interest rate, use this financing instead.

Variation: The salesman offers a very appealing price for a buyer's trade-in in addition to a competitive price on a new car. When the deal is nearly done, the salesperson apologetically says he cannot offer nearly as much for the trade-in as promised because the dealership's service department discovered the vehicle had a hidden mechanical problem. Either walk away from the deal or pull the trade-in out of the deal and sell this used car through the classifieds or Craigslist.com.

•**"But everyone pays the vehicle-prep fee."** If a savvy car buyer won't pay a steep purchase price, the salesperson might move to plan B—agree to a fair price, then tack on hundreds of dollars in extra fees at the last minute when you are about to sign the papers. If the buyer protests, the salesperson will act surprised and claim that these fees are standard and unavoidable.

What to do: Well before you are about to sign the final papers, ask the dealership to quote you an "out-the-door price" that includes absolutely all charges. Some fees, including destination charges and tax, title and licensing fees, are truly unavoidable. Many dealerships also refuse to budge on a "documentation" fee, which covers processing the paperwork for the title and registration, although it is worth at least trying to negotiate this fee if it is significantly above $50. Many other fees, however, are negotiable, especially if you threaten to walk away. This includes dealer prep fees…delivery fees in excess of factory destination charges…and charges for add-ons you did not request and that are not necessary, such as vehicle identification number (VIN) etching on the windshield. Any fees that are charged should have been included in the out-the-door price you were quoted.

•**"If you buy a car, we'll pay off your loan on your trade-in."** The dealership might try to roll your current loan into your new one. Or it might delay paying off your loan, sticking you with late-payment penalties while it enjoys what amounts to an interest-free loan.

What to do: Check the total amount being financed in the new loan contract to confirm that the balance on your existing loan has not been rolled into it. Confirm that the contract stipulates that the dealership will pay off your loan by your next payment deadline.

USED-CAR SALES TACTIC

In a tactic that applies only to used cars, the car salesperson says…

"This used car is in great shape—I'll even show you the Carfax." Salespeople know that sophisticated used-car buyers are likely to check a vehicle's Carfax report before buying. This report lists the vehicle's accident records and certain other aspects of its history. So salespeople steer sophisticated buyers to vehicles that have clean Carfax reports, then offer to provide these reports for free. This creates the impression that the salesperson is honest and that the car is problem-free. In reality, the salesperson might be using the buyer's faith in the Carfax report to trick him/her into failing to take prudent steps to uncover other significant issues. Automotive problems that do not result in insurance claims often do not find their way onto Carfax reports.

What to do: Pay an independent mechanic $200 to $400 to give a used car a prepurchase inspection before buying even if it has a clean Carfax report.

The Hybrid-Battery Lie

John Voelcker, editor of GreenCarReports.com. He is a member of the screening committee for the World Green Car of the Year award.

Hybrid car batteries have proved to be long-lasting, but they don't last forever. And when hybrid batteries fail, car owners can be in for a shock. If the battery is no longer under warranty, it likely will cost well into four figures to have a replacement installed. For the popular Toyota Prius, it is something in the neighborhood of $3,000—but with most other hybrids, the price is likely to be upward of $4,000 and, in some cases, close to $10,000.

Fortunately, you might not need to pay that much. First, confirm that the hybrid battery—not the far-less-expensive 12-volt battery—truly is the problem. AAA or an independent garage should be able to test your 12-volt battery. If the 12-volt battery is not the problem, have the vehicle towed to a garage that specializes in hybrids for a second opinion. There is a chance that an inexpensive fix to the battery pack is all that's needed, but this is something the average auto mechanic might not know how to do. Dealership mechanics might recommend replacing an entire unit—the easiest but most expensive option—even when a cheaper solution might be available.

If you can't find a garage in your area that specializes in hybrids, look for a shop advertising expertise with the Toyota Prius. The Prius is by far the most common hybrid car, and shops that work on it often can solve battery problems with other hybrids as well.

If the battery must be replaced, one option is to buy a used pack pulled from a vehicle that has been totaled. This could cost anywhere from about $400 to $2,000 or more. A mechanic who specializes in hybrids might know where to acquire a used pack, or a local salvage yard could have one. If not, enter the make and model of your vehicle and the phrase "battery pack" into eBay—battery packs often sell for $500 to $1,500 on that auction website. Labor costs to have the battery installed are likely to add at least a few hundred dollars.

If you're buying a used battery, get proof of the car's year and mileage. It is wise to look for a battery that is less than eight years old with fewer than 100,000 miles.

Warning: Never repair or replace a hybrid vehicle's battery pack on your own. These high-voltage systems are potentially lethal.

To Cool Cars Quickly…

Bottom Line Personal.

To draw out hot air, open one window. Then open and close the door on the opposite side about five times.

Variation: Open all windows. Then go around the car twice, opening each door on the first circuit and closing each door on the second.

3 Club Soda Tricks

Reader's Digest. RD.com

Three reasons you should always have club soda on hand…

- **Pour club soda into a spray bottle, and keep it in your car**—a quick spritz dissolves bird droppings quickly so they're easy to wipe away.
- **Drizzle it over a screw that's rusted stuck, and wait about five minutes**—the rust will dissolve so that the screw is easy to turn.
- **Pour a bit into a glass, and soak jewelry with gemstones overnight**—by morning, they'll be sparkling again.

Rental Car Rip-Off: Steep Fees for Road and Bridge Tolls

Christopher Elliott, a consumer advocate specializing in the travel industry. His latest book is *How to Be the World's Smartest Traveler.* Elliott.org

Rental car companies such as Avis and Hertz are offering automatic toll-paying devices such as E-ZPass and FasTrak. But some companies charge as much as $4.95 per day even if you don't use the device…and they charge the regular cash rate for all tolls, not the discounted rate that device owners often get.

Self-defense: Decline the device and pay cash… or bring the automatic toll device from your own car if it covers the area.

How to Find Affordable Parking…Even Free

Roundup of experts on parking, reported in USA Today.

Easy ways to find a parking spot—and save money. Park a rental car for free at one of the rental company's locations. Some rental firms offer discounted parking if you ask for it. ParkingPanda.com locates garage spaces and lets you reserve and pay for them in advance. Recently it found $16/day spaces in Washington, DC—saving one user $9/day. It is available in more than 40 US cities. Parkopedia.com is the Wikipedia of parking information with more than 8,000 cities in 75 countries. ParkWhiz.com specializes in events where parking can be costly and difficult to find. It lets you reserve and pay for a spot in advance.

Beware These Flood-Damaged Cars

Tom McParland, who operates New Jersey–based Automatch Consulting, reported by Karen Larson, former editor, *Bottom Line Personal.*

A friend is looking for a used car, but with the recent natural disasters, he's wary of getting stuck with a flood-damaged vehicle. He's right to be concerned—flooded vehicles often later experience massive problems with their electronics and other systems.

The titles of flood-damaged vehicles often are branded "salvage" or "flood." But that doesn't always happen…and unscrupulous sellers have tricks for obtaining new "clean" titles when it does.

Car buyers in storm-ravaged regions are not the only ones at risk. "Cars damaged during hurricanes in the south will be sold in places such as Nebraska where buyers are not as on guard about flood damage," warns Tom McParland, who operates New Jersey–based Automatch Consulting. *What to do…*

•**Look under the spare tire for mud, water or rust.** Unethical resellers of flood-damaged vehicles typically try to remove evidence of the immersion, but McParland says they often don't bother to take the spare out of the trunk and clean underneath.

•**Check for discolored or replaced carpeting.** Slide the front seats all the way forward and back. It could suggest flood damage if the carpeting under the seats is discolored. Related red flags include brand-new carpeting in an older car…or sections of carpeting that have been replaced.

•**Get the vehicle history report.** Go to Carfax.com ($39.99) or AutoCheck.com ($24.99). Proceed with extreme caution if the vehicle came from an area with flooding. If shopping on a used-car lot, ask the salesperson to provide at no charge one of these reports—be suspicious if he/she resists.

14

Crime Concerns

Get Out Alive! Strategies to Survive Life-Threatening Crime Scenes

Clint Emerson, a retired Navy SEAL who spent 20 years conducting special-ops missions. He is also author of *100 Deadly Skills: Survival Edition* and founding partner of Escape the Wolf, a crisis-management and risk-mitigation company based in Frisco, Texas. EscapetheWolf.com

When a crime occurs, you don't always have the time or opportunity to call 911 and wait for someone to come to your rescue. It pays to plan ahead. Here, Clint Emerson, a retired Navy SEAL who spent 20 years conducting special-ops missions, shares his strategies for surviving two terrifying emergencies...

CARJACKING

Before there's a problem: If you are in a high-crime area, leave at least one car length's space between your vehicle and the vehicle in front of yours when you come to a stop at a red light or stop sign. This greatly improves the odds that you will have sufficient room to speed away in an emergency. While stopped in traffic, keep your car doors locked, windows up and transmission in drive (or in first gear if the car has a standard transmission). Monitor your side and rearview mirrors, and glance out the side windows. Drivers who focus only on the traffic light or who become distracted by their phones or radios at stops are more likely to be targeted by carjackers.

Also, pay close attention to your surroundings when in parking garages and when pulling up to drive-through ATMs—these are common carjacking locations. If you see anyone lurking, drive away and find a different parking place or ATM. After using an ATM, don't stop to count your cash or put it in your wallet—drive away quickly.

During an emergency: The best response depends on how the carjacking occurs...

•**If you are walking in a parking area when someone demands your keys, locate an exit for an escape on foot and then toss the keys as far as you can in the direction opposite this exit to allow yourself time to run.** What you hope will happen is that while you are making your escape, the criminal will go in the other direction to pick up your car keys and then simply will take your car. If there is no nearby exit, toss the keys and take cover behind a solid obstacle such as a concrete pillar. The carjacker will get your car, but removing yourself as a factor as best you can decreases the odds that you will be kidnapped or harmed.

•**If you are stopped at a stop sign or red light when you see someone approaching with a weapon,** drive away even if this means going up on a sidewalk or running a red light (assuming that you can do so without causing an accident or running over a pedestrian).

•**If a carjacker gets into the passenger seat of your car while you are stopped, immediately jump out and run.** If he shows a gun and orders you to drive, offer to surrender the vehicle. If this offer is rejected, speed up, then slam on the brakes and quickly get out and run, ideally toward nearby people or into a building.

•**If a carjacker sticks a gun or knife through your driver's side window while you are stopped, offer to surrender the car.** If the carjacker refuses and orders you to slide over to the passenger seat, raise your arms slowly as if in surrender and then suddenly use your raised arms to push the carjacker's arm forward into your dashboard while simultaneously flooring the gas. The carjacker will not expect this, and his attention will immediately shift from stealing your car to not being hurt by your car.

HOME INVASION

Before there's a problem: Identify escape routes from your home. These should not just lead out of your house but also off your property. The ideal route exits your home only a short distance from a tree line or a neighbor's home that can shield you from view. Your escape route should conclude at a "rally point"—a predetermined place where family members can gather safely.

Keep your car keys, cell phone and flashlight near your bedside at night. These can come in handy (see below).

During an emergency: Resist the urge to turn on a light if you think someone has broken into your home at night. Light might make you feel safer, but turning on a light actually shows the home invader which room you are in. It also robs you of a tactical advantage—you know your home's layout better than the home invader does, so you can navigate it in the dark better than he can.

Grab your cell phone, car keys and flashlight… gather other members of the household…and head for your escape route. Sometimes it is not possible for everyone to move together as a family, so everyone, including children, should know that escape is the priority. What you don't want is your family waiting around while Mom or Dad confronts the intruder. If your car keys have a fob with a panic button, press this—the sound of your car alarm might scare off the home invader. Even if it doesn't, the alarm may provide a distraction that buys you time to escape while also alerting your neighbors. If you have a home-security system with a panic button, press this, too. (You should have a wall keypad or remote alarm button in your bedroom.)

Dial 911 as you proceed along your escape route or when you reach a safe spot—do not halt your escape to make this call. Do not hide inside your home unless you see no way to escape and/or there is a secure safe room in the home. Running is better than hiding because people who hide usually are found.

Warning about guns: If you are proficient with a gun, use it. But if it sits in your nightstand and you never use it, you should run rather than pull your gun—the last thing you want is to shoot a round through a few walls and injure or kill a family member or have the gun used against you.

FLASHLIGHTS CAN BE TACTICAL TOOLS

A flashlight can do more than light your way during an emergency. *You also can…*

•**Shine a flashlight into a neighbor's window or at passing cars to signal for help if,** for example, you are pinned down inside your home.

•**Disorient a home invader by shining a flashlight in his/her eyes in a dark room.** Then quickly turn the flashlight back off and run—the light burst should temporarily rob him of his ability to see in low light.

•**Use a flashlight as a club.** This requires a big metal flashlight loaded with heavy D-cell batteries. It can be an effective weapon or can be used to break a window.

Do-It-Yourself Home Security Systems

Ry Crist, a senior associate editor for CNET, the consumer-electronics website. He specializes in smart and automated home electronics products and systems. CNET.com

About 20% of US homes have professionally installed and monitored security systems. These services, with maintenance and monitoring fees that add up to several hundred dollars a year, are beyond the budgets of many people. Also, many existing homes would require custom installation and wiring.

But a different type of home security has been catching on—do-it-yourself (DIY) systems that have no contracts and, in most but not all cases, no additional fees beyond the cost of the equipment and no professional monitoring. Instead of requiring wires in the walls, DIY systems typically use the existing Wi-Fi network in your home...wireless door and window sensors...an app on your smartphone or tablet to control the system...and optional wireless cameras. You can install, customize and monitor these systems yourself.

DIY systems aren't right for everyone, especially if you don't want to figure out where to put sensors and/or you are unwilling to sacrifice the added security of professional outside monitors to contact authorities when you are away or under threat. But for home owners willing to do without that extra layer of security, DIY systems can provide some peace of mind without a lot of the extra cost.

HOW IT WORKS

The centerpiece of a DIY home security system typically is a base station that connects to your home's Wi-Fi router. The base station usually contains a built-in, very loud 110-decibel alarm and communicates with various sensors, including motion detectors for rooms and contact sensors for doors and windows, all of which can be attached with double-sided tape. The wireless motion-detecting video cameras that also can be used in these systems tend to get a lot of attention—there's a certain gee-whiz factor using your smartphone or tablet to see what's going on in your living room from anywhere in the world—but video cameras are not as important as the other components for actually deterring break-ins.

With most DIY systems, you choose whether to receive a text message, an automated phone call or both whenever a sensor or video camera is triggered. Many also can be controlled manually with a wireless keypad that you affix near an entranceway and/or with a key-chain remote.

Drawback: Most DIY systems depend on the Wi-Fi network in your home, so they might not fully function if you lose electrical power unless they have a battery backup.

A basic, entry-level DIY system starts at about $200, while an elaborate system with lots of additional sensors and cameras can run several thousand dollars. A comparable entry-level professional home security service for a small house typically charges a $99 installation fee and a $40 monthly monitoring fee with a mandatory 36-month contract (that is a savings of $1,340 with the average DIY system).

WHAT TO BUY

There are more than two dozen companies offering DIY home security systems, ranging from well-known brands to start-ups. *Consider these three factors when you choose...*

●**Price.** Most DIY systems are cheaper than a professional home security service when you consider that with DIY, you might not have any outside monitoring to pay for. But there is a wide range of how much you can spend.

●**Size of your house.** For a small apartment, a very limited DIY system with base station and contact sensor on the front door may be enough. A large house may require a system that's easy and affordable to expand and offers you options such as range extenders that strengthen Wi-Fi signals to reach rooms far from the router.

●**Type of protection you need.** Most systems offer a basic security package and let you customize it to your needs by adding additional sensors, sirens, cameras and remotes. But you may want a system that also offers additional types of protection beyond break-ins. For example, some systems have carbon monoxide sensors and flood sensors. Others have key-chain remotes that elderly parents can carry around in the house to alert you via smartphone if they have an emergency.

My favorite DIY systems now…

•**iSmartAlarm.** Best very basic, inexpensive system. The starter package comes with a base station, two door/window sensors, a motion sensor and two key-chain remotes. It took me just 15 minutes to open the box and get the system up and running.

Cost: $199.*

Note: The starter package does not include a camera, but you can buy one for an additional $150. iSmartAlarm.com

•**Piper Pro.** Best for home owners who want a system that provides more flexibility and greater potential coverage. You get a base station with a Piper NV night-vision video camera and your choice of three other items (for example, you can choose door/window sensors or smart plugs that plug into existing electrical outlets and allow you to automate lights and appliances and turn them on and off remotely).

Cost: $300. GetPiper.com

•**Iris by Lowe's.** Best for a larger house or if you want home automation as well as security. To use Iris for security and/or home automation, you'll need to buy the Smart Hub—the brains of the system—and then add on what you want. The basic home security package comes with a motion detector, two door/window sensors and an alarm keypad. What sets Iris apart is the wealth of affordable options—more than 60 add-on devices for security and home automation, including a programmable thermostat ($79.99)…smart plugs ($37.99)…a wireless video camera ($89).

Cost: $69 for the hub…$99 for the basic security package. An optional $14.95/month plan gives you more advanced controls and lets you have up to six people notified when an alert is triggered. IrisByLowes.com

•**SimpliSafe.** Best if you don't want to monitor the security system yourself but want low monitoring costs. This is a hybrid DIY/professional offering with no contract. You install the system, but it

*Prices subject to change.

is professionally monitored, so when an alarm is triggered, the system makes a cellular phone call to a dispatcher. The Economy package consists of a base station, a wireless keypad, three door/window sensors, one motion sensor and a key-chain remote. Extra sensors are available, and there is a battery backup for the base station and a cellular backup in case the power goes out.

Cost: $259.95 for equipment plus a $14.99 to $24.99/month fee, depending on the options you want. SimpliSafe.com

Credit Card Scam: Stealing Security Codes

Curtis Arnold, founder of the news and review websites CardRatings.com and BestPrepaidDebitCards.com. He is author of *How You Can Profit from Credit Cards.*

The three- or four-digit security codes printed on credit and debit cards are meant to protect you from criminals who want to charge purchases to your account. But criminals—who already have their hands on millions of stolen card account numbers—are tricking cardholders into revealing the codes as well.

The scam works like this: You receive a phone call from someone who claims to work in your card issuer's fraud-prevention department. The caller reads your credit card account number to you and says that suspicious transactions have been identified on the account, then asks you to confirm whether you made a particular purchase. When you say you did not, the caller tells you not to worry because a new account number will be issued and you won't be responsible for any fraudulent charges. But first you have to provide the security code to prove that the card still is in your possession. If it is not, you might be responsible for some of the fraudulent charges, the caller claims.

Even savvy consumers fall for this scam because the caller already knows the card account number, making it easier to convince you that it is the card issuer calling.

What to do: If a caller claims to be from your card issuer's fraud-prevention department, ask for the caller's name and/or employee ID, hang up, then call the 800-number on the back of your card and ask to speak to the fraud-prevention department or that particular employee. If the call was not from the card issuer, explain that your account number likely has been stolen. The issuer will give you a new card with a new number.

• **Visit Nomorobo.com** to find out if its free robocall-blocking service is available for your landline and/or cell-phone carrier. Nomorobo was a winner of an FTC contest that sought ways to block robocalls.

• **Download a robocall-blocking app to your smartphone**…or buy a robocall blocker for your landline from a retailer or Internet shopping website that sells electronics.

The Fake Survey

Bikram Bandy, an attorney with the Federal Trade Commission, Washington, DC, and program coordinator of the federal Do-Not-Call Program. DoNotCall.gov

An automated call that claims to want your opinion actually might be after your money. Phone surveys are exempt from rules that ban automated "robocalls" and calls to numbers on the federal Do Not Call Registry. Some companies believe, incorrectly, that beginning an automated sales call with survey questions makes it legal. The Florida company Caribbean Cruise Line agreed to pay $500,000 to settle claims that it robocalled millions of phone numbers with what seemed to be a political survey. People who responded were told that they could receive a free two-day Bahamas cruise for their trouble—but when they tried to claim this reward, they were connected to a salesperson who tried to talk them into paying for parts of the "free" cruise.

This fake survey has been shut down, but other companies use similar tactics.

What to do: If someone tries to sell you something during a phone survey, hang up immediately.

If a robocall tells you to press a button on your keypad to be removed from the call list, don't do it. Pressing this is likely to increase the number of calls you receive. *Instead…*

• **Visit DoNotCall.gov** to confirm that your phone number is on the Do Not Call Registry. This will reduce sales calls.

Cyber-Crooks Could Crack Your Nest Egg: How to Protect Your Financial Accounts

Gary Miliefsky, founder of SnoopWall (now NetShield), a counter-intelligence technology company. He is a member of the advisory board of the Center for the Study of Counter-Terrorism and Cyber Crime, based at Norwich University in Vermont. He previously served as editor of *Cyber Defense Magazine* and advised the US Department of Homeland Security's National Infrastructure Advisory Council.

High-tech thieves are trying to crack your nest egg. An incredible 88% of brokerages and 74% of investment advisory firms say that they have been targets of cyber attacks, in most cases involving malware or fraudulent e-mails, according to a recent SEC report.

In many of the attacks involving fraudulent e-mails, the financial firms were tricked into transferring to scammers amounts ranging from $5,000 to $75,000.

There are no laws requiring investment firms to compensate investors for cyber-theft losses, although in many cases the companies do. However, if a high-tech thief manages to transfer your life savings to his own offshore account, that money might be gone for good—even if it is your investment firm's lax security that allows the crime to happen.

Investment companies are working to beef up their security. A recent survey by the consulting firm PricewaterhouseCoopers found that US financial services companies are rapidly increasing their cyber-security spending. Citigroup now spends more than $300 million per year. JPMorgan Chase plans to double its spending from $250 million to $500 million over the next five years, following a 2014 data breach that put 76 million JPMorgan customers at risk and a 2013 incident in which prepaid cards were accessed by hackers.

But while financial companies are spending huge amounts on cyber-security technology and staff, successful attacks remain common. *Here's why the firms remain vulnerable and what you can do to protect your money…*

THE FLAWS THAT REMAIN

Two of the biggest vulnerabilities…

•**Investment company employees fall for the same identity-theft tricks that trip up individuals.** Investment companies warn their customers to be wary about clicking on links in e-mails or opening attached files—the e-mails might be from cyber-criminals trying to steal account information. However, employees at those companies sometimes fall for the same scam, accidentally giving cyber-criminals access to computers containing customer information.

•**Account information is not always encrypted.** If you ask an investment company whether it encrypts customer data, it likely will assure you that it does, then tell you about "128-bit Secure Sockets Layer (SSL)" encryption or something similar. But this means only that digital communications between your computer and the company are encrypted. Most companies don't encrypt account information when it is stored on the company's hard drives or used internally…or confirm that it is encrypted when it is shared with corporate partners or vendors.

If investment firms would practice end-to-end encryption, it wouldn't be such a big deal when hackers break into their systems—the hackers would not be able to read the encrypted files.

Why don't investment companies do this? Because end-to-end encryption is not only expensive, it also makes life more difficult for executives and employees. And even though end-to-end encryption can be useful, companies that use it often make mistakes that expose account information long enough for lurking hackers to pounce.

HOW TO EVALUATE SECURITY

The daunting reality is that no investment firm or investment account is completely safe from cyber-criminals—but some are safer than others. *Here's how to tell whether your investment companies are doing everything possible to protect your assets and how to decide which of the security options they offer are worth the trouble…*

•**Can you get an extra security code sent to your phone? Roughly half of large financial companies now offer two-factor authentication.** If you opt to get this protection, your investment firm will text a onetime-use code to your cell phone (or give you a key-fob-size "token" that displays a code) each time you try to log in. You must enter this code on the company's website to access your account. This greatly improves account security—cyber-criminals are unlikely to have access to your phone (or token) even if they get their hands on your account information.

Among the firms that offer it: Bank of America, Charles Schwab, E*Trade, Fidelity, Goldman Sachs, Merrill Edge, T. Rowe Price, USAA, Vanguard.

Helpful: If you want the security of two-factor authentication without having to check a phone or token for a code each time you log in, find out whether the company offers the option of requiring authentication only when logging into the account from a computer other than the one you normally use, as many firms do.

•**Is there a history of hacks?** If your investment firm has had customer accounts breached repeatedly in recent years, it could be a sign that its cyber defenses are especially weak. If it has suffered any major breach in the past 12 months, it still might be in disaster-recovery mode—it can take a full year for a company to figure out exactly what happened and to confirm that hackers are 100% flushed from its systems.

The Privacy Rights Clearinghouse maintains an online database of known data breaches. At Privacy Rights.org, click "Data Breaches," then enter the financial company's name into the box labeled

"Search for a company or organization by name." Finally, under "Select Year(s)," click on "Select All."

Examples: Schwab and Scottrade both had breaches in the past few years.

•**Will the company make good on cyber-theft losses?** If investment companies cannot protect their customers from online criminals, they should at least repay any money that is stolen. An increasing number now offer online security guarantees that promise to do this, although these guarantees usually have limitations.

Examples: Ameriprise, Fidelity and TD Ameritrade promise to cover losses that occur "through no fault of your own." Scottrade and Vanguard customers must follow a checklist of security procedures, such as using up-to-date security software, to remain eligible for reimbursement guarantees. Charles Schwab and E*Trade impose relatively few restrictions. Schwab asks customers to safeguard account-access information and to report unauthorized transactions as quickly as possible, while E*Trade asks them just to not share user IDs and passwords and to review statements and report unauthorized trades promptly. American Funds, Franklin Templeton, Pimco and T. Rowe Price do not currently have written cyber-security guarantees (though they still might compensate investors for cyber-crime losses if the customer is not to blame).

If you can't find a cyber-theft guarantee on a financial company's website, type the company's name and the words "online security guarantee" or "online fraud policy" into a search engine…or call the company's customer service department.

Helpful: See whether the company has cyber-theft insurance to compensate customers if there are large-scale losses.

Dial-Back Scam Hits Cell Phones

Scambusters.org

With this con, a scammer leaves a phone message saying that there has been a death in your family and to call for details. The message asks you to add *72 to the beginning of the call-back number. When you dial a number beginning with the *72 code, you are telling your cell-phone service to forward all future calls to the number after that code. This lets anyone call the crook by using your number—and you are charged for each call, which you don't realize until the bill arrives.

Self-defense: Do not use *72 or any other code before calling a number that you do not know or do not recognize.

<h1 style="text-align: center;">15</h1>

House and Home

Make Your Home Look More Upscale

Hilary Farr, cohost of *Love It or List It*, which airs on *HGTV*. She is president of Toronto-based interior design company Hilary Farr Design. HilaryFarr.com

The trouble with upscale home upgrades is that they tend to come with up-market price tags. But there are home projects that can bring a sense of class and distinction to a home for $1,000 or less—sometimes much less. These upgrades won't just impress your guests and make your house a more appealing place to live—they also could help attract buyers when you sell. We asked Hilary Farr, cohost of the popular HGTV show *Love It or List It*, for inexpensive ways to make a home appear more upscale inside. *Here are six of her favorite ways to get an expensive look for less...*

• **Install crown molding,** a decorative strip traditionally made from plaster or wood that runs along the tops of interior walls. This molding creates a visual transition between wall and ceiling and adds design detail, making a home feel more upscale. (It also hides drywall imperfections where walls and ceilings meet.)

Hiring a skilled plasterer to install a traditional plaster crown molding would be very costly...as would hiring a carpenter to put in an elaborate wood molding. There are less expensive, preformed moldings made from fiberboard, but those are very heavy and difficult to install well. Fortunately, there's a fourth option—install polystyrene foam moldings, which can be glued in place. Unlike wood moldings, polystyrene moldings do not expand and contract with changes in temperature, so cracks and gaps will not develop over time, and unlike fiberboard moldings, they are not very difficult to install. They are quite sturdy and can be lightly sanded and painted.

Select a crown molding that is at least five inches in height—anything smaller won't make enough of an impression to be worth the trouble.

Cost estimate: Expect to pay about $2 per linear foot—that's less than $200 for a 20-foot-by-20-foot room. If you opt for professional installation, it might add up to $200 more per room to your bottom line, depending on the amount of molding and local labor rates.

Related project: Beef up your baseboards. Replace the insubstantial-looking molding found along the bottoms of most walls with baseboards that are five-and-a-half to six inches tall. These should match the room's crown molding in color and style, but they should be made of wood, which can take the beating that baseboards can get over time.

•**Expand the trim around interior window frames to make windows seem grander.** Windows are the single most important feature in the typical room—our eyes are drawn to them. The easiest, least expensive way to make windows appear more upscale and impressive from the inside is to expand the trim around them. Just add a "backband"—a three-quarter- to one-and-a-quarter-inch strip of wood that is nailed in place around the outer perimeter of the existing interior window trim and painted to match.

If you're willing to tackle a larger project, you could remove the existing window trim and replace it with something more substantial. This will look even better and save the effort of searching for a backband that will work with the existing trim. If you want to improve your home's curb appeal, upgrading the trim around the exterior of windows is worth considering, too.

Cost estimate: Backband molding made of paint-grade wood such as poplar for interior use or pine for exterior use typically costs just $1 to $2 per linear foot, so even factoring in the price of paint and finish nails, this project should cost no more than $30 to $50 per window.

Related project: Expand your window dressing. Purchase curtain rods that extend six to 18 inches beyond the edges of your windows on each side. Install these rods at least four inches above the tops of the windows and ideally all the way up near the ceiling or crown molding. Purchase curtains that extend all the way from this rod to the floor—they should just touch the floor, not stop a few inches above it. This also makes windows of modest size seem grand.

•**Install subway tile in your bathrooms and/or kitchen.** Home owners who want tile that seems upscale and special have three choices. They can pay up for expensive tile …they can choose unusual colors or patterns that stand out but that might later go out of style or alienate future home buyers…or they can install subway tile.

Subway tile is rectangular—typically three inches by six inches—so it is more eye-catching than ordinary square household tile. It has been in use for well over 100 years but is timeless and has never gone out

of style. White subway tile with black grout or black subway tile with white grout produces a particularly upscale result. A staggered "brick" tile pattern creates a traditional look…a straight-line tile-on-top-of-tile "stack" pattern creates a more modern look…while chevron and herringbone patterns, created by laying the tiles on a diagonal, are distinctive.

Cost estimate: Three-by-six-inch ceramic subway tile often costs just $2 to $3 per square foot. A typical kitchen backsplash of 15-to-20 square feet could be done for less than $200 per backsplash if you do it yourself. Professional installation can add $5 to $10 per square foot.

•**Upgrade interior doors.** High-end homes do not just look more upscale than other homes, they also feel more upscale. Their components are solid and substantial to the touch. One simple way to make a conventional home feel more solid and substantial is to replace its hollow-core wood interior doors with solid-core wood doors. This works because doors are among the parts of the home that are handled most frequently by home owners and guests.

When doors open with some weightiness and close with a subtle thunk, the whole house feels more upscale. Also, solid-core doors keep out noise better than hollow-core doors.

Cost estimate: Solid-core wood interior doors can be found for around $200 apiece. One way to control the cost of this project is to upgrade just the doors that you and your guests use most often, such as guest bathroom doors and/or master bedroom doors.

Related project: Upgrade doorknobs. Select new knobs based on their solid feel, not just their appealing looks. You can get a good-quality doorknob for $20 to $30.

•**Transform entryways from clutter receptacles into visual greetings.** In many homes, entryways are ad-hoc storage areas. Shoes and umbrellas are lined up near the front door…keys, mail and other clutter rest on any available flat surface. Clutter is inelegant, especially as a first impression. Your home instantly will seem more upscale if you remove all clutter that can be seen from its entryway. If necessary, purchase closet organizing products to make it easier to stow entryway clutter in the hall closet…and/or an elegant, understated cabinet or a small table for the entryway featuring drawers to hide small clutter including keys and mail. Use the surface of this cabinet or table to place a beautiful element of welcome such as a vase containing one fresh flower.

• **Install laminate kitchen countertops that look like quartz, marble or granite.** Quartz, marble and granite countertops make homes look upscale because they are upscale—they typically cost $75 to $100 or more per square foot, installed. But these days, there are laminate countertops that do an excellent job of mimicking the look of those desirable, high-end materials for less than half the cost.

Examples: Wilsonart HD laminates (Wilson art.com)…and Formica 180fx laminates (Formica. com).

Take a close look at the edge of laminate countertops in showrooms before buying. Some do a wonderful job mimicking high-end materials when you look only at the top but ruin the illusion by looking like laminates along the edge

Cost estimate: $30 per square foot, installed, for laminate countertop.

New Ways to Get More When You Sell Your Home

Stan Humphries, chief analytics officer at Zillow, the real estate information service based in Seattle, which has a database of more than 110 million US homes. He is coauthor of *Zillow Talk: Rewriting the Rules of Real Estate.* Zillow.com

---

The housing market is finally getting back to normal. But real estate economist Stan Humphries says that some of the conventional wisdom about buying and selling a home has changed drastically. That's partly because people have become much more wary about the future of real estate prices in the wake of the 2007–2009 housing-price meltdown…and partly because of the growing role of technology, especially the Internet, in real estate shopping. Humphries has analyzed millions of home listings, as well as data gathered from millions of monthly visitors to the Zillow real estate website. He has developed insights that can earn you thousands of dollars more on the sale of your home.

Conventional wisdom says that as a seller, you should overprice your home by 5% to 10% to leave yourself some wiggle room in negotiations…renovate your kitchen to add the most value to your house…and list early in the year to catch the spring and early-summer home-buying rush.

But here's what national and local housing data say are the rules that work better now…

RULE 1: **Price a home as close as possible to fair market value.** About half of all sellers still price their homes too high and have to make cuts to attract potential buyers. Zillow studied more than a million homes listed for sale and tracked price changes until they sold. Homes that required a 10% price cut spent an average of 220 days on the market and sold for 2% less than their estimated value. That's because buyers bargain more aggressively when a listing sits on the market a long time. Homes that were correctly priced to begin with needed no price cut to sell, spent an average of 107 days on the market and, best of all, sold for 2% more than their estimated value.

Best way to determine fair market value: Have a real estate agent prepare a market analysis of the recent selling prices of comparable homes in your area to help establish fair market value.

RULE 2: **Make sure the last non-zero digit in your original asking price is a nine.** This is the same kind of psychological pricing that works in retail stores, and it leads to faster, more lucrative sales for homes at every price level.

For example, the average US home that was listed initially for $449,000 wound up selling for about $4,000 more than a home listed at $450,000. What's more, comparable homes priced $1,000 lower than their counterparts sold four days faster on average.

Why it works: Consumers are conditioned to see prices ending in nine as signifying an attractive discount. That kind of pricing attracts more attention to your home's listing, which often translates into higher offers.

RULE 3: **Make modest upgrades to your home that restore the basic functioning of the house.** Modest upgrades have a much bigger relative impact on your home's value than renovations that add fashionable but frivolous luxuries. For example, upgrading a bathroom from poor to decent shape completely changes the livability of the property and appeals to just about everyone. But taking a fully functional bathroom and adding high-end elements, such as fancy jet-massage showerheads or dramatic tiling, actually may turn off many prospective buyers. Based on Zillow's analysis, a $3,000, mid-range bathroom remodel—with such steps as replacing the toilet...updating lighting fixtures...adding a double sink...and painting or putting up wallpaper—resulted in a $1.71 increase in home value for every $1 spent on renovation. But plunking down $12,000 for a complete bathroom overhaul, including replacing the floor and moving plumbing, resulted in only an 87-cent increase in value per dollar spent.

Note: In contrast to conventional wisdom, kitchen renovations have a lower return than many other home-improvement investments, with a cost recovery of just 50 cents per $1 spent regardless of the scope of the remodeling.

Reason: Prospective buyers are very particular about what constitutes a dream kitchen. They won't be excited about a kitchen renovation if it doesn't happen to match their needs and tastes.

Rule 4: **List your home for sale in late March or later.** Many home sellers choose to list early in the year, starting in late January or in February. They do this in order to have plenty of time to catch the spring and early-summer home-buying rush. But Zillow's data indicates that listing very early in the year has become so popular that you're better off waiting until after the first few weeks of March or even the second week in April in some markets, such as Boston. The average US home put on the market in late March, for example, sold for over 2% more than the average home listed earlier in the year.

Reason: Your house doesn't get lost in a sea of new listings. That leads to more attention and potentially more offers.

RULE 5: **Write long, carefully worded listings.** Although the Internet allows home sellers to upload videos and lots of photographs of their homes, the data shows that homes with written descriptions longer than the median length of 50-to-70 words routinely sell for more than their asking prices, while homes with shorter written descriptions don't. Prospective buyers want details, and those extra words give them additional information that makes a home worth seeing in person.

Note: After a listing reaches 250 words, additional length did not seem to help the sale price.

What to write: Avoid words in your listing that connote "small," "nothing special" or "needs work." These words include cute...charming...potential... quaint...needs TLC...and unique. Such words turn off buyers and can reduce the selling price by as much as 2% to 7% of the asking price.

On the positive side, lower-priced homes described in listings as "luxurious" beat their original asking prices by 8%, on average...and using "impeccable" beat their original asking prices by 6%. In more expensive homes, listings with the word "captivating" boosted the sale price by 6.5%, on average, and the word "gentle" (typically referring to the property description such as gentle rolling hills) was worth an additional 2.3%, on average. Words such as "remodeled" pushed up the selling prices of homes in every price range by an average of 1.7% to 2.9% and "landscaped" by 1.5% to 4.2%.

HOW TO BUY A HOME THAT SOARS IN VALUE

People choose to buy particular homes for a variety of reasons that have little to do with money. But if one of your primary goals in choosing a home is price appreciation, the data is clear—look at properties in up-and-coming neighborhoods.

If you can get to one of these neighborhoods within the first five years of it becoming hot, you have a chance of snatching a property at a much lower price point than in areas that are already well-regarded.

How to spot these soon-to-be hot neighborhoods...

●**Use the Halo Effect.** Look for less developed areas adjacent to premier neighborhoods that already have taken off and have ample restaurants, cafés, parks and nightlife.

●**Look for a Starbucks.** Believe it or not, having a location of the popular coffee shop within a quarter mile of a house has proved to be one of the strongest, most reliable indicators of neighborhood gentrification and rapidly appreciating home prices. Between 1997 and 2014, US homes appreciated 65%, on average. But properties near a Starbucks appreciated 96%, on average, and they recovered much more quickly from the housing bust.

Reason: Starbucks has an army of analysts and geographic information specialists dedicated to finding the next hot neighborhood, assessing everything from traffic patterns to the kinds of new businesses opening in the area. In addition, the iconic coffee shop is seen as a proxy for gentrification by other potential upscale businesses.

How to Keep a Vacation Home in Your Family for Generations

David S. Fry, Esq., an attorney in Rockford, Michigan, who specializes in vacation-property succession planning. He is coauthor of *Saving the Family Cottage: A Guide to Succession Planning for Your Cottage, Cabin, Camp or Vacation Home.* CottageLaw.com

A vacation home can be the setting for an extended family's fondest memories. Whether it's a cabin in the mountains or a cottage by a lake, this is a place for grown kids and young cousins to reunite and relax.

Vacation-home owners might imagine that these properties will be enjoyed by their descendants for decades to come—but that's usually not what happens. Problems often start as soon as the following generation inherits and attempts to share ownership. Even if all the adult kids are well-meaning,

they inevitably have divergent ideas about the care and use of the property. That leads to disagreements, ill will and, sooner than you might ever have expected, the property's sale.

If you want your vacation property to be enjoyed by your family after you are gone and to be a positive force, it's up to you to avoid the big mistakes that vacation-home owners typically make when they leave homes to the next generation...

MISTAKE: **Using the wrong method to transfer the property to heirs.** Many vacation-home owners sow the seeds of family discord by the legal means they use to hand down the properties...

●**Leaving a property in a will.** This is very easy—but it's a mistake if there is more than one child. Consider how hard it can be to agree with one's own spouse about how and when to spend money maintaining and improving a home. Now consider how challenging this would become if, as happens when ownership is divvied up in a will, several siblings had to agree—siblings who might have very different budgets and priorities, plus their own spouses to answer to.

●**Leaving a property through a trust.** This can be a reasonable option, but it, too, can lead to discord. Often some descendants become convinced that the descendant who was named trustee is taking unfair advantage of his/her power. And if someone other than a descendant is named trustee, all the heirs might bristle at their lack of control. In addition, using a trust may not provide adequate protection against the claims of your heirs' creditors—and family ownership of the property might therefore be threatened.

●**Using a tenancy in common.** This legal arrangement of ownership allows two or more people to hold shares in a property. But this is a terrible choice if your goal is to keep the property in the family. In most states, any of the "tenants" has the right to force the sale of the property, virtually guaranteeing that it won't remain in the family long.

BETTER: In most cases, the best route to leave a vacation home to your descendants is to transfer ownership to a limited liability company (LLC) set up for this purpose during your lifetime. With an LLC, you get to design an "operating agreement" that lays out descendants' rights and obligations if they wish to continue owning shares of the property. Laying out these rules now saves your heirs from bickering over them later. An LLC can continue in perpetuity, making it simple for your descendants eventually to leave the property to their descendants…spelling out the rules if they decide to sell (more on this below)…and limiting your heirs' exposure in any lawsuits related to the property.

Each "branch" of your family—that is, the families of each of your children—typically names one representative to the LLC's "management council," which functions like a corporate board of directors. This way, all feel that their voices are being heard, and disagreements can be settled through a preselected process such as a management council vote.

An estate-planning attorney might be able to set up an LLC of this sort for as little as $1,000, though costs could be several times that amount in high-cost areas or with complex arrangements. There also are certain tax-filing requirements for LLCs. If there is a mortgage on the property, the lender might block the transfer of ownership to the LLC, and owning a property through an LLC could interfere with your ability to deduct its mortgage interest. You can work through all these wrinkles with your attorney or accountant.

MISTAKE: **Failing to restrict ownership to descendants.** If you do not take steps to prevent it, one of your descendants could sell his share in your vacation property to someone outside the family…or lose control of his share in a divorce or lawsuit.

BETTER: Ask your attorney to include language in the LLC operating agreement (described above) stating that the only people eligible to be partial owners are "lineal descendants" of you and your spouse—this phrase means that only people who can trace their ancestry directly back to you are eligible. (It's worth specifying that adopted descendants and/or stepchildren can become partial owners, too.)

MISTAKE: **Failing to think through future sales prices.** At some point, some of your heirs will want to sell their shares of the vacation property. If you do not plan for this, it could become a source of tremendous family conflict.

For the property to remain in your family, sellers must be restricted to selling to other family members—but that means relatives will be on opposite sides of the table with thousands of dollars at stake. Sellers want to get fair market value…while buyers argue that surrendering a share of a family property is different from selling on the open market. Often everyone ends up angry.

BETTER: Provide a specific formula for determining how much heirs receive when selling to other heirs. One good way to do this is to mandate that future generations should start with the property's most recent municipal assessment…adjust that assessed value to reflect the actual property value, if necessary (in some locales, assessed value is 50% of fair market value, for example)…and then apply a discount rate and payment schedule of your choosing. Typically, this discount is between 25% and 50% and the payment period is five or 10 years. The higher the discount rate and the longer the payment period, the greater the odds that the property will remain in your family because selling becomes less attractive and buying becomes more attractive. Descendants typically are required to buy out those who decide to sell. Because of this obligation to buy, it is critical that the operating agreement provide a formula for establishing favorable purchase price and payment terms.

To prevent a situation where a well-off heir buys out the other heirs and then sells the house on the open market for a large profit, the rules can include a provision that if the property is sold outside the family within a certain time after an heir sells to another heir, the share-selling heir is to receive a certain percentage of what he/she would have received if the intrafamily sale had not occurred.

MISTAKE: **Making descendants shoulder the full costs of ownership.** Owning a vacation home with its property taxes, insurance premiums, utility bills and upkeep can be costly. These costs are among the most common reasons that descendants decide to sell.

BETTER: If you can afford to, set up an endowment fund to cover ownership costs. Go back through your records to determine your approximate annual costs, divide this figure by 0.03 and, if possible, put that amount in a low-risk mutual fund or some other investment that is likely to pay annual returns of at least 3%. This will require a very significant amount of money, however—it comes to $333,333 even with relatively modest annual expenses of $10,000. But, when feasible, it is a way to ensure that your descendants who have limited financial resources can continue to own a share in the property.

If you cannot afford this full endowment, put a smaller amount of money aside to pay ownership costs. This buys your heirs time to figure out whether they can afford to own the property.

MISTAKE: **Establishing a schedule for use of the home rather than a flexible system for creating a schedule.** Heirs won't always want multifamily reunions at the house—they'll want individual family time as well. But if you try to assign certain descendants certain weeks, as many benefactors have done, some heirs inevitably will feel that they're getting the short end of the stick.

BETTER: The property's operating agreement should divide the peak season into "use periods" of between one and three weeks and instruct heirs to take turns picking periods. Which heir gets first pick should rotate annually.

MISTAKE: **Letting heirs be "half in."** An heir who uses the property only rarely might not want to have a full ownership share but might not want to sell his entire share either. In situations like this, it can be tempting to create "partial shares" or other complicated ownership distinctions. Don't do it. Doing so will only open the door for other descendants to angle for their own special arrangements, forcing remaining heirs to buy up an ever-larger percentage of the property and pay a huge portion of the expenses.

BETTER: Give descendants just two options—in or out. An heir who wants to use the property only very rarely could be allowed to sell his share to another heir and then visit occasionally as a guest.

8 Ways to Warm Up a Cold Spot in Your Home

Richard Trethewey, heating, ventilation and air-conditioning (HVAC) expert for the PBS-TV series *This Old House* since 1979. He is founder and owner of RST Thermal, which provides energy-efficient solutions for home heating and cooling to home owners and businesses in New England. He is based in Westwood, Massachusetts. ThisOldHouse.com

Is one room or area in your home much colder than others? There are various ways to solve the problem, some of them simple and inexpensive…others involving greater effort and expense.

Heating expert Richard Trethewey explains how you can figure out what's wrong and what to do about it…

SIMPLE SOLUTIONS

Home owners often think that they have to live with temperature inconsistencies in different parts of their homes because they are reluctant to spend tens of thousands of dollars to upgrade their heating systems and insulation. *But in many cases, the solutions are so simple and inexpensive that people may overlook them…*

● **Check the arrangement of the furniture and drapes to make sure that heating vents or radiators are not blocked.**

● **Shut the damper in the fireplace firmly when you aren't using it.**

● **Feel for drafts along windows** by holding a lit candle along the gap between the window and the trim. Watch if the flame bends or flickers, indicating a leak, and then caulk or weather-strip to close the gap. If a window still feels drafty, pry off the interior wall trim around the window and spray foam sealant between the wall and window frame. Then press the trim back into place.

● **If you need to heat only a specific part of a room** such as the desk area in a home office or a couch near a TV, get an energy-efficient, 1,500-watt portable electric space heater such as the Holmes Eco Smart Energy Saving Portable Heater, which weighs less than five pounds, stands 7.5 inches high and costs about $35 but produces as much heat as larger models.

BIGGER PROBLEMS

Here, cold-spot problems and cost-effective solutions…

Problem: **Major heat loss through exterior walls.** Does one wall or part of a wall feel cold all the time in the winter? Traditional fiberglass insulation in the wall may be inadequate because it has broken down over time or has left gaps around electrical boxes or light fixtures, creating drafts.

Solution: **Blow Icynene into the walls.** Icynene is a new type of expanding foam insulation that is injected into wall cavities through small holes. It's much denser than fiberglass and reduces air infiltration with double the effectiveness of fiberglass. Icynene can be sprayed in without removing the fiberglass and directly onto electrical and plumbing work. (If you need to access pipes and wires for repair in the future, the Icynene foam can be cut away). For more information and to find a licensed Icynene contractor, go to Icynene.com.

Cost: About $4 per square foot for the material and installation.

Problem: **Heat from your furnace is not making it to the room that is cold.** If you have a forced-air heating system and the airflow out of a room's vent feels weak, you may be losing heat to tiny cracks and gaps in the ductwork in your walls. In older homes, as much as 20% of the heat never makes it to rooms, especially those farthest from the furnace. Trying to seal ductwork yourself with mastic tape often is ineffective because leaks can be hard to identify and much of the ductwork in a house is not accessible.

Solution: **Use Aeroseal duct sealant,** a nontoxic polymer spray that contractors pump into both rigid and flexible ducts, sealing gaps from the inside of the ducts. This product received a Best New Product award from *This Old House* magazine. It has proved so effective at improving heat flow (and saving on heating costs) that it's worth doing in your entire home. Go to Aeroseal.com to locate a dealer near you.

Cost: About $1,000 to treat the ductwork of a 2,000-square-foot home.

Problem: **Your thermostat is poorly positioned.** If your thermostat is in a sunny room that cools slowly, there will be a delay before the heat kicks in. If the room warms quickly, it shuts off the furnace too early.

Solution: **Add a wireless thermostat in the chilly room.** You can easily replace your old wall thermostat with a wireless receiver and place a wireless thermostat, which contains the temperature sensor, anywhere in the house. These units transmit up to 500 feet through walls, ceilings and floors.

Recommended: ZoneFirst Wireless Thermostat and Receiver (ZoneFirst.com).

Cost: About $200 plus a one-hour service call from an electrician.

Note: If moving your traditional thermostat wiring to a chilly room is easy to do, consider installing the Nest thermostat (Nest.com) instead. It's not wireless, but it can be linked to your computer and/or smartphone so that you can control it remotely, adjusting the temperature up or down on short notice even when you are not at home. The Nest also can learn your daily patterns, so it can turn down the temperature when you leave the house.

Cost: $250 plus a one-hour service call from an electrician.

Problem: **Heat from a warmer room is not dispersing into an adjoining colder room.** Rooms with an additional heating source (for example, a stove or a fireplace), as well as rooms on the south side of a house that get a lot of sun, tend to be warmer than the rest of the house.

Solution: **Install a room-to-room ventilator.** These ultraquiet fan systems are positioned between rooms right in the wall. One side of the ventilator draws heat from the warm room…the other side disperses it into the cold room. Ventilators run off of a manual wall switch or an automatic thermostat.

Cost: About $100, depending on the size of the ventilator, plus two to three hours for an electrician to open up your wall and install the ventilator.

Problem: **You just want to add extra heat to an entire room without having to turn up the thermostat for the whole house.**

Solutions: **Put in a ceiling fan that includes a space heater.** The Reiker Room Conditioner with remote control installs and functions just like a regular ceiling fan. But in the winter, with the heater engaged, the fan blades circulate heat quickly through the room.

Cost: $350 plus a two-hour installation service call from an electrician.

Install radiant-floor heating, especially for rooms with cold, ceramic tile floors such as bathrooms, mudrooms and kitchens. Radiant-floor heating consists of ultrathin heating cables in mesh mats—not unlike the wires in an electric blanket—that are installed underneath your flooring.

Drawback: Because the heating system must be installed under the tile, this option is best reserved for when you are planning to redo your floors anyway.

Cost: About $6 per square foot for materials and installation.

If these solutions don't work, your problems may be more complex and you may need a professional energy audit.

Don't Call a Plumber for a Clogged Sink Until You Try This First

Men's Health. MensHealth.com

Fill an empty milk jug or a two-liter soda bottle with water. Cover the overflow drain of the sink with duct tape (to stop air from escaping). In one quick motion, jam the top of the bottle into the drain and squeeze the bottle hard to send a jet of water into the drain. Remove the duct tape, and run the water to see if the clog is gone. If not, you can repeat these steps up to three times. If that doesn't work, it's time to call a plumber.

16

Fall Asleep in 7 Minutes!

Overcome Insomnia in 7 Minutes

Loren Fishman, MD, assistant clinical professor, Columbia University College of Physicians and Surgeons, and physical and rehabilitative specialist, both in New York City. He is author of *Yoga for Osteoporosis*.

C an't sleep? Here's an antidote to tossing and turning…a routine of sleep-inducing moves that will help you drift off in no time.

You don't even have to get out of bed to do them! And you can do them whether you wake in the middle of the night…or can't conk out in the first place. In fact, you might even fall asleep (or fall back asleep) before you complete the whole routine.

This routine, inspired by yoga poses, works 80% to 90% of the time.

PART 1: DO RECLINING HAND TO BIG TOE POSE

This yoga pose stretches the hamstrings, causing them to relax, and brings on a sense of floating to the legs that signals the entire central nervous system to relax.

What to do: While on your back, lengthen your body by stretching your heels away from your hips and the back of your head away from your shoulders. Symmetrically position your shoulder blades fairly close to the spine. Keep your spine straight.

Bending your right knee, lift your right thigh until it is perpendicular to your back. Keep your left leg firmly on the bed as you

Photo credit: Maura Rhodes

straighten your right knee, and grasp your right foot with both hands and pull it toward your forehead. Tighten your quadriceps (the muscles on the front of your thigh) to make your knee truly straight—a reflex will automatically relax your hamstrings.

Hold for 20 to 30 seconds, taking slow, deep breaths. Then lower your right leg, and repeat the move with your left leg. (If you can't reach your foot with your hands, loop a belt or towel over your foot and hold on to that.)

PART 2: BREATHE SLOWLY AND EVENLY

While still on your back with your legs back down on the bed, close your eyes and breathe normally until you feel settled. Then exhale and take a good normal breath, puffing out your chest.

Now here comes the tricky part. Retaining the puffed-out chest, exhale as much air as you can. Then inhale in three small equal segments with a pause of two to five seconds between segments. Don't use your throat or mouth or tongue to stop inhaling in each of the three segments. Just halt the downward movement of your diaphragm. When you've completed the three segments and held your breath for five to 10 seconds, exhale and take a normal breath.

Repeat the process two more times, with a normal breath between each time.

Now do it in reverse—fill your lungs, puff out your chest and then exhale in three equal segments with two-to-five-second pauses between segments, retaining the puffed-out chest throughout the exercise.

Take a normal breath before repeating the entire exhalation exercise two more times.

PART 3: AN ABBREVIATED RELAXATION RESPONSE

Start with your toes. Let them relax…let the spaces between your toes breathe. Move up the relaxation to your calves, then your thighs, then all the way to your navel. Then relax your fingers as you did your toes. Starting at the tips of your fingers and thumbs…move up to your forearms…upper arms… shoulders and shoulder blades…neck and face.

Enjoy the peace…you may even feel tingling. Then focus on your navel moving up and down as you breathe.

Last, imagine total peace, or your favorite place and/or time in your life.

To Sleep Better, Press Your Thumb Right Here

Deborah Flanagan, certified reflexologist, founder of the Center for True Health in New York City and a member of the Reflexology Association of America.

If you have trouble sleeping, try this simple do-it-yourself reflexology move.

Reflexology involves applying mild pressure to specific spots on the hands and feet believed to correspond with different body organs. While there isn't good scientific evidence that reflexology can treat diseases such as asthma and diabetes (as some people claim), there are some small studies that find that it can help with insomnia…and there's no harm if it doesn't help.

Deborah Flanagan, a certified reflexologist and founder of the Center for True Health in New York City, offers a do-it-yourself approach…

● **Locate the middle of the "whorl" of your right thumbprint.** In reflexology, this corresponds to the pituitary gland, which helps regulate sleep.

● **Press the side of your left thumbnail into the center of the whorl and hold it for 45 seconds.**

● **Switch thumbs and hold for another 45 seconds.**

● **Do this two to three times per day.**

You can also try this "in the middle of the night if you wake up and have trouble getting back to sleep," says Flanagan.

This Blanket May Help You Sleep

Study titled "Positive Effects of a Weighted Blanket on Insomnia" by researchers at University of Gothenburg, Sweden, published in *Journal of Sleep Medicine & Disorders.*

Michael J. Breus, PhD, a sleep specialist in Manhattan Beach, California. His latest book is *The Power of When.* TheSleepDoctor.com

Brett Scotch, DO, an osteopathic physician specializing in sleep medicine and otolaryngology and director of Scotch Institute, Wesley Chapel, Florida.

Karen Moore, OTR, an occupational therapist and founder of The Sensory Connection Program in Franconia, New Hampshire.

Move over sleep meds—there's a new solution in town. Weighted blankets.

The comforting heavy covers, filled with small plastic balls that are sewn into compartments for even distribution, have been used for years to treat children with anxiety, ADHD, autism spectrum disorders and other disorders. Parents swear by them, especially to help kids sleep.

Now they're catching on as a simple DIY solution for healthy adults with sleep problems. The theory is that they provide "deep pressure" that helps you feel calmer and more relaxed, making it easier to fall asleep and stay asleep. Think of it as a kind of swaddling for grown-ups.

LESSONS FROM INSOMNIAC SWEDES

A recent study from the University of Gothenburg in Sweden looked at the effect of weighted blankets in 33 normal healthy adult men and women with chronic insomnia. Participants wore "actigraph" watches, which recorded the pattern of their movements when they went to bed, and they also kept sleep diaries. In the first week, they slept their usual way. Then for two weeks, they slept under weighted blankets of their choice, which ranged in weight from 13 pounds to 22 pounds—at least 12% of their body weight. During the fourth week, they went back to their normal sleeping conditions.

Results: When they used the weighted blankets, the sleepers spent more time in each phase of sleep, including truly restful deep sleep, and they moved around less during the night. According to their diaries, they found it easier to settle down to sleep, had better quality sleep and felt more refreshed in the morning.

While the Swedish study didn't take anxiety into account, the blankets have a documented calming effect, which may help explain how they enhance sleep, according to sleep expert Michael Breus, PhD. "Most people who have insomnia have some level of anxiety," he said. The sympathetic nervous system, which regulates the "fight or flight" reflex, is often easily aroused in people who have trouble sleeping, he explained. "A weighted blanket puts pressure on the mechanoreceptors—nerve endings under the skin—which sense pressure and signal muscles to relax. That makes us feel safe and supported."

SNUGGLING TIPS

Who's a good candidate to try a weighted blanket? Anyone who is in good health but has trouble falling asleep or staying asleep, according to Dr. Breus.

Who isn't: Anyone with a respiratory disorder (such as severe asthma) or a circulatory disorder, according to Brett Scotch, DO, an osteopathic physician specializing in sleep medicine and otolaryngology in Wesley Chapel, Florida. "The weight on your chest may impede your ability to breathe or decrease cir-

culation to your extremities," he warned. (If you have any serious health condition, consult your doctor before sleeping with a weighted blanket.)

If you do decide to try getting under heavy covers, look for a blanket that weighs about 10% of your body weight or more, has a material that feels good to you and distributes the weight evenly to provide firm, constant tactile stimulation across your body. The blankets are widely available online, from companies such as Sommerfly (Sommerfly.com/default. asp) and Mosaic Weighted Blankets (Mosaicweighted blankets.com), and cost around $140. "If you're claustrophobic, you may want to start with a lighter one and give it a chance," said Karen Moore, OTR, an occupational therapist and founder of The Sensory Connection Program in Franconia, New Hampshire.

Will it work for you? The Swedish study is relatively small and short-term, so this is not the definitive solution to insomnia. Ultimately, the only way to find out if a weighted blanket will help you get better shut-eye is to try it.

The good news: It's safe and free of side effects. And unlike with prescription sleep medications, there's no "rebound" problem—except, perhaps, to your wallet—if you decide it's not for you.

Sleep Better with Cognitive Behavioral Therapy for Insomnia

Donn Posner, PhD, CBSM (Certified in Behavioral Sleep Medicine), psychologist, Palo Alto VA Medical Center, Palo Alto, California. A former clinical associate professor of psychiatry and human behavior at The Warren Alpert Medical School of Brown University, Providence, he is co-author of *Cognitive Behavioral Treatment of Insomnia: A Session-by-Session Guide.*

Do you lie awake night after night, struggling to catch the sleep that eludes you… then feel exhausted and miserable during the day? Don't just suffer stoically—insomnia is serious! It increases the risk for high blood pressure, obesity, diabetes, anxiety and substance abuse. What's more, although insomnia often is considered a sign of depression, recent research reveals that the insomnia can come first and double a person's risk of developing depression.

Sleeping pills may seem like a quick fix, but don't be too hasty in taking that route. Though these drugs do help some people, they also can have bad side effects…and according to one study, long-term use is associated with increased risk for early death.

There's a much better option that can get you the deep, blissful sleep you need. It's completely safe and drug-free, and because it addresses the underlying causes of insomnia (unlike medication), its benefits persist even long after treatment ends. It's called cognitive behavioral therapy for insomnia (CBT-I), and just a few sessions can go a long way to restore normal sleep patterns. CBT-I has been shown to relieve insomnia for a wide variety of people, including older adults and those who suffer from chronic pain, fibromyalgia, cardiovascular disease, mood disorders and other health problems. It can even help people who have been taking sleeping pills for years. *Here's what you should know about CBT-I…*

IS THIS SLEEP SOLUTION RIGHT FOR YOU?

A few restless nights should not be considered insomnia (important to know so that you don't feel overly stressed about an occasional bad night!).

True chronic insomnia means difficulty initiating or maintaining sleep, despite adequate opportunity to sleep, that occurs at least three times a week and lasts for at least three months. How long can it take you to fall asleep before it's a problem? Most experts in the field consider 30 minutes of lying awake, either before first falling asleep or after having woken up in the middle of the night, as the cut-off. In addition, insomnia leads to some daytime consequences—for instance, fatigue, memory problems, difficulty concentrating, poor work performance or even anxiety about being unable to fall sleep. Insomnia is not just a nighttime disorder…it's a 24-hour disorder.

If you think that your sleep pattern fits the above description of insomnia, talk to your doctor—a medical problem could be interfering with your slumber,

and you may find that sleep comes more easily once that underlying condition is addressed. If your insomnia persists, however, you should strongly consider trying CBT-I.

WHAT TO EXPECT DURING TREATMENT

The first step with CBT-I is for you to find a sleep specialist who offers it. To do this, ask your doctor for a referral to a qualified professional with expertise in CBT-I…or find a practitioner through the Society of Behavioral Sleep Medicine (Behav ioralSleep.org) or contact the nearest certified sleep center and say that you're interested in CBT-I.

Once you choose a sleep specialist, you can expect to undergo a thorough evaluation of all areas of functioning to determine all the factors that are contributing to your sleep problems. Genetic makeup, internal rhythm, social life, home life and work life are all evaluated…and you are instructed to keep a sleep diary to help pinpoint problematic patterns. Your therapist also tries to determine whether an emotional issue or even another sleep disorder precipitated your insomnia. When the evaluation is complete, the therapist creates an individualized treatment plan, typically consisting of four to six weekly one-hour sessions.

Then the real work begins. As the name implies, CBT-I involves both behavioral and cognitive elements. *Though therapy is tailored to each patient, a typical protocol includes the following…*

•**Sleep restriction.** You may be instructed to stop napping…stay active in the evening to avoid dozing off in front of the TV…go to bed later than you usually do…and get out of bed at precisely the same time every morning regardless of how well you slept. Your sleep therapist also may restrict the amount of time you spend in bed, for instance, by allowing you only 30 minutes more than your actual sleeping time—so if you usually get just five hours of sleep, you'll be told to spend no more than five and a half hours in bed. Only as your "sleep efficiency" improves do you start going to bed earlier and staying in bed longer. The idea is for you to be very sleepy at bedtime…which makes it much easier to fall asleep.

●**Stimulus control.** You are cautioned against using your bed at any time of day for anything other than sleeping or sex. That means no lounging on the bed to read, watch TV, talk on the phone or surf the Internet. For times when you do go to bed and do not fall asleep (or fall back to sleep) within 15 to 20 minutes, you are told to get up and go do something in another room, returning to bed only when you feel sleepy again—and repeating this instruction as many times as necessary.

The rationale: When a person habitually struggles to fall asleep, he/she "works" at what should be a natural process…and he becomes conditioned to associate the bed with anxiety, frustration and effort. In contrast, by getting out of bed whenever he cannot sleep, he gives up that struggle. If he applies this rule consistently, over time the bed becomes a trigger for sleep rather than for wakefulness. That association between bed and sleep is further reinforced when he avoids using the bed at all while awake. The only exception is sex. If we asked people to give up the bed as a place for sex, they wouldn't comply anyway. But more importantly, during sex you presumably are not trying to sleep, so it doesn't present the same problem as, say, reading in bed with the intention of getting to sleep. It is really sleep effort above all that we try to eliminate.

●**Sleep hygiene.** Typically patients are advised to avoid caffeine after noon…and to avoid exercise, alcohol, heavy meals and nicotine within two hours of bedtime. Your sleep therapist also reviews your bedroom environment to make sure it is dark and cool enough to be conducive to sleep. (Many people keep their bedrooms too warm for good sleep.)

●**Anxiety abatement.** The therapist teaches you how to deal with the anxiety you may feel before heading to bed. For instance, you may often think, I'll be a wreck if I don't get to sleep…or I can't stand lying awake like this! As you learn to counteract that "catastrophic thinking" with rational thoughts—*I can function OK even if I don't sleep for eight hours*…or *Insomnia is unpleasant but hardly unbearable*—your anxiety lessens and sleep comes more easily. You also may be shown relaxation techniques to practice during the day and at bedtime. And you learn to avoid staring compulsively at the clock, which only makes you fret more as you calculate how much sleep you're losing. If you need an alarm clock, you may be told to use one without illumination…or to place the clock under your bed where you can't keep checking it.

Commitment is key: Too many people try one or two of the techniques for a few nights, and then if they don't immediately start sleeping better, they get frustrated and give up. There is nothing magic that will work tonight. It takes dedication and commitment to make CBT-I work because you have to rebuild your innate sleep drive and realign your body's natural rhythms before you'll be able to sleep well. Be forewarned—during treatment, sleep problems often get worse before they get better…but that's a sign that the protocol is working. It can take a week or two to start seeing real progress. Given that most people with chronic insomnia have had the problem for years, a couple weeks of work should be a good trade.

Covering the costs: The Affordable Care Act currently requires insurance companies to cover behavioral health treatments, but benefits vary depending on the state you live in, your insurance plan and your sleep therapist's professional degree. The price for a course of CBT-I treatment averages about $460 for up to six sessions. It's also worth noting that you may end up saving money in the long run. A recent study showed that older adults with insomnia spent an average of $1,100 more on health care over a six-month period compared with those who did not have insomnia—and that, after completing as few as three sessions of CBT-I, participants' total health-care costs dropped significantly.

So even if you have to pay out of pocket, you may want to consider CBT-I an investment in yourself. Chances are good that it will end up saving you anxiety, aggravation and money…promoting optimal health overall.

Foods That Sabotage Sleep

Bonnie Taub-Dix, RDN, CDN, a registered dietitian and director and owner of BTD Nutrition Consultants, LLC, on Long Island and in New York City. She is author of *Read It Before You Eat It*. Follow her on Twitter @eatsmartbd. Bonnie TaubDix.com

Y ou know that an evening coffee can leave you tossing and turning in the wee hours. *But other foods hurt sleep, too....*

•**Premium ice cream.** Brace yourself for a restless night if you indulge in Häagen-Dazs or Ben & Jerry's late at night. The richness of these wonderful treats comes mainly from fat—16 to 17 grams (g) of fat in half a cup of vanilla and who eats just half a cup?

Your body digests fat more slowly than it digests proteins or carbohydrates. When you eat a high-fat food within an hour or two of bedtime, your digestion will still be "active" when you lie down—and that can disturb sleep.

Also, the combination of stomach acid, stomach contractions and a horizontal position increases the risk for reflux, the upsurge of digestive juices into the esophagus that causes heartburn—which can disturb sleep.

•**Chocolate.** Some types of chocolate can jolt you awake almost as much as a cup of coffee. Dark chocolate, in particular, has shocking amounts of caffeine.

Example: Half a bar of Dagoba Eclipse Extra Dark has 41 milligrams of caffeine, close to what you'd get in a shot of mild espresso.

Chocolate also contains theobromine, another stimulant, which is never a good choice near bedtime.

•**Beans.** Beans are one of the healthiest foods. But a helping or two of beans—or broccoli, cauliflower, cabbage or other gas-producing foods—close to bedtime can make your night, well, a little noisier than usual. No one sleeps well when suffering from gas pains. You can reduce the "backtalk" by drinking a mug of chamomile or peppermint tea at bedtime. They're carminative herbs that aid digestion and help prevent gas.

•**Spicy foods.** Spicy foods temporarily speed up your metabolism. They are associated with taking longer to fall asleep and with more time spent awake at night. This may be caused by the capsaicin found in chile peppers, which affect body temperature and disrupt sleep. Also, in some people, spicy foods can lead to sleep-disturbing gas, stomach cramps and heartburn.